LOVE
BY DESIGN

LOVE
BY DESIGN

6 Ingredients
to Build a
Lifetime of Love

SARA NASSERZADEH, PhD, DipPST, CSC

balance

New York   Boston

Balance
Hachette Book Group
1290 Avenue of the Americas
New York, NY 10104
GCP-Balance.com
Twitter.com/GCPBalance
Instagram.com/GCPBalance

First edition: February 2024

Balance is an imprint of Grand Central Publishing. The Balance name and logo are trademarks of Hachette Book Group, Inc.

The publisher is not responsible for websites (or their content) that are not owned by the publisher.

Balance books may be purchased in bulk for business, educational, or promotional use. For information, please contact your local bookseller or the Hachette Book Group Special Markets Department at special.markets@hbgusa.com.

Illustrations by Giovanna Castro
Thinkocrats and Relationship Panoramic are Registered Trademarks in the US.

Library of Congress Cataloging-in-Publication Data
Names: Nasserzadeh, Sara, author.
Title: Love by design : 6 ingredients to build a lifetime of love / Sara Nasserzadeh.
Description: First edition. | New York : Balance, 2024. | Includes bibliographical references. |
Identifiers: LCCN 2023040976 | ISBN 9781538742914 (hardcover) | ISBN 9781538742938 (ebook)
Subjects: LCSH: Love. | Marriage. | Interpersonal relations.
Classification: LCC BF575.L8 N376 2024 | DDC 152.4/1—dc23/eng/20230928
LC record available at https://lccn.loc.gov/2023040976

ISBNs: 9781538742914 (hardcover), 9781538742938 (ebook)

Printed in the United States of America

LSC-C

Printing 1, 2023

*To Pejman, my co-designer of our inspiring Emergent Love.
You are the driving force behind my pursuit of meaning in life.*

Contents

Introduction

When I was a child, I remember hearing my parents say, "Marriage is like a watermelon. You don't know what it will look like until you open it up. Will it be tasteless, or red and juicy? Marriage is the same." To me, that made no sense. What if you ended up with one of the tasteless ones? Was there nothing you could do? Surely that could not be what they meant.

I grew up in an intercultural, interfaith household in Tehran. My mother had also grown up in Tehran, and my father moved there as a young adult. My mother was a social scientist and my father started his career as a social worker, and they met when he went to intern for an organization where my mother was, at that time, the director. He brought my mother's favorite flower (wintersweet, also called Japanese allspice) to her office every week during the winter with a note that said, "From your secret admirer." It took my mom a while to figure out who her admirer was, but once she did, the rest was history. They fell in love and were married.

My parents grew up speaking different languages and followed different cultural rituals. My mother did not engage in any physical activity, not even dancing, and my father was a professional athlete most of his life who turned heads on the dance floor. My mother enjoyed many types of arts and creative engagements, and my father liked getting his intellectual stimulation from his books. Over the years, I and my three siblings observed how they often needed to clarify to each other what a certain gesture, word, or act meant when the other had misunderstood. We also observed how they laughed together, showed up for each other, went out of their way to please each other (like recording a show the other liked), played games with each other (their favorite still is backgammon), and worked to incorporate each other's family of origin. I don't remember ever seeing them kiss on the lips in front of us; but hugs, back rubs, and taking care of the other when they were sick were all common practice. They rarely used their keys to come into the house when they knew someone was at home, and always greeted each other at the door with two kisses on the cheeks.

I remember having conversations with them in which I would ask impertinent questions (as many children do, trying to make sense of the relationships around them). "Why did you marry each other?" Their answers were usually along the lines of, "It was destiny," or "When you feel something in your heart for the other person, you have a strong foundation to build other things." Like the watermelon analogy, it seemed like they were telling me that it was all a matter of luck. I didn't like these elements of unintentionality and chance, so sometimes I would press the issue. "But why *him*? Why *her*?" My mother would say things like, "Your father was handsome, loyal, reliable, and in love." My father would say, "She was beautiful, intelligent, successful, and courageous." In my young mind, I thought that maybe there was more to marriage than destiny, feelings, and luck, but it also seemed like those things were never mentioned unless I asked, as if they were somehow less important than the notes from a secret admirer. It was all very confusing for my young mind.

In most parts of the world today people marry for love, and my parents were no exception. Of course, many of us have at least a vague awareness that other things are also important—things like compatibility, shared interests, and good communication skills—but no one ever questions the idea that love is non-negotiable. And it's not just any love, either. You need to be *in love*. The greater the passion and intensity of that love, the thinking goes, the more likely the marriage will succeed. You will be able to work out your differences and endure any hardship.

We talk about love as if it is the Great Panacea, here to heal personal struggles, cure our existential loneliness, and make us whole. We read about how to find our Soulmate, or how to know that she's The One. We place all our hopes for a lifetime of relational bliss on the feeling of being in love. We tell ourselves that love is all you need, that love can move mountains, that love conquers all. And we expect it to last, and to maintain its intensity, for the life of the couple.

At the same time, most of us today want so much more from committed coupledom than just the feeling of being in love. A soulmate, a helpmate, a roommate, a lover, and a best friend are just a few of the roles our partners are expected to fulfill. We begin our relationships in a swell of passion, holding firmly to the belief that love is enough, and we are so often disappointed when reality fails to live up to our expectations. "He wasn't who I thought he was." "After a while I just sort of lost feelings. It wasn't anybody's fault, it just happened." "I was so in love with them when we married, and now we can hardly get through a day without fighting." "He is so irresponsible it makes me crazy." "She cares about her career more than she cares about me." "My in-laws are impossible."

Love may or may not be all we need, but it is certainly not all we want. Still, we're so committed to the idea of the love-first marriage that any dissenting opinion is immediately shut down. People who marry for resources, or to gain access to the opportunities a partner might provide, are "gold diggers." Even people who marry for compatibility or friendship are seen as "settling." True Love, we believe, is the only viable option. But, let's be honest: How has that served us so far? How has it served *you*?

If you're reading this book, I suspect that you are struggling with some aspect of your romantic relationships. Maybe you're facing some challenges in your relationship that you don't know how to navigate, or you're wondering whether your current partner is a good choice for the long term. Perhaps you've had your heart broken a time or two, or more, and you're struggling to trust that committed coupledom can ever be a mutually satisfying experience.

Of course, being in a fulfilling, supportive relationship isn't just a nice thing to have. Our romantic relationships have a major impact on our lives. Being in unsatisfying relationships is correlated with a whole range of negative physical and mental health outcomes for both partners—high blood pressure, heart disease, depression, and anxiety (to name a few).[1] Children raised by high-conflict couples experience greater psychological distress than those raised by low-conflict couples,[2] and, for most people, divorce and separation are financially destabilizing, particularly to women, and they are frequently devastating to mothers who don't have a college degree.³ Though the statistic that 50 percent of marriages will end in divorce is not exactly true—statistics are skewed by people who marry and divorce many times, as well as by committed couples who do not marry at all—the number does hover around 35 percent.⁴ And what about the miserable marriages that endure, sometimes for decades? Few of us today would categorize that as successful coupledom.

Maybe you're one of the lucky ones: You've hit the relationship jackpot and found the love of your life, and it's been smooth going and seamless ever since. You are reading this book to strengthen your bonds. Fantastic! Or maybe you're pretty sure you know what love is, you're pretty sure you know what it takes to be happy, but each of your last relationships has ended in disappointment, and you aren't sure what you're doing "wrong." Is there really no way to tell what that watermelon is going to look like before I open it up?

Whatever it is that brought you here, I'm so excited to be able to offer you a new way to look at loving relationships—one that is designed to give your heart a break, and not another heartbreak. I believe that mutually satisfying relationships have to be based on more than just luck, chance, or the feeling of being in love. In fact, after more than two decades of working with couples and a decade's worth of research, I think it's safe to say I'm sure of it.

I didn't start out as a researcher. I went to graduate school to become a couples counselor and psychosexual therapist, and I began working with couples in private practice in London. But as my clinical practice developed, I realized that I was not the only one with unanswered questions: How do you know when you've found the one? What should you look for in a partner? What really matters? Why do so many people end up getting divorced? Is love just a feeling, or is there more to it than that? How do you know? That's when I decided to devote my academic life to studying relationships of all kinds, from bedrooms to boardrooms. After completing a master's degree in research methodology, which gave me the skills I needed to make sense of my observations in a more scientific way, I earned a PhD in social psychology to be able to make sense of social constructs and conduct research on a larger scale. Later on, when we moved to California, I did another master's degree in counseling with the focus on marriage and family therapy to deepen my knowledge and update my skills.

I began my study on what would become the Emergent Love Model because I wanted real, evidence-informed answers to my questions about how to cultivate love in committed coupledom. I was looking for a model for loving relationships that included a sense of individual agency, choice, and creativity.

I began my research by conducting a retrospective qualitative analysis of more than 300 couples I had worked with in my global practice in the previous decade. Even today, my clients come from all walks of life and every continent except Antarctica. Some are married, some live together, some are dating, some are single. They are gay and straight and bisexual, cisgender and transgender and genderqueer. They range in age from eighteen to eighty-six. They are monogamous, monogamish,* and polyamorous. There is tremendous variety in terms of their strengths, levels of ability, and resources—financial, physical, and otherwise. The only things they have in common are their humanity, their desire to be in a loving relationship, and the privilege that they offer me to work with them.

As I sifted through the mountain of notes I had taken, certain themes began to crystallize. Words like "trust," "intimacy," and "respect" appeared over and over again. I looked at the problems couples brought to my office, and at the interventions and exercises I offered that seemed to help. I compared the words partners used at the beginning of our work together to the words they used when our work was concluded. I wanted to know what proved to be effective, what didn't, and why.

Part of conducting this research involved framing the right questions. When I stopped asking, "Why do relationships fail?" and started asking, "Why do relationships succeed?" many of the pieces started to fall into place. I realized I needed to understand what successful relationships

---

* Couples in monogamish relationships are emotionally exclusive but have occasional sexual encounters with others outside of their coupledom. The term "monogamish" was first used by the journalist and author Dan Savage (July 2011).

looked like in terms of the partners' behaviors rather than their feelings. Once I had this framework, I was able to isolate and analyze the specific attitudes and behaviors of each partner which, in combination, create a sustainable context for love.

By the time I was finished, I had identified the conditions that must be present so that love has a chance to emerge. In the years that followed, I partnered with the founder of Thinkocrats to conduct a more rigorous quantitative analysis, so that I could be certain that my working hypothesis was supported by concrete evidence. What we found is that relationships based on mutual attraction, respect, trust, and commitment, where partners share a vision for the future and are intentional about the way they express their love, report the greatest levels of satisfaction both within their coupledom and also in their individual lives.

Inspired by the pioneers of Systems Thinking, I started to see that love wasn't a static entity, but rather something that was built and sustained by a couple's day-to-day interactions. In his book *Systems Thinking: Managing Chaos and Complexity,* Jamshid Gharajedaghi talks about love as an emergent entity that comes into being only if all the elements that make it possible are present and the context is nurturing.[5] He gives the example of a spark and a log coming together in a conducive context (the presence of oxygen) to make a fire. As long as these conditions are present, the fire exists, but as soon as you take away even one of the elements, the emergent entity (in this case fire) ceases to exist. Love is the same: It emerges only under the right conditions, and will continue to exist only as long as the conditions that make it possible are present. In other words, if you want to experience all the fulfillment that coupledom can offer, you need to shift your focus from how you feel to how you are and what you do.

This is a far cry from what I was taught about love. Chances are, it isn't what you learned, either. Emergent Love is not just a matter of luck, and it certainly doesn't happen by chance. Instead, Emergent Love is a collaborative effort. It is something that you build with your partner day by day. There are concrete skills involved—like listening, clarifying expectations, and maintaining boundaries—and they can be practiced and mastered over time. It is the hopeful and sustainable alternative to romantic passion that burns hot then fizzles out. Instead of fading over time, Emergent Love gets stronger.

I began researching loving relationships as a way to answer some of my own questions about what it means to love and be loved. As I got deeper into the subject, and the research began to take on a life of its own, I started to think about how I might share some of our findings with others. The first time I presented the results of our research was at Stanford University in 2015. When I was finished, a woman stood up and started clapping and crying at the same time. I was so moved by her emotions that I offered her the mic. She said, "You just reversed everything I ever believed about love! Where were you twenty years ago?" My answer, in utter empathy, was "I was in your shoes twenty years ago."

I was not one of those teenagers who fantasizes about getting married; I actually wasn't even looking for that. I remember when I was fifteen, I read in a magazine that 50 percent of marriages ended in divorce. Later on I learned that this was just a perpetuated misbelief and a mere projection that was made about the marriages that were formed after World War II. At the time I didn't know that and those odds seemed dangerous. My solution? I stopped going to weddings. I couldn't understand why anyone would be foolish enough to want to celebrate them. Marriage, to my fifteen-year-old thinking, was a gamble that was best avoided.

Then I met my husband, Pejman. As in Dr. Pejman Azarmina, a medical doctor and researcher who founded Thinkocrats. As we started dating, I began to reconsider my position on marriage. I set about unlocking "the secret of a happy marriage" and, after I was sure I knew the answers and had a plan in place, we were married. Pejman and I navigated a lot in the first years of our marriage, from graduate schools to multiple immigrations. But the turning point in our relationship, and also the origin story of this research, happened several years into our marriage when I had a panic attack when sharing a ride with my friends. This was definitely not part of the plan.

When I went for a consult with a psychologist, he suggested we take a look at some of my close relationships, especially my marriage; I was deeply offended. How dare he question my perfect relationship! In the months that followed, I came to understand how Pejman and I were fused into each other, as if the two of us had become one entity with one brain and one heart. Immigrating to a whole new country meant that we relied on each other even more, both for practical reasons and also to avoid losing ourselves and our sense of identity in the new context. Our relationship reminded us who we were and what our place was in the world. It was the place we knew.

The long road from fusion and codependence to interdependence took time, and it wasn't always a walk in the park. When we initially started to regain parts of ourselves that we had completely forgone we both felt a sense of loss at times, or anger toward ourselves or the other for letting go of those parts that had made us the individuals we were before we got together. I acknowledge that, as humans, we naturally undergo growth and transformation over time. However, experiencing the loss of key aspects of your identity is an entirely distinct and profound sensation. Sometimes one or both of us felt unseen by the other, and it took a while to figure out how to share ourselves without losing ourselves again. I remember feeling embarrassed that I had not figured it out after all (remember, I had a plan!), and I think we both felt some frustration toward the world, because it seemed like none of the resources we had access to could offer a different path. I once spoke with my father about this and, as usual, he said, "You don't see it? Create it." So I did.

It took that panic attack for me to realize that almost everything I thought I knew about love was wrong. For many of my clients, that moment of clarity happened during the COVID-19 pandemic. The mandate to sequester in place and severely limit contact with people outside one's home put an enormous strain on those living alone, many of whom reported spending days, weeks, and even months with no face-to-face contact. The real damages of skin hunger (insufficient human touch) became one of the topics of conversation in our professional Zoom meetings with colleagues. Partnering up with someone, and being able to make it work, took on a new urgency, and compromises that had once seemed impossible were suddenly more appealing. My client Dave told me, "I'm thirty-six years old, and I haven't touched another human being in three months.

I've had relationships—one for three years in college, one for seven, and this last one for about five—and they were all kind, decent women. But none of them felt like *The One*. Only I'm starting to think that maybe I've been wrong this whole time, looking for something impossible. I don't want to be alone for the rest of my life."

For people who were quarantined with a partner—sometimes referred to as *bisolation*—the cost of the romantic ideal was a little bit different. All the minor pet peeves and annoyances that were easily overlooked pre-pandemic, when there were so many other demands on their time and attention, became horribly magnified under the constant scrutiny of forced togetherness. My client Janie described it to me so poignantly when she said, "It's like how you feel at the end of a great movie. For two hours you've been completely wrapped up in this idyllic world, but then the credits roll, the fluorescent lights come up, and you remember that you're actually in a theater in Queens with your sneakers stuck to the floor and popcorn all over your sweater." Spending six months confined to their tiny apartment, Janie and her wife realized that they had slowly grown apart in the ten years since their wedding. Fortunately for them, the pandemic provided vast stretches of unstructured time together—something they sorely needed but hadn't realized they were missing.

As with everything in life, nothing is all bad or good; real life is in the nuances in between. For some couples, being sequestered together gave them an opportunity to reevaluate and reprioritize their relationship. They were grateful to have someone to quarantine with and began to develop a new appreciation for traits that they hadn't thought about in a while—things like patience, being a good listener, or having a playful sense of humor. Taking care of themselves and each other took on a new significance and underscored their commitment. Some got to observe things for the first time such as how a partner is with the children or, from hearing their work calls, manages stressors at work.

Many others had a very different experience, and the partners discovered that the foundation of their relationship just wasn't strong enough to withstand the pressure. I worked with several couples who asked me to facilitate their separation, because they had finally come face to face with what they had deliberately chosen not to see in their pre-pandemic time by distracting themselves, outsourcing their emotional needs, or avoiding their partner altogether. Many people told me that their near-death experience with potential COVID contraction made them reprioritize and rethink what they wanted from life. Some told me that they were forced to choose one partner to quarantine with and let the other partner(s) go. Some discovered an ongoing affair, some lost their coping mechanisms (traveling, going to the gym, seeing friends) and broke down, and others found their partner's parenting style unacceptable.

We don't have to wait for the next pandemic to start re-examining the way we think of committed coupledom. Within these pages, you'll find timely wisdom for the here and now. Wisdom stands the test of time while gracefully accommodating individual contexts. Whether you are a Baby Boomer, Gen X, Millennial, or Gen Z, I am sure you will find something that strikes a chord with you. As the Persian poet Hafiz said in the fourteenth century: "Every heart deserves the embrace of love, for within it resides the longing to be held by another soul's tender devotion."

My hope is that this book can lead you on a path toward the love you desire *and* deserve. In part one we'll start by deconstructing modern coupledom to see how we fell into our current ideas about romantic love, and why we remain so committed to them. We'll also take a look at the impact this has had on our personal lives and on society as a whole. I'll introduce you to the core findings of our research with thriving couples, present the model of loving relationships that grew out of the research, and explain how the pieces fit together. In part two we'll explore each of the six ingredients of Emergent Love to better understand each one, why it matters, and how it can be cultivated. This section includes an abundance of exercises and practical tools that you can put in place in your relationship right away. I want to say up front that I do not intend for any of these tools to be a one-size-fits-all prescription. Rather, I hope to provide a clear scaffold around which you can shape your own version of what is recommended. I invite you to work through the exercises as suggested first, but don't be afraid to adjust or adapt them so that they can be meaningful for your own life and relationships. Particularly depending on your physical, mental, emotional, or social contexts, you may need to choose to try different versions of what I've suggested—and that's completely okay! As long as the two of you can agree about what is being practiced and why, then you will most likely benefit.

In part three we'll focus on how Emergent Love can support some of the key life arenas and what that looks like in action. I will guide you through some of the daily rituals and happenings of a couple—sex, conflict, and planning the future—to make sure you not only have the material (literacy) but also walk away with a clear idea of how to sustain the love and relationship you have designed (fluency).

I will play multiple roles as I accompany you on this journey. I won't just talk the talk, as your thinking partner, I'll walk you through it step by step. Sometimes I will come in as the expert, sometimes as a facilitator of your thoughts, sometimes I will delegate tasks to deepen your understanding and help you figure things out, and sometimes I will demonstrate how I (or other people) have done things so you have examples to refer to. By the end of this book, you will have the tools and mindset changes you need to stop just surviving in your coupledom and, instead, to thrive in it. There is also a webpage dedicated to further resources which you can access at any time while you are reading *Love by Design.**

It is my firm belief that you deserve a loving relationship. You deserve to experience a coupledom where you feel and see that you are desired, respected, and loved in ways that are meaningful to you. You trust your partner and are trusted by them. You hold a space in your heart for your partner's suffering without being overburdened by it, you give them the benefit of the doubt in any situation, and you know that they will do the same for you. You express your love in ways that are specific and intentional. You have tremendous self-literacy. Your bond is secure; you don't spend time worrying about the relationship. You feel loved, seen, and fulfilled. You can name and refer to why you feel this way instead of referring to an abstract concept, guessing, or hoping.

Drastic and dramatic emotional states are not a baseline in Emergent

---

* www.lovebydesignbook.com

Love—intense rages, sobbing reconciliations, bitter resentments, makeup sex, anxiety about being smothered or abandoned—but this does not mean that it is boring or monotonous. The opposite of tumult is not boredom. It is peace of heart and clarity of mind. It is a continuous yet subtle calibration of needs and resources that maintains equilibrium even as it shifts from day to day. Your interdependency ebbs and flows, like waves at the beach or like the breath moving in and out of your body. You're aware and honest about your needs, desires, and limitations (at least with yourself). You are not striving for excitability, unpredictability, or perfection but for balance, a deep sense of fulfillment, and strength. When something happens to throw you off balance, you are able to resolve the issue and restore it. You have clear boundaries and know where to compromise and when to stand your ground lovingly and firmly.

Like a young child, when your primary bond is secure you are free to turn your focus outward and engage with the world. When people feel emotionally depleted by the drama in their primary relationship, they rarely have the bandwidth for much else. Perhaps this is one reason satisfying relationships are correlated with a whole host of positive outcomes: financial security, professional accomplishment, better physical and mental health, and an overall sense of thriving. Wouldn't it be great if more people could experience these? Let this be a gift from me to you. My liberation is yours. Let's design the love you desire together.

PART I

FALLING IN LOVE

CHAPTER 1

Modern Coupledom

Love is composed of a single soul inhabiting two bodies.

—Aristotle

M ost of us have heard a story that goes something like this: One day, when you least expect it, you will meet a special someone. They will be your Soulmate, The One, your Other Half (or Better Half). They will complete you.

You will know that this is Your Person because of the butterflies in your stomach when you meet them for the first time. You spend some time together, then more time, then all of your time. They really *get* you. You tell each other everything. You've never felt so happy, so alive, so optimistic about the future. You're so in tune you finish each other's sentences. You have so much in common. You can't stop thinking about them. When you feel like you can't get enough, and you can't take your hands off each other, you realize you are *in love*. If it's reciprocated at some level then, after a period, you might move in together. If things continue to go well, you either propose or wait anxiously for a proposal. You get engaged, plan a lavish wedding to celebrate your love, and get married. You trust that your love, as powerful as it is, will endure for all the years that follow, through good times and bad. True love, when you find it, is eternal, and can overcome any obstacle.

I can almost hear some of you scoff or even laugh out loud. "Yeah, right," you say. Nowadays, basic relationship literacy is such that most of us have at least some skepticism when it comes to this romantic ideal. We understand that *Cinderella* is a fairy tale, and we're wise to the ways the media supports and encourages unrealistic expectations of relational bliss. We've come to accept that relationships take work, and we have legions of experts to offer advice for when, inevitably, the butterflies start to wane. There are books, articles, podcasts, reality programs—you name it!—that cover everything from rekindling passion to deciding whose turn it is to cook. Perhaps that's because so few of us feel confident that we know what the real work of a loving relationship entails. How *do* you keep love alive? Romantic partnership has become a job with no job description. We know we need to put in time and effort, but what exactly are we supposed to be doing? And what are we putting in to build what we want to build?

Committed coupledom has undergone dramatic changes in the past century, and an increasing number of people no longer see a marriage license as an absolute requirement for cohabitation, or starting a family, or emigrating together, or purchasing property—things that would have been well outside the norm even fifty years ago. Today we marry later or not at all, choosing to dispense with the legalities and express our commitment in other ways. We needn't share the same religion, racial identity, ethnic or cultural background, education level, socioeconomic status, or heteronormative identity. The institution of marriage has expanded in many places to include same-sex and genderqueer couples who can increasingly expect all of the benefits of legally acknowledged partnership.

All these changes have something in common: They are inclusive and serve to expand the range of options for love-based commitment. Today we are more free to follow our hearts and partner for love than ever before in human history.

We believe deeply in true love, and this belief is reflected and reinforced in everything from our legal system to the fairy tales we read to kids. And let's face it: Most of us, deep down, still long for that perfect other who will complete our lives. We delight in the feeling of falling in love, and we want it in our lives. But does it serve us to believe that love conquers all? That it offers us the best possible foundation for a lifelong partnership?

In this chapter I hope to do three things. First, I want to engage you in a critical examination of romantic love. If being in love is non-negotiable for committed relationships, it's probably a good idea to explore this slippery concept. Second, I want to take you on a brief historical tour of some of the origins of our modern ideals of committed coupledom. The way we think about love and partnership is deeply embedded in our social and historical context. Understanding what we mean by love, the language we attach to it, and where those ideas came from is a necessary beginning for all the chapters that follow. Finally, we'll take a look at the state of coupledom today. What does it mean to be a partner? What is that supposed to look like, and how is it supposed to feel? Let's dig in.

WHAT DO WE TALK ABOUT WHEN WE TALK ABOUT LOVE?

In a thought-provoking TED talk, French philosopher Yann Dall'Aglio asks, "What is love? It's a hard term to define in so far as it has a very wide application. I can love jogging. I can love a book, a movie. I can love escalope. I can love my wife."[1] We use the word *love* to describe an infinite variety of relationships with both animate and inanimate objects. Obviously, here we're talking about romantic love—the kind of love that leads to committed partnership—rather than the love we feel for dogs or friends or ice cream. But narrowing our focus does little to simplify the definition of love.

When clients tell me they are in love, I like to ask, "How do you know?" There is often a pause as people really consider this question, sometimes for the very first time. Many reply, "I don't know how I know; I just know. It just feels so right. I'm so happy." Others report a kind of mysterious and indescribable physical, mental, and emotional state of being that they have come to identify as being in love: part obsession and part euphoria with a lot of sexual desire in the mix. "I can't stop thinking about her," "I want to be with them all the time," "I can't take my hands off of him," "I'm out of control." And though some people speak of certain qualities in the beloved that they perceive to be valuable, like intelligence, kindness, and physical beauty, almost everyone eventually circles back to the way they *feel*. Being in love is most frequently described in early relationships as a *feeling*.

Over the years, as I've listened to thousands of people describe their own personal experience of falling in love, certain ideas appear over and over again.

1. *Romantic love is something that just happens to you.* Falling in love is beyond our control, and in this way it is fundamentally passive. Love cannot be willed or demanded. The heart wants what it wants.

2. *Love is all-encompassing.* It is not enough to love someone, we must be "in love" with them. Through love we are transformed. Love, in this case, is more than a feeling; it is a state of being. There is a tinge of obsession, even madness, that accompanies romantic love. We are not ourselves.

3. *Love is dangerous.* Love is passionate, volatile, and unpredictable, which makes it dangerous and exciting at the same time. We do crazy things in the name of love. What's more, romantic love always includes the risk that our beloved might not return the feeling, or might not return it with enough intensity, or in the right way, or for a long enough time. When this happens the pain is indescribable. Our hearts are broken.

4. *Love is all you need.* Romantic love is capable of overcoming all obstacles both within and outside of the relationship—it transcends both interpersonal problems and also social conventions. Nothing, we believe, can or should stand in the way of True Love.

Taken individually, none of the items on this list seems especially bizarre or nonsensical. But when you consider them as a whole, suddenly love sounds like a highly unstable state of being that is both completely beyond your control and also the single most important criterion for your future happiness. *Indescribable pain? Fundamentally passive?*

What?

This is the essential paradox of modern coupledom: Love is both unstable and also the best possible foundation for lifelong commitment. It is idealized and idealistic while also being an ordinary part of everyday life. We talk of love as being dangerous, painful, and unpredictable, and in the same breath we talk of love as a kind of safe haven where we feel accepted and understood. Falling in love is a spontaneous event that just happens, but maintaining love takes intentional effort. Love is easy. Love is the hardest entity in the world. It is both exquisite and exquisitely painful.

Our thinking about romantic love is really all over the place. Perhaps this is why we have a tendency to talk about it in such ambiguous ways. Like Rumi's tale of the elephant in the dark, we can only describe one part of the whole. We use myths and parables, classic fairy tales and the modern fairy tales of Hollywood and social media, to try to grasp and deconstruct the possible meanings. One of the ways we try to make meaning is through the use of metaphors. We may not know what love *is*, but we can always talk about what it's *like*.

In the book *Metaphors We Live By*, George Lakoff and Mark Johnson explore the notion that we use metaphors to help us conceptualize ideas that are otherwise difficult to understand.[2] Our lived experience is reflected in these metaphors, and they help us make sense of the world. At the same time, our lived experience is directly *shaped* by these metaphors. After hearing the stories so many times, we *expect* love to "just happen" to us, to change us, to break our hearts, to be a roller coaster, to be all-consuming.

One phrase that really captures the passivity and chance that we've built up in our romantic ideals is "falling in love." Think about it. Falling is accidental, unplanned, sudden, and often painful. It happens against our will when we're not paying attention.[3] This is how we describe a new relationship, and what we have come to expect. We don't choose love, at least not initially. And we "fall out of love" in much the same way. Today partners say they've "lost feelings" for each other, as though love you experience toward another human being is no more robust than the love you once had for a favorite sweater—something so fragile it is subject to

change on a whim, or may even vanish completely. How many relationships end with the phrase "I love you, but I'm not in love with you anymore"? Lakoff and Johnson take a slightly different view of this passivity
with the metaphor that love is magical: In love we are spellbound, hyp-
notized, entranced, bewitched.[4] The metaphor of being struck by Cupid's
arrow is another manifestation of the idea that love is largely passive.

In the West, and particularly in the United States, where we place
such a high value on individual freedom, it seems incredible that so many
people gladly embrace the idea that, when it comes to love, we have no
choice. The capricious nature of love becomes a scapegoat and an excuse
for all sorts of behavior that otherwise would be unacceptable. We break
our commitments, stay with partners who batter or humiliate us, and justify otherwise toxic relationships. We kill in the name of love, act up in
the name of love, come together in the name of love, and divorce in the
name of love. Being in love becomes the universal justifier for all actions,
both rational and irrational.

If all this sounds irrational, it's supposed to. Love makes us crazy. We
think about our beloved all the time. We don't eat, don't sleep, and feel
like we can do anything. We are euphoric, elated, insane. The ancient
Greeks called this type of love *mania*. In fact, falling in love looks a lot
like the mania of bipolar disorder, with its elevated mood, inflated self-
esteem, decreased need for sleep, persistent and intrusive thoughts, pressure to keep talking, distractibility, agitation, and excessive involvement
in pleasurable activities.[5] In Arabic, al-*hoyam* describes passion that has
drifted into obsession, madness, and total loss of reason.[6] In Hindi, *asakti*
translates roughly into being lost in or consumed by love.[7] Everyone, from
Plato to Patsy Cline, Mike Batt, and Beyoncé knows that love makes you
crazy.

One of the more damaging metaphors that both reflects and shapes
our expectations of love is the association between love and pain. Let's
really consider this one for a minute: We expect love to be painful. In
1975 the Scottish hard rock band Nazareth released their single "Love
Hurts."[8] It became an international hit, the number one song in six countries and the band's only song to go platinum and make it to the US

Top 10; it stayed on the Norwegian chart for more than a year.[9] Love hurts when it is unrequited, when we are separated from our beloved, when we fight, when we misunderstand each other, when we are betrayed, and most especially when it ends. People come to my office physically ill with heartache, doubled over in pain, and say, "I must really love him if it hurts this bad."

Writer Mandy Len Catron puts it this way: "In love we fall. We are struck; we are crushed; we swoon. We burn with passion. Love makes us crazy, and it makes us sick; our hearts ache, and then they break."[10] Catron has a point. If the way we talk about love not only reflects our experiences but also helps to shape them, what does it mean that we all accept the idea that pain is part of love? Think how different it would be if, instead, we believed the opposite: Love is not supposed to hurt.

The idea that love is unstable, even dangerous, is the logical outcome of the view that love is both beyond our control and also potentially devastating. Falling in love is like being struck by lightning. We talk about love as a whirlwind, a storm, a tornado. Love is a derailed train that has gone off the tracks, a ship in a storm. We are cautioned to put on the brakes because we are going too fast. We use metaphors that are violent and combative: We are winners and losers on a battlefield. We make advances, strategize, conquer, and are conquered in turn. We are annihilated, obliterated, destroyed. Perhaps the danger is part of what makes the experience of modern love so intense. Our anxiety around it mobilizes and sometimes paralyzes us!

In case you can't tell by now, I am fascinated by language. I love to explore the nuances, the way our words shape cognition, and the evolution of ideas as they are traced through language. The idea of a soulmate, for instance, first appears in Plato's *Symposium* in the form of a parable. Socrates explains that human beings originally had two heads, four arms, and four legs. They were cleft in two by an angry Zeus, and so we are forever forced to search the world for our other half. Mythology is filled with these kinds of stories, and many of our most dearly held beliefs can be traced back through millennia.

Despite love being seen as a maddening, painful, and dangerous force that we cannot control, the idea that true love is transcendent and enduring has persisted for centuries. Love is the only criteria for modern coupledom that is both necessary and also sufficient. More practical matters, like where to live, how to earn and spend money, what to experience and what to build, matter less than the existence of love. Dramatic differences in temperament, social class, interests, education level, earning capacity, religious beliefs, cumulative impact of past traumatic experiences, and anything else you can think of can all be overcome if there is enough love. There is a kind of bizarre logic that emerges from this belief that true love is all you need for a relationship to last forever: If true love can never die, then if it dies it must not have been true love. The objection proves the rule. Our metaphors provide some insight into *how* we conceptualize romantic love, but they tell us little about *why* we think of love in this way. In order to answer that question we have to go back in time, all the way back, and start by looking at how we evolved as a species. Love is in our DNA.

THE BIOLOGY OF UNION

Biologically speaking, we humans are hardwired to arrange ourselves into pairs. In evolutionary terms, pair bonding meant survival for *Homo sapiens*. Our ancestors who bonded into couples increased the chances that their offspring would survive, and those genes were passed on to the next generation. While other species developed fur and feathers, teeth and claws and gills, we developed communities (and also gigantic brains). In the words of author Mark Manson, "At some point during evolution between plankton and Bon Jovi, apes evolved the ability to become emotionally attached to one another."[11] Attachment is part of our biology.

Sex, too, is part of our biology. Intense physical attraction is powerful stuff. It's part anxiety and part excitement—I call it "nervited"—and it feels significantly different than our baseline: anxious because you don't know what might come out of it and excited because you want to go ahead and find out anyway. If these moments of sexual reactivity happen in the right place (a friend's wedding, say, or across the room at a nightclub) and they include a person who also happens to be available and interested and physically attracted to you, it can feel like you've just won the lottery. What typically follows is all the heady excitement and obsessiveness that we have come to identify with "being in love" or "love at first sight."

Dr. Helen Fisher is an anthropologist who studies sexual chemistry at the biological level. She calls this stage "sexual infatuation."[12] Some people only stay with this feeling for a night or two; others continue for a more extended time and have what we call a "honeymoon phase." We feel invincible in our coupledom as our brains experience an explosion of passion and lust, marked by the chemical release of phenylethylamine—also known as one of the "feel good" hormones—which in turn increases levels of endorphins, dopamine, and norepinephrine. Simply put, we feel *great*. In fact, we feel so great that we aggrandize our partner's more positive traits (she's so generous!), minimize their more negative ones (she spent her student loan on a motorcycle for her friend!), and enter into a mental and emotional state that somewhat resembles a range of clinical diagnoses of mental health issues.[13] We think about our beloved all the time, stop noticing if we're tired or hungry, have seemingly limitless energy, and feel like we can do anything. Our brains light up with a rush of dopamine. We crave more and more of this feeling. We never want it to end. Today we talk about being addicted to love, and we're not far off the mark. In this phase, sexual encounters happen within this nutrient-rich broth of neurotransmitters, and you get something that feels incredible. Dopamine, in addition to increasing pleasure, also can increase testosterone, which, in both men and women, amplifies sexual desire.[14]

If all this sounds good to you, you're not alone. There is something about being swept away, overcome, recklessly verging on out of control, that we recognize on a primal level as something we want because it feels so overwhelmingly good. Yet romantic love is far more complicated than sexual attraction and the initial chemistry that we feel with someone. Yes, we evolved to bond, to mate, and to reproduce, and all this hormonal activity ensures that we will. But how did we come to identify this specific physiological phenomenon as love? Why not simply call it lust and be done with it? That part is far more complicated.

THE EVOLUTION OF MODERN COUPLEDOM

Though many of our ideas about love are uniquely Western and originated in Europe, the idea of coupledom is universal. In cultures across the world, I have observed that there is a strong distinction between a person who has ever been in a romantic relationship or married and one who has remained single. In cemeteries across the Middle East and in some African countries, the graves of the unmarried and "unfulfilled" are decorated differently than those who died with the privilege of experiencing loving connection and consummated their marriage at least once. In Kurdistan, the gravestone of an unmarried person (presumably a virgin) is decorated with black and red nets to differentiate them from the graves of those considered more fortunate. The best wish one could receive was (and this is still true in many cultures) to find someone and settle down, share your life, and keep each other company. And the worst curse was (and still is in many cultures) to end up lonely and unloved. Marriage, or committed coupledom, is a milestone on the path to adulthood that is universally recognized and celebrated. Why is that?

The idea of the love-based marriage, which the vast majority of us subscribe to, is actually a fairly recent development in human history and is uniquely Western (though it has been exported to and absorbed by much of the world at this point). The first *Homo sapiens* appeared roughly 300,000 years ago, but our current ideas about romantic love date back only to the eleventh century and the emergence of *amour courtois,* or courtly love, among European nobility.

A thousand years ago (the blink of an eye in evolutionary terms), marriage was primarily a political and practical decision aimed at forging alliances and ensuring paternity. Marital sex was all about procreation, and passion was reserved for extramarital affairs as it was considered far too destructive for marriage. Courtly love transformed the lustful passion of illicit sex by ennobling it with ideas like virtue, honor, and respect. The result was that sex and love became inextricably attached in a way they never had been before, and romance was born. It's important to note here that courtly love still remained outside the bonds of holy matrimony—though the lovers might be married, they were not married to each other.

In the book *Talk of Love*, sociologist Ann Swidler traces modern love back in time to try to understand the way we talk about love today. She explains that the courtly lover was besieged with a sudden and intense passion for an idealized other. This love transformed the lover, whose feelings could be proven by acts of virtue and honor. And because the beloved was usually married to someone else, the love was forbidden, causing the lovers to defy social conventions in order to pursue fulfillment.

Does this sound familiar? Courtly love was involuntary, idealistic, all-encompassing, life-altering, virtuous, and worthy of any and all sacrifices. It remained an idealized version of love among European nobility for centuries. Then, in the late 1700s, the industrial revolution in Europe heralded both the rise of capitalism and the emergence of a bourgeois middle class. Ann Swidler believes that these two forces transformed courtly love, this time introducing individualism and choice into the mix. Love became a matter of integrity, a clear and unwavering choice for a specific other, a one and only.[15] Courtly love became True Love and was invited into the confines of matrimony and marked by permanent exclusivity. By the mid 1800s, Jane Austen and Charlotte Brontë were rewarding their heroines' virtue and integrity with happy and successful marriages, often to very wealthy men (though never *because* they were very wealthy men). The idea of marriage based on romantic love has besieged us ever since.

In fact, our basic assumptions about romantic love have changed very little since the 1850s. Philosopher Simon May, in his brilliant book *Love: A History*, suggests that a time-traveler from the nineteenth century would have no trouble with our modern ideas about love, though he would recognize little else about modern life. Our ideas about parenting, sexual orientation, freedom, the role of women, race, religion, and art have all evolved; only love remains unchanged.[16] We are, in fact, so convinced of this version of love that we refuse to consider any others. Laura Kipnis, in her book *Against Love: A Polemic*, argues that the rigidness of our ideas limits discourse rather than freeing it. She asks, "Isn't there something a bit worrisome about all this uniformity of opinion? Is this the one subject about which no disagreement will be entertained, about which one truth alone is permissible?"[17]

ROMANTIC LOVE IN THE MODERN AGE

Did you ever wonder why it is that we remain so committed to the romantic ideal of marrying for love, even as our actual marriages fall apart? Perhaps it is because the romantic ideals of the 1850s just aren't up to the demands of modern coupledom.

Once upon a time, in most countries throughout the post-industrial Western world, people married within a few years of completing their education. They left their childhood homes to create a new family that was financially separate. According to the US Census Bureau,[18] in 1950 the *average* age at marriage was twenty for women and twenty-two for men. For the generation born between 1930 and 1950, the traditional markers associated with adulthood had usually been achieved by the time they were twenty-five: They had finished school, found full-time employment that paid a livable wage (if they were men), were married, had children, and lived independently from their parents—though often geographically nearby. Gender roles were strictly enforced, with middle-class women performing unpaid labor in the home and men performing paid labor outside the home until they retired, usually with a pension provided by their employer.

In most of the world today, that is the exception rather than the rule. Urbanization, globalization, the rising costs of higher education and housing, and wages that have failed to keep up with the cost of living have made the single-income nuclear family virtually impossible, financially speaking, for anyone under thirty (and for most people over thirty as well).

In addition to these dramatic socioeconomic shifts, the way we partner has also undergone a profound change. Marriage, as an institution, has been on the rocks in the United States for decades. The introduction of birth control pills in 1960 separated sex and reproduction. Before then, engaging in premarital sex had such disastrous consequences (pregnancy, single parenthood, social ostracism, forced marriage, maternal death) that people avoided it—not by remaining abstinent, but by marrying young. Today, rather than being a gateway to sex, marriage is more likely to be seen as the end of sexual freedom. The decade after the pill was introduced we saw the legalization of the "no fault" divorce, in 1969, which allowed partners to leave a marriage *without evidence of mistreatment*. The civil rights movement, the women's movement, gay rights, and free love became the cultural zeitgeist of the 1960s and 1970s in the United States and around the world. Sex had broken free of the bonds of marriage, and has remained at liberty ever since. The average age at marriage has crept up incrementally over the years, right alongside these larger cultural shifts. By 2022, the average age at marriage was twenty-eight for women and thirty for men.[19]

One of the results of all this change is that we have freed ourselves of the strict gender roles of the past. Women have more power today than ever before in history, and most expect an egalitarian partnership in which their own needs, goals, and ambitions are given equal importance. On the heels of the #MeToo movement, we have clarified new boundaries around sexual encounters even beyond the borders of romantic partnerships. Just as women are no longer stuck at home, men are increasingly invited back into the home. Most men no longer assume they'll have to be the sole breadwinner for the family and spend the vast majority of their adult lives at work. Today being a husband or a father is a hands-on affair, and most men expect to participate in activities involving caring for children and maintaining the home. Anyone can change a diaper, mop the floor, or be the primary earner—something same-sex couples have known for years. Furthermore, fulfilling the role of a parental figure does not require being a man or a woman, either.

It has been decades since marriage was seen as a sacred vow of life-long commitment meant to ensure procreation, property rights, and social acceptance.[20] Today many of us enter relationships for their own sake, and we expect them to be mutually satisfying, fair, and rewarding.[21] But these very ideals also make our relationships more fragile.[22] Almost no one today sees committed partnership as a social contract between two people embedded in their community and society. Traditional communities have eroded, and we are increasingly mobile and increasingly isolated. Today many couples are *alone together* instead, and look only to each other for most of their needs. And our needs are legion.

Single people today approach relationships with a list of criteria that would have made our grandparents laugh. In addition to romance, sexual chemistry, and the thrill of falling in love, we also look to our partners for stability, companionship, friendship, sanctuary, financial security, and an equitable division of labor and resources. Our partners are meant to be both best friend and passionate lover, confidant, business partner, co-parent, confessor, personal assistant, social organizer, witness, playmate, and soulmate. We look for unconditional love, forgiveness, total transparency, emotional support, and a collaborator to help us process our deep feelings and heal our trauma. And we want that most elusive quality of all: happiness.

In the past fifty years the demands placed on romantic love have increased exponentially. Simon May argues that we now look to love to provide what was once provided by religion: love that is unconditional, eternal, and "the ultimate source of belonging and redemption."[23] It is no wonder that so many couples collapse under the weight of all these expectations.

Though we may still be willing to suffer for love, we are no longer willing to suffer for marriage. Our relationships today have to last only as long as we feel in love. And when we reach a state that we are no longer in love, as we inevitably do, we become disillusioned. We question our choice of partner and conclude that perhaps it's time to cut our losses and try with someone new. And there are so many options out there.

Online dating has increased our access to potential mates (or extramarital liaisons) by a factor of thousands. We now have seemingly infinite choices when it comes to finding a new partner, which feeds into the idea that maybe we'll have better luck with someone else. Most of our parents only had access to a handful of suitable mates: people they met at school or on the job, friends of friends, or maybe a stranger they met in a bar or coffee shop. Today we have dating apps so loaded with potential mates that we actually need to filter the selection.

A NEW ROMANTIC FRONTIER

With the emergence of artificial intelligence, we are moving from the Eliza Effect (people often tend to interpret more meaning from computer-generated strings of symbols, like words, than what is actually there)[24] to using generative AI chatbots such as Replika that learn from the user about them and act as their companion. Do you remember the movie HER that was released in 2013 where Theodore (played by Joaquin Phoenix) fell in love with Samantha, an enchanting voice of an operating system (played by Scarlett Johansson)? A decade later, this is no longer a sci-fi fantasy. People are really finding romance and marriages with AIs. Rosanna Ramos, a thirty-six-year-old mother from the Bronx, New York, was the first person reported to have married the AI-powered boyfriend Eren Kartal, whom she created in 2022. Ramos is still dating in the real world, too. Maybe outsourcing our needs for emotional bond to an AI knight in shining armor, and leaving the rest to our coupledoms, will be the norm in the future!

It is wonderful not to be limited by proximity when we choose a partner, but it is also overwhelming. It is so much easier to choose the best of three options than to choose the best of 10,000 options. Our human brains are not made for this level of filtering. The dizzying array of decisions we make every day (for everything from shampoo to dinner to partners) is not only overwhelming, it also promotes dissatisfaction. In the book *The Paradox of Choice*, Barry Schwartz explains that the more choices you have, the more likely you are to be dissatisfied, because you will always wonder about the missed opportunities and what-ifs rather than the positive aspects of the choice you did make.[25] Perhaps this is why so many newly decoupled partners have a tendency to reach back in time to reacquaint themselves with former lovers, thinking, "If I had married Jack instead of Jane maybe I wouldn't be so unhappy."

We are so committed to the ideals of romantic love that we cling to them even when our partnerships fail, repeatedly, to live up to the fantasy. Rather than questioning the model, we reject the partnership, declare that the love wasn't "true enough," and try again with someone new, hoping for a better outcome.

If anything, the idea of romantic love as the basis of marriage has become *more* popular since the 1960s, not less. In 1967, researchers found that 75 percent of women (and 35 percent of men) would marry a person who had all the qualities they were looking for in a partner even if they were not in love; by 1984 that number was down to 20 percent for both men and women.[26] Four out of five adults would not marry someone unless they were "in love," even if that person was otherwise a great fit. It seems our parents and grandparents may have believed in romance back in the late sixties, but they didn't believe that it was the sole criterion for marriage.

Today, marrying for love, and love alone, has become a mandate. Anything else is suspect. Those who marry for money or status are derided as "gold diggers." Those who marry for the opportunities or other resources a partner might provide are accused of being mercenary. And those who turn down a potential partner because they are looking for compatibility in education, socioeconomic class, ethnic and racial belonging, immigration status, and career prospects are equally cold and calculating. Those foolish enough to admit to "ulterior motives" become targets of our collective derision.

A couple of years ago, while visiting my esteemed colleagues Elaine Hatfield and Richard Rapson (the authors of *Love and Sex: Cross-Cultural Perspectives*) at the University of Hawaii, Dr. Hatfield shared her experience this way: "You can tell people what will work or not all you want. You can even show them the research. They're still going to want the thrill of being in love, getting their hearts broken, and getting up and doing it all over again!" If this is your choice, I will cheer you all the way. But I'm writing these words so you know that it is possible to choose otherwise. There is another way. I honestly think love should give your heart a break, not another heartbreak!

The idea of wanting love in our lives is not new, but we do need new narratives to match and express our current experiences in our modern lives. There is so much that we hold on to from old narratives that has no merit in our lives. Most of us would rather take the road that is already there, even if it's full of potholes that will give us flat tires, than to create one that actually suits our vehicle and the speed we want to operate in. Do you still tell your children to eat their carrots because they're good for your eyes? Well, carrots are a super source of beta-carotene, which is a type of vitamin A; however, the idea that they are a super-vegetable that will keep your vision healthy is a leftover from World War II propaganda that still gets circulated like a fact. Do you still think your child is hyperactive because they had sugar, or that cracking your knuckles will give you arthritis? Do you still religiously drink eight glasses of water a day? These are all fictions disguised as facts, and none are backed up by evidence from solid scientific research. These misbeliefs are perpetuated within societies like invasive shrubs; they catch us all at different times and find their ways into our belief system. One time I received a gift of a matchbox with the caption, "Every time you masturbate, God kills a kitten." Some people still fact-check this with me when I am interviewed.* Hopefully, you have researched this one on your own and know it to be false, or there would be no kittens left on earth.

With this in mind, I want to ask you to do something for me: Suspend your current beliefs, just for a moment. Set aside what you think love is supposed to look like, what you've been taught or told or have read online about how to get a man or how to drive women wild or how to make anyone fall in love with you. What I'm about to tell you is most likely *not* what you were taught. So try to keep an open mind as we explore, together, the meaning of love. I promise your life and pursuit of love will never be the same!

---

* I first heard this in Mexico when I was given a matchbox that had this written on it! The phrase originally appeared in 1996 as the headline "Fact: Every Time You Masturbate, God Kills a Kitten. How Many More Have to Die?" along with a kitten photo, on the cover of *The Gonzo*, a satirical publication produced by students at Georgetown University.

CHAPTER 2

A New Model: Emergent Love

Life is the flower for which love is the honey.
— Victor Hugo

In the performance that won her the title of American Idol in 2002, Kelly Clarkson sang passionately about finding true love after waiting for so long. The song, "A Moment Like This," is an anthem for modern love.[1] But when this doesn't happen, or it doesn't happen in exactly this way, I am left sitting with people in my office in pain, in confusion, trying to find a glimmer of hope to help them move forward.

As you are reading through these words, it must be obvious to you that as a social psychologist I am always interested in how our experiences and expressions of love are shaped and whether they are serving us in our relational spaces or not. But as someone who works with individuals in search of a lifelong partner as well as couples in crisis, I also see the results of our romantic ideals up close and personal. What I have observed is that our large-scale cultural confusion around love directly impacts our individual experiences in loving relationships, and usually not in a pleasant way.

It is heartbreaking to watch people try to navigate the aftermath of basing the most important decision of their lives on a feeling. Only when the relationship starts to break down do they begin to acknowledge the red flags, many of which were there from the beginning. Some are practicalities that seemed minor at first: One expects to spend every weekend together, the other wants to go solo camping; one is nomadic and likes to move every few years, while the other has lived in the same city all his or her life; one wants to stay home full-time and the other expects a second income; one comes from wealth, the other struggled to make ends meet; one is messy, the other tidy; one saves easily, one spends easily. And there are often deeper misalignments around values attached to commitment, fidelity, religion, cultural identifications, parenting, the role of the family of origin, political ideologies, work, and money. Things that seemed unimportant in the first flush of romance can become huge problems later on. The passion that was supposed to smooth over all the bumps has proven insufficient to the task at hand. Elna and Josh are a good illustration of this type of early-stage disillusionment.

1 + 1 = 1: A LOVE STORY

When Josh and Elna first walked into my office in New York, they were hand-in-hand, all laughter and smiles. As they approached the couch I have for my clients, they were mindful of each other, offering the other first dibs on seating. They were comfortable together, and soon with me, too. Elna even asked if she could take off her shoes and put her feet up.

Elna and Josh had been together for almost three years. As they told me the story of their courtship, they continued to hold hands, smiling at their happy memories. But when they got to the part of the story that brought them to my office, the sense of levity left the room. For so long, they had been wrapped up in what they'd thought was the warm embrace of love. They shared a love of travel and had spent a lot of time having adventures. In fact, they spent so much of their time together that they felt disoriented when apart. They didn't see the need (nor did they have the desire) to be with their other friends, so, over time, they only got invited to couples' gatherings, and their individual friends didn't include them in events as much as before. This was fine with them because they preferred to be together anyway. They both worked full-time and kept their spare time for each other. "This is what it means to be in a loving relationship, isn't it?" They'd gotten to a point where what mattered to one person automatically mattered to the other, so much so that they no longer knew whose idea it was in the first place. You may have felt this at some point in your life, too. Many of us do, especially at the beginning of a relationship when the urge to merge is very strong.

But now, although they acknowledged loving each other, they worried that they were no longer *in love*. Elna had tears in her eyes as she told me about this shift in their relationship. She thought she had found her soulmate, and now she was not so sure. As she shared her doubts with me, she curled into herself on the couch away from Josh. Josh, for his part, felt compelled to comfort Elna. At the same time, he was dealing with his own sorrow. Lately, he had been feeling rejected in the life they had built for themselves. And in the retelling of their story, he was feeling rejected anew.

Their pain was so familiar to me. I have seen it over and over again in my office as I witness the grief and sorrow that couples share in our conversations. I wanted to give Josh and Elna a different way of thinking about their coupledom—beyond just talking about it with me—so I invited them to disengage from language and engage with their visual senses instead. Sometimes shifting the focus of our engagement from words to images (or other sensory input) also helps clients to shift the way they see their situation.

I presented them with a variety of images to choose from to show how their love used to feel. They selected an illustration of two astronauts, hand in hand, lost in space and surrounded by a giant heart. They explained that this image captured that floating feeling both had experienced at the beginning of their relationship—a sense that they were so in love their feet barely touched the ground. Instead, they'd glided along in a protective "love bubble." As long as they were safely ensconced in this love bubble, they didn't think much about the future or worry about where they were going. Elna sighed. "I was not initially taken by Josh. He's not my type, but our sexual chemistry was great and he was so persistent and loving that eventually I felt the spark. I really want that back."

I asked them when they first noticed the change, and they said it was all gradual. Using the astronaut image, they shared that they began to drift apart when their feet started to touch the ground again. Elna became distant and detached, almost depressed. She was seeing her own therapist when we met. She mainly cuddled with their dog and cried more often. Josh noticed that something was off. Elna was not interested in being physically close, touch became less and less frequent, and even when they were making love it felt distant and cold.

"Elna," I asked, "what is it that brings you joy?" She glanced at Josh as if looking for the answer. "I am asking you," I said, giving her a gentle nudge, "not Josh." She struggled to find an answer. They both struggled. Neither of them could remember a time when either had done something that was purely for him- or herself, something that did not involve the other or was not for the other. I see this way too often in my office: people who have merged so completely with each other that they've lost track of who they are as individuals.

Many of us learn that this is what real love is supposed to look like. If we feel differently than the other or like something different, it is a sign of divergence and lack of unity. What we are not taught is that there are many, many ways to organize a relationship, and that we can have a lot of choices in how we build our love. Because of the stories we've been told about love and romance, we may imagine that all successful relationships should look and feel the same. But they don't! In any one relationship, there are three active parts: you, your partner, and the coupledom. How you arrange those three is completely up to you and will depend on the context that you live and operate in.

Some of the most common relational models that emerged from my research look like the seven types illustrated below. Almost everyone who works with me will, at some point, see a laminated sheet that looks like the image below. I find it incredibly helpful both to understand where we are and to create a pathway for where we want to be. See if it resonates with you as well. It is good to have a framework.

When I offer these diagrams to couples, I rely heavily on the visual aspect of the images. In setting goals for our work, I ask them to identify

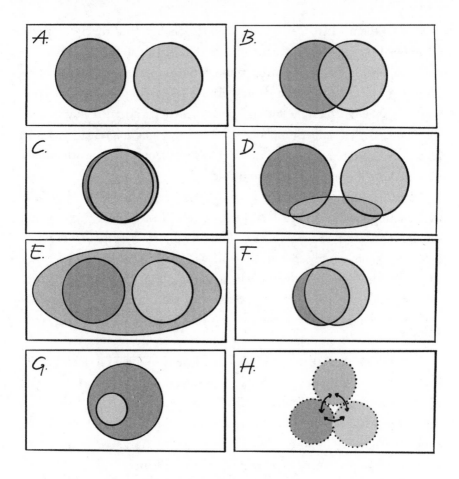

where they think their coupledom is and then where they want to see themselves if our work is successful. Sometimes partners choose different models, which gives us a starting point for conversations about expectations and the vision that each has for their coupledom. As you read this, think about which of these models describes your own relationship (whether actual or aspirational). Would your partner pick the same?

For our purposes, and for the sake of clarity, I gave each dynamic a name and a brief description so you can remember it easily. These configurations will reappear throughout our time together here.

A. **Friends with benefits:** These partnerships are usually shaped around sharing experiences, and commitment to building something shared is notably absent. Individuals maintain total independence. The currency exchanges are often clear and understood by both parties (for example, sex, adventure, plus one in social engagements, sounding board, financial backups). They can usually continue until one party decides to exit the agreement for reasons such as one person meeting a new partner, one person wanting more, etc.

B. **Contemporary couples:** This is the most popular visual chosen by post-honeymoon, long-term couples. This is what mad and passionate romance is expected to become as it mellows over time in its ideal form. Partners have some independence with some shared space—this can be what they manage together or their interests and feelings—but not much of a sense of their coupledom as a separate entity. These relationships tend to involve a lot of negotiating when boundaries become blurred around power dynamics, allocation of resources, and division of labor, particularly if there are children (or other labor-intensive projects or people) involved. Tensions around fairness and equality are common.

C. **Submerged couples:** Partners have very low levels of autonomy and primarily identify as one half of a couple. Individuals tend to have a less developed sense of self and difficulty establishing and maintaining boundaries. Typical of early relationship infatuation, these couples risk developing codependent dynamics over time if they don't evolve to more of an interdependent status.

D. **Leftover couples:** Two groups fall into this category. The first consists of partners who maintain high levels of independence. Resources of time, energy, attention, and money are prioritized to the individual partners rather than to the couple. They may seem like the golden couples who "have it all" in their social circles and on social media, but they often feel disconnected from each other on an intimate level. The second group are the couples whose competing priorities are not a matter of choice but are a matter of context; they can only give each other and their relationship whatever they have left. Both groups see their relationship as a separate entity from themselves but relegate it to just one more item on the to-do list.

E. **Constitutionally bound couples:** This is most typical of long-term coupledom in collectivistic societies where the approval, welfare, and judgment of the community supersede the individual. Roles are usually clearly defined, and there is a high level of determination to stay together. The relationship is deeply embedded within the couple's community, and it often serves a higher purpose, whether demanded (e.g., in collectivistic cultures or tight-knit kinship and family groups), created (e.g., perfect couple on social media, public image for public figures), needed (e.g., financial arrangements, social status, or sense of self-worth), or enforced (e.g., orthodox and/or very religious groups and in the case of immigrants who need this to stay in the country). Forgiveness, tolerance, and acceptance exist at high levels, and the survival of the relationship as a whole is stressed above the needs of the individual.

F. **Get-in-where-you-fit-in couples:** In these relationships, one person goes out of their way to accommodate the other's needs, wants, and lifestyle. In most cases, there is barely enough expectation of mutuality and reciprocity to call this configuration a relationship since, by definition, relationships require both. High levels of doubt and frustration are common from the party required to be the most flexible, as are threats to leave. In this dynamic, the couple's relationship expectations are not aligned (e.g., one wants more quality time and wants to be prioritized while the other believes what is offered is sufficient and even more than necessary). The majority of these relationships are based on unmet needs rather than wants.

G. **Parent and child relationship:** I have also had couples label it as Mentor-Protégé or Shield-Bearer relationship. This is not much of a partnership, as it is often based on one person's need for security, guidance, and stability and the other's need to protect, mentor, and rescue. While this relationship is not necessarily abusive and in some social systems might even be encouraged, the downside is that when the couple's social status or personal context changes, divorce is more common. (An example would be a couple that moves from a society that encourages clear gender roles and submission of one partner to one with a more egalitarian cultural, social, and legal system.) There can be a visible difference between privileges or power dynamic of these couples (such as financial imbalance; age, race, or gender difference; or immigration status).

H. **Emergent Love couples:** Partners are independent entities and ready to enter an interdependent partnership with healthy and clear boundaries. Boundaries are considered to be invitations and liberating assets rather than defensive or offensive tactics. The couple is connected, but they also view their relationship as a distinct entity in which each partner participates in ways that are suited to their strengths, and partners are intentionally directed at solidifying their bond with the other. The relationship is based on equity and not equality or tit for tat. The six ingredients of Emergent Love are present and love emerges as the result. They give to the relationship and receive from it, too.

None of these configurations is categorically "right" or "wrong," they are simply different arrangements that I have seen meet different needs and have different outcomes. It's also common for couples to shift from one configuration to another during the life of their coupledom.

Josh and Elna reflected a classic C, which is exactly what they chose. Submergent love is all about two individuals merging all they can of their lives with each other to become a single unit: 1 + 1 = 1. The "deeper" in love they are, the less room there is for the individual. It looks something like the illustration on page 28.

Over time, partners no longer know where one ends and the other begins. Elna's depression becomes Josh's depression, and also his problem to fix. When she is angry, he becomes angry. His favorite band becomes her favorite band. And both experience any bid for autonomy by the other as a rejection. When people talk to me about how their partner is not the

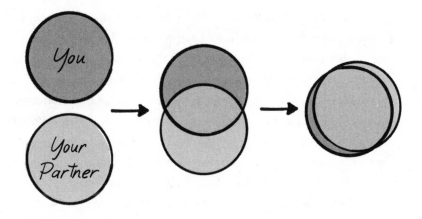

Submergent Love 1+1=1

person they once fell in love with, they are usually referring to this kind of merging. There is no "other" anymore to be witnessed and attracted to!

In many ways, this submerged state is the natural outcome of the hormonal rush that accompanies budding romance. Remember, in this stage the rational brain is short-circuited by the evolutionary imperative to breed. Partners really are pulled together as if by a magnet, and they really don't want to be with anyone else. The world lights up when they're together and is dull and faded when they separate. The physical presence of the partner brings on a flood of feel-good neurotransmitters, and their absence can feel like withdrawal. The urge to merge (or submerge) is an attempt to maintain this heightened state of well-being—to make something permanent that is inherently temporary.

Submergent love is measured in its power and intensity by how people involved *feel* when they're together—the hormonal rush that accompanies budding romance. But it is also a static entity that relies on our feelings remaining the same forever. If you subscribe to this version of love, everything is fine…as long as the feelings don't change. But what happens when they do settle down, as the evidence assures us they will?

The partner who was once so spontaneous is now seen as irresponsible;

the partner who was unique and quirky is now too weird to bring to the company holiday party; the interesting relatives become the crazy in-laws; the artistic rebel who defies social convention is now just unemployed and a weight around your neck. In a way, points of attraction become points of annoyance. When the shine of chemical romance wears off and reality sets in, couples find that they aren't as compatible as they once thought. Things that seemed relatively unimportant in the beginning become enormous problems that they don't know how to resolve.

At the beginning of their relationship, Elna and Josh's sexual chemistry overshadowed everything else, and they imagined it would be powerful enough to remove any obstacles in their way. Now that those feelings have subsided, they're noticing that they're not as aligned as they thought. They come from very different backgrounds—Josh's family is wealthy and not at all religious, while Elna's family is middle-class and places a high value on being of service in their religious community. These seemingly insignificant differences impact their core values, their political affiliations, their expectations of each other and of the relationship, and their ideas about what they want their lives to look like in the future. They, like many other couples, assumed that their sexual chemistry would be there forever, fueling a lifetime of great sex and guaranteeing seamless negotiations in all other areas of their lives as well.

The fairy tale of submergent love may always include happily ever after, but the narrative itself ends at the wedding—often a gala affair complete with princess gown and a waltz across an empty ballroom with all eyes on the loving couple. Think about it: The wedding is the end of the story rather than the beginning. The story doesn't accommodate change, or growth, or any of the realities of building a life with another person. It is all about a whirlwind journey that culminates in the majestic experience of matrimony.

Of course, in this day and age most people have some idea that relationships take work, but few of us really understand what that work entails and where the efforts must be directed. No one talks about Cinderella at forty-two, juggling teenagers and a job, taking an Uber to work because Prince Charming needed the car for a visit to the doctor where he is getting fitted for a CPAP so he doesn't keep her up all night with his snoring. No one talks about how much energy, flexibility, and generosity are required for that particular scenario. In fact, most people spend more time planning the wedding than they do thinking about what a mutually satisfying relationship will look like on a day-to-day basis.

When single people tell me that they're looking for their True Love, I like to do this exercise with them. I ask, "Imagine that I have a magic wand. I'm going to swing it around your head and tomorrow morning, magically, you'll wake up with the person of your dreams in your ideal relationship. Now, tell me how your life would be different." The initial response I typically hear is about feelings. "I'd be a lot happier," "I'd feel more secure," "I'd feel loved, and I would love them, too." But when I press them by asking, "Yes, but how would your life be different? Who is doing what? Where? How do you interact with each other? How do you know your partner loves you? Respects you? Trusts you? What do you talk about? What might you argue about? How will you handle disagreements? In-laws? Children?" they don't know how to answer because they've never thought about it. It all goes back to figuring it out together with the power of love they have for each other. I want to tell them that it's great to have the fuel, but if the other parts of the car are broken you will not go far, my dears.

When the idyllic fantasy of True Love is confronted with the limitations of reality, disillusionment sets in. The partner is, after all, only human, with all the attendant flaws and shortcomings humans share. If the couple is well suited and given the right guidance to begin with, they may be able to move through this stage and come out on the other side. But if there are serious misalignments, and the couple is not equipped with the right mindset and tools they need, the unfortunate result is a relationship that is unsatisfying on many different levels.

This is usually when people seek me out for advice, and why the courses on rekindling desire sell so well. That waning of intensity is seen as a sign that partners have fallen *out* of love. They start questioning the veracity of their love and the strength of their bond. The belief and hope is that if they can get that feeling back, it will all be okay again.

I don't subscribe to the idea that true love is something (or someone) that finds us when we're not looking. I also don't think it's a mysterious emotional state we achieve and then that's it, we're done, all set for a lifetime of bliss. Instead, love is the result of a dynamic balancing act of supporting and maintaining the critical ingredients that must be present if love is to exist. It includes paying attention to the currencies we exchange on a daily basis and throughout the different phases of our life as a couple.

EMERGENT LOVE

Have a look at the figure below, the Disenchanted Love we know. When we place the intense emotions of courtship at the foundation of our relationships, those relationships become inverted pyramids, unbalanced and destined to collapse under the pressures of everyday life. Love is at the bottom of the pyramid, and is expected to sustain (and survive) a

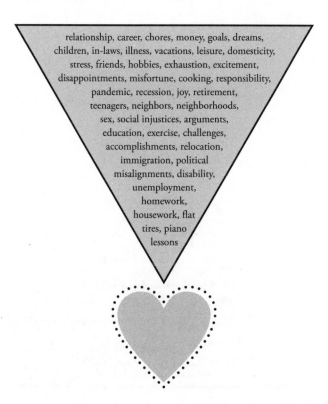

relationship, career, chores, money, goals, dreams, children, in-laws, illness, vacations, leisure, domesticity, stress, friends, hobbies, exhaustion, excitement, disappointments, misfortune, cooking, responsibility, pandemic, recession, joy, retirement, teenagers, neighbors, neighborhoods, sex, social injustices, arguments, education, exercise, challenges, accomplishments, relocation, immigration, political misalignments, disability, unemployment, homework, housework, flat tires, piano lessons lifetime of experiences: your relationship with your partner, your children (if you choose to have any), extended families and in-laws, your career, other friendships, pets, hobbies, financial recessions, political elections, global pandemics, other unexpected challenges, expected challenges, social life, illness and aging, all your hopes and dreams, all your expectations, and everything you want to build, accomplish, and experience. The pyramid also includes all the misunderstandings, arguments, disagreements, and negotiations involved in such an awesome project. It all goes in there. How long do you think that the feeling of being in love will be able to support all the rest of your life before it comes tumbling down?

Now I'd like you to consider, for a moment, what would happen if we flipped that pyramid on its head. What would a relationship feel like if the base of the pyramid was firmly grounded and stable, able to support the whole structure with ease?

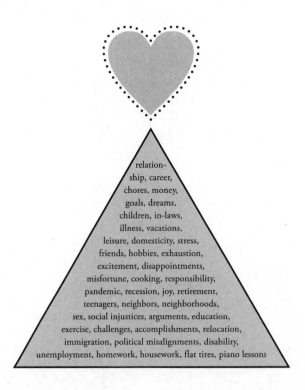

relationship, career, chores, money, goals, dreams, children, in-laws, illness, vacations, leisure, domesticity, stress, friends, hobbies, exhaustion, excitement, disappointments, misfortune, cooking, responsibility, pandemic, recession, joy, retirement, teenagers, neighbors, neighborhoods, sex, social injustices, arguments, education, exercise, challenges, accomplishments, relocation, immigration, political misalignments, disability, unemployment, homework, housework, flat tires, piano lessons

Love is a byproduct of the relationship rather than the sole foundation, something that grows slowly, over time, and is built every single day in a thousand small and specific interactions. This kind of love is less like a lightning bolt or a whirlwind or a raging storm and more of a cumulative process, like building your home one brick at a time, designing and redesigning it while it continues to provide you with a warm shelter, cozy comfort, and exciting memories. Even at a glance you can tell which one is more stable and likely to last without burnout, constant uncertainty, and debilitating anxiety.

This second pyramid is the path of Emergent Love, the fundamental idea of which is that long-lasting, generative, nourishing love is an emergent property. It comes into being as the result of a couple's intention to choose *attraction, respect, trust, compassion, commitment*, and *being loving* toward each other on an ongoing basis. Each of these ingredients is something that we can practice; a way of being and a skill that we can hone and build mutually in our partnership. When these building blocks are in place, love comes into being on its own. It's like having a log, a spark, and enough oxygen: When these come together, they produce something new, fire, which is *of* them but not identical *to* any of them. This fire will be created in your own unique way and will last as long as all the components are present and in continuous exchanges with one another.

In Submergent Love, 1 + 1 = 1. You find another person and in adding them you aren't even two—you just get a bigger "1." In Emergent Love, 1 + 1 = 3. This model includes the idea that each person is unique, a separate individual with independent thoughts, feelings, desires, and needs. (This is less an ideal than it is a reflection of reality: When we try to be inclusive of the other fully, we tend to lose the boundaries around our own selfhood, and in turn we lose the diversity that brought us together in the first place.) The partnership, then, becomes a separate entity unto itself, a "relational space" that each participates in with intention. There is You, there is Me, and there is We. One of my clients described it as two birds building a nest together: Each brings materials and weaves them with the other's into a safe space for their future. I love this analogy. Partners may continue to design and redesign their home, but their roles, their skills, and the way they show up remains true to their capacities and their commitment to a shared vision. Rather than being a passive experience that just happens to you, Emergent Love is consciously designed and intentionally cultivated.

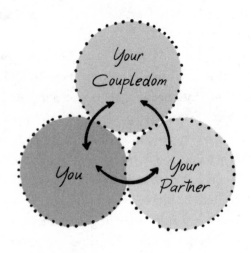

Emergent Love 1+1=3

Cultivated is the key word here. These relational spaces don't happen on their own: They're built and nurtured. It is a mutually empowering, sustainable, and liberating experience that contrasts sharply with submergent, enmeshed, codependent, misconstrued, fleeting, dramatic, and abstract types of love. Emergent Love is a collaborative act to create something new that is yours, mine, and ours.

In this model, love is not experienced as lust, sexual excitement, need, or even want. Because it is built on behaviors, more so than feelings, it is something that can be taught. This is good news for anyone who walks into my office (and anyone reading this book) believing that, at some level, they have failed at love. In this way Emergent Love offers a fresh and hopeful framework for experiencing long-term, thriving relationships.

THE ORIGINS OF EMERGENT LOVE

The seeds of Emergent Love were initially sown back in London in 2007, while I was working as a psychosexual therapist. I began to notice similarities in the words my clients used to describe the satisfaction they felt in their relationships. A decade later, with my researcher hat on, I conducted a ten-year retrospective study of 312 couples I had seen in my global private practice, both in person and online.* These original couples hailed from twenty-one countries in Europe, the Americas, Africa, Asia, and Australia. They were Black, white, Middle Eastern, European, Asian, Latinx, Indigenous, or a mix of one or more ethnic and racial groups. They were gay and straight, cisgender and transgender and nonbinary and queer. Most, but not all, were in monogamous relationships. A few were in consensually non-monogamous relationships, and some were polyamorous. They were dating, engaged, married (or otherwise committed), separating, decoupling, and divorced. Several were in relationships with someone from a different country, race, culture, or religion. They came into my offices with a wide range of hopes, issues, and concerns.[2]

After reviewing years of notes and transcripts of sessions, certain patterns started to emerge. While there are an infinite number of variables that might lead to struggles or crises in a couple, there are far fewer variables when it comes to couples who think of themselves as thriving. Satisfied couples have more in common with one another than unsatisfied couples. I'm reminded of the first line of *Anna Karenina*, where Tolstoy writes, "Happy families are all alike. Every unhappy family is unhappy in its own way."[3] By focusing exclusively on these satisfied couples, I was

---

* The way I describe the work I do in my private practice, and the titles I use, depends on the local regulations where I am practicing, what I am offering, or where my clients live. I am alternately called a doctor, therapist, professor, consultant, counselor, coach, psychosexual therapist, couples therapist, and a few other terms besides, depending on the context. Regardless of where in the world I am practicing, and in what context, I tend to refer to all my clients as "clients" because I do believe that the wisdom lies within them, and I would like to acknowledge their sense of agency over making the life they desire happen.

able to isolate and identify the themes that would eventually become the building blocks of Emergent Love.

I have met many couples who identify themselves as satisfied in their relationships—whether through personal interviews, through my work, or through their willingness to participate in our research. Most of them talk less about excitement and more about being a good fit, being there for each other, being seen and appreciated by the other person, and feeling like they have someone who knows them in all the ways that matter most to them. They like each other and are drawn to each other over and over again because being with the other feels rewarding on multiple levels. They talk about thriving as individuals and couples, and describe their partnerships using words like secure, caring, interdependent, engaging, inspiring, affectionate, and safe. They describe their partners as respectful, trustworthy, interesting and interested, loyal, and compassionate.

When you look closer, the partners tend to have similar values and a compatible vision (that is clear but not rigid) for both the future of the relationship and the future of their individual lives. They are deliberate and intentional in their words and behaviors. They are kind to each other. And, what is most noticeable to me, they are usually able to describe in detail the specific behaviors of both themselves and their partners that demonstrate these qualities every single day. Partners have a variety of ways they show up for the other, and by doing so they create a mutually fulfilling experience. In other words, thriving couples think of love more as a range of behaviors than as a feeling.

In these relationships, each partner demonstrates a sense of individual accountability and agency, and each puts the same level of emphasis on what matters for the health of the relationship. There is an intentionality behind time, energy, attention, and other resources that each brings to the table. These might not be exactly the same at all times—it is not a tit-for-tat or an exercise in keeping score—but the overall feeling is that each partner gives and receives equitably. This makes their dynamic fulfilling and nurturing for both. They don't stop at the surface with happiness and they express a sense of deeper fulfillment. Stressors, in the relationship and in life, are also handled with intention. Partners manage their own stress cycles and know when and what to bring to the other person or to the relational space. They know how and when to rely on each other, and when to seek support elsewhere to keep the relational resources for what matters most to the coupledom. They usually do not react to situations but instead are able to be responsive when disagreements arise. They know how to repair after any ruptures (which are inevitable in a relationship), they grow together, and they find new ways of being attracted to each other. And they're aware of the reciprocity they need to deepen their bond over time.

When all the elements are in place and balanced, the outcome is a sense of individual and mutual satisfaction, thriving, health, and, yes, love. Partners are not preoccupied, insecure, or overly anxious about being loved, being fulfilled, or wasting their life with the "wrong one." They have clear minds and peaceful hearts, and tend to be more fulfilled in other parts of their lives as well. Emergent Love is dynamic; it grows with you and adjusts to what you bring to the mix. It is realistic and adapts based on what is needed and what is possible. It is resilient. It allows you to immerse yourself in the deepest sense of pleasure, growth, and fulfill-ment that a coupledom can offer. That is why I say that everyone deserves to be in their desired loving relationship. Because it is achievable for all.

THE LIFE-CHANGING RESEARCH: THE SIX INGREDIENTS OF EMERGENT LOVE

As I was mining a decade's worth of data, I had a good idea of what I was trying to measure. But so far, my research had been restricted to the couples I knew and had worked with personally. If the research was to be useful for everyone it had to be credible, or as we say in the research world, validated and reliable, which meant that my ideas had to be tested rigorously. That is when I partnered with Dr. Pejman Azarmina, founder of Thinkocrats, who is a medical doctor and a genius researcher. I should know because I live with him!

Over the course of several years, we narrowed the focus of my Emergent Love qualitative research to the three domains that seemed most significant in relationship outcomes: Individual Fundamentals, Dyadic Fundamentals, and Interpersonal Dynamics. For our purposes, the short version is that individual fundamentals include everything you bring into the relationship with you—these are qualities that are present regardless of a person's relationship status. We looked at things like how you connect to other people, your thinking style, your personal and moral values, how you handle money, and your general outlook on life (i.e., positive thoughts and emotions).

Dyadic fundamentals are what we commonly think of as "compatibility," and encompass all the areas of a relationship where being in alignment is essential if love is to be created and nurtured over time. These include things like being attracted to each other, having compatible goals for the future, having similar values, and having compatible attitudes toward managing your finances.

The third category is the couple's interpersonal dynamics, which are all about how the partners interact on a daily basis. These are what I think of as the ingredients of Emergent Love, and what we will be discussing in the coming chapters. Interpersonal dynamics are twofold—they are both expressed and received—and they must be mutual and reciprocal. These include attraction, respect, trust, shared vision, compassion, and loving behaviors.

Since we were looking for measurable results in this research, we created a list of questions designed to assess these main elements, and incorporated validated scales and measures that were already in existence wherever that was possible.[4] We tested this on a sample group of forty couples, including psychologists and other subject matter experts, in 2018. Thanks to them, we made critical revisions based on their feedback and tested again in 2019, this time with 159 couples who were representative of the US population, to ensure that our results were both valid and that the test results could be replicated regardless of participants' demographic information.

The end result was the Relationship Panoramic Inventory (RPI), a 360-degree tool that provides a comprehensive assessment of a couple's relationship.* The questions address a whole range of subjects that are important to the health of the relationship, including lifestyle habits,

---

* For those of you who are interested, you can learn more about the RPI or even take the inventory on the website https://relationship-panoramic.com.

sexual health and well-being, conflict management style, general religious and political interests, temperament and circadian rhythms, positive and negative emotions, individual identity, and many other domains that are too numerous to list here. We designed the inventory as a tool for couples to make an annual review of their coupledom. It is a strengths-based model, so it doesn't measure pathology or offer diagnoses or prognosis. Instead, it is meant to help couples learn about what they do well and identify areas that might need some attention—like an X-ray that shows what is in place, what is cracked but still holding, and what needs immediate attention.

We also included questions that assess each partner's overall sense of satisfaction, fit, and thriving within the relationship. So not only did the RPI provide useful information for each specific couple, it told us a lot about what all thriving couples have in common. And the research revealed what I had long suspected: The partners' reported satisfaction is strongly correlated with an identifiable set of skills, attitudes, and behaviors. While it's certainly important to have your own house in order (individual fundamentals) and to have enough in common to make a go of it (dyadic fundamentals), the way partners interact with each other on a daily basis has an enormous impact on their sense of satisfaction in the relationship. These are the six specific dynamics that emerged in our research:

Attraction: Recognizing the evolving roles and attributes you find appealing in your partner.

Respect: Having high regard for your partner and keeping their needs and priorities in mind.

Trust: Believing that your partner will show up for you consistently and in the ways that matter to you and you do the same for them.

Shared Vision: Making a commitment to go somewhere or build something together with shared priorities.

Compassion: The capacity to show up fully for your partner without making it about yourself.

Loving Behaviors: Manifesting love through specific, exclusive, and tender actions toward your partner. Making each other feel special.

Each of these elements has a role to play in how relationships are created, sustained, and experienced as fulfilling for all parties involved. When all six of the interpersonal dynamics are functioning, couples report the highest levels of satisfaction in terms of their overall sense of fit, their sense of thriving, their sexual connection and physical connection, and their lifestyle. They also report the highest level of global satisfaction in both their relationships and their lives. This outcome is what I call Emergent Love. It is something two people build together over the course of their relationship.

———

Emergent Love is the robust and fulfilling alternative to relationships based on butterflies, chemistry, luck, chance, and the temporary insanity of hormones. Because the ingredients of Emergent Love are based on behaviors and skills, rather than feelings, they can be studied, practiced, and strengthened. There is a sense of agency behind it. Remember above where I talked about how love has become a job with no job description? Well, this is the job description. We have far more control over manifesting love in our relationships than we have been led to believe. There is nothing passive about it. In fact, it takes a lot of effort. Some of you might be thinking, "Ugh! More work!" Believe me, I get it. But it's not like you haven't been putting any work into this; it's just that I am afraid the efforts were put on the least fertile grounds! The payoff here is enormous, and improving your primary relationship will benefit all areas of your life. I'm reminded of the saying, "The best time to plant a tree is ten years ago; the second best time is now."

CHAPTER 3

What We Bring to Love

To find out what is truly individual in ourselves, profound reflection is needed; and suddenly we realize how uncommonly difficult the discovery of individuality is.

—Carl Jung[1]

Katrina came to see me in my New York office one summer day. A charming, attractive young woman in her late twenties, Katrina grew up in North Carolina in an Irish Catholic family of seven. Her father worked in business; her mother stayed home to take care of the five children. Katrina, a certified yoga instructor, had become so successful through her online classes that she was able to live anywhere in the world, provided there was internet. I asked her what brought her to New York, and she answered, "I moved here for love." She showed me the pendant she wore around her neck, a silver heart with a keyhole in the center. She smiled gracefully and said, "I am open and ready and know that I will find the key to my heart in this city. This is something that keeps me focused and reminds me of my mission in life on a daily basis: to find love that lasts."

My own heart sank. In that moment I was secretly hoping that Katrina did not belong to the camp who believed that love would *happen* to you. Maybe her words had another meaning? But as we explored her history of romantic relationships, she revealed several heartbreaks. Two relationships ended when her boyfriends cheated on her, claiming that she was "too uptight." She dated a woman after that, hoping the problem was men, and only realized she was not as much into women when she "fell in love" with Mitchell, her most recent boyfriend. Though her relationship with Mitchell was filled with passion, he was compulsively jealous and controlling and made her life a "living hell." I'll spare you the details, but the police got involved to get her out of that relationship. Hoping some distance would help, she left Asheville to visit a friend in Brooklyn, who suggested that maybe it was time for a change of scenery. She moved less than a year later, in part because she thought her opportunities to find love would be better among so many people. "This time I'm going to do it right," she explained, "which is why I've come to be coached." She came to see me because at some level she must have known that just changing her context, creating space in her life, and putting herself out there might not be the most effective pathway to the kind of relationship she so eagerly desired.

As a first step to help Katrina understand her patterns I showed her my relationship models chart. You're probably not surprised to learn that Katrina chose Submergent Love to describe both her past relationships and also her ideal for any future relationships. "So you're looking for a relationship like the ones you've had in the past?" I asked her. "Noooooo," she lamented. She looked confused, then started laughing uncomfortably, then admitted, "I don't understand; what's wrong with me?"

"Nothing! You've heard the saying 'We can't solve problems with the same thinking that created them,' right?" I asked her. "Well, that applies here. Instead of thinking about your ideal relationship as something out there"—I waved to the window—"that's going to find you, let's talk a little bit about why you want to be in a relationship in the first place, why you think you're ready, what you hope it will be like, and how it would feel day-to-day."

In the previous chapter I gave you a brief outline of the three separate domains that our research indicates lead to more satisfying relationships: fundamentals that we need to develop in ourselves (individual fundamentals), areas for couples' compatibilities (dyadic fundamentals), and the fluency and consistency in which all of these are communicated on a daily basis (interpersonal dynamics). In the remainder of this book we will talk primarily about the interpersonal dynamics that are the building blocks of Emergent Love—attraction, respect, commitment, compassion, trust, and being loving. Those are, after all, the ingredients that we want to cultivate in our relationships. But before we get to that, I want to invite you to take a closer look at some of the fundamental elements that must be in place, both within yourself and between you as a couple, that make Emergent Love possible. I also want to acknowledge that many of you are reading these words without having a partner, or without having a partner who is on board. While it is impossible to build or completely transform a relationship without *both* partners being brought into the process, there are things we can work on in ourselves to do our part and to create a ripple effect that could bring positive changes into the coupledom. At the end of the day, your own attitude and behavior are the only things you can reliably control.

IT ALL STARTS WITH YOU

I began with Katrina by asking about herself, as I begin with all of my single and coupled clients who come to me wanting to understand why they are not in the loving relationship that they desire. It's hard to share yourself with someone if you don't have a fully developed sense of who you are. So let me ask you, too, "How well do you know yourself?"

Most of us have at least some idea of how to answer this question by the time we reach adulthood. We know what we're good at, our strengths and weaknesses, what we like, dislike, and absolutely cannot tolerate. But when it comes to relational spaces and romantic relationships specifically, we lack *relational self-awareness*[2] or as I would like to call it, self-literacy. Any languages that I have learned first started with a level of literacy and then led to fluency, which meant that I could apply them in various contexts to either express myself or ask for what I wanted or needed. Here it is very similar. We may have theories about how our unique history has helped to shape the person we have become. We know what bothers us and maybe what's important to us, what we feel we must have in our lives, and what we can comfortably do without. A lot of you have also done greater work to perhaps be able to name areas that were sources of pride or shame, left a scar, and made you the person that you are today. As Sara Kuburic, the author of *It's On Me: Accept Hard Truths, Discover Your Self, and Change Your Life*, says, this is necessary work to give you capacities to be intimate with another person. I like to think of it this way, intimacy is "into-me-I-see" and "into-me-you-see."[3] (I first heard this expression during a conversation with Dr. Christopher Walling.[4])

Whatever level of self-literacy that you bring to us today, throughout the book I will provide practical exercises designed to help you increase your self-literacy and come to a deeper understanding of how your life experiences have shaped your expectations, desires, fears, and longings around love and beyond. In this section I'll guide you through some questions that will help you start thinking about what you bring to the shared relational space. Taking a look at your sensitivities, quirks, and pet peeves is a good place to begin.

Sensitivities, Quirks, and Pet Peeves

Your *sensitivities* are aspects of yourself or your life that are particularly sensitive for you, or are more sensitive for you than for others. All of us have areas of sensitivity—we'd hardly be human and barely unique if we didn't. Sometimes they appear as a chip on your shoulder, a past resentment, or an injustice that you're having a hard time letting go of. Maybe you grew up in a household where resources were prioritized for your siblings but not for you, and today you have a sensitivity around things being fair and equitable. Or maybe you grew up in a home where money was tight, and now you find that you're afraid of not having enough or you harbor a resentment toward those who grew up in better circumstances.

Sensitivities can also appear as areas of insecurity. Let's say in your childhood or in a previous relationship the person that you trusted most betrayed you, and now your ability to trust is a little bit bruised, and you are more sensitive in that area than the average person out there. If you had a trauma in the past that activated your trauma responses, you might be hyperaware or hypervigilant about certain things. Sometimes aspects of yourself that are simply different from the norm can be experienced as sensitivities, like having different physical abilities or any other attributes that put you in the minority, or being an extreme introvert, being cognitively atypical (for example, being gifted or neurodiverse), and so on.

Your *quirks* are behaviors that serve you in some ways, but they could be sources of irritation for people who interact with you, and particularly the people who share your living space. Most of us are not always fully aware of these, and sometimes we even think they're cute and make us who we are. For example, maybe you hum all the time, or curl your hair around your fingers, or need to have your clothes color-coordinated in your closet. Do you put pillows around you when you sleep? Or do you think that there's a right way and a wrong way to make coffee, load a dishwasher, or fold clothes? Maybe you like the clicking sound that you make when you're thinking, or you like the way you laugh. Maybe you like the smell of your sweat after a workout, or you have a tendency to find peace in chaos and leave a mess behind you when you cook, or you're seriously grumpy in the morning. Generally speaking, your quirks are not necessarily problems or challenges you've faced. Instead, they are the specific behaviors that other people might associate with you. They become issues when people around you experience them as annoying, obnoxious, or otherwise disrespectful.

Your *pet peeves* are things that really annoy you about other people or about your environment. If something makes your blood boil or sends shivers down your spine, that's a pet peeve. Sometimes they are how you feel when you are on the receiving end of someone else's quirks! Like quirks, they're highly idiosyncratic. John might not care that Mary leaves wet towels on the bathroom floor, but it drives Edward absolutely nuts. Certain types of music, people who talk a lot and never seem to get to the point, finding a wet tissue on the kitchen counter or whiskers in the bathroom sink, interrupting when someone is speaking, giving wet kisses on the cheek, speaking with your mouth full of food, bad breath, loud chewing noises, picking a pimple or passing gas, seeing someone pick their nose or spit in public are all examples of pet peeves. At the beginning of a relationship, we usually notice these but either think they are cute and endearing or don't think they matter too much. These are usually relatively minor issues, but they could become major issues over time, especially if one person's quirk is the other's pet peeve. I know many of you are chuckling and nodding, because these are among the recurring complaints that I hear from couples when they declare that they are no longer in love with the other person. They are often even embarrassed to talk about these with me, because they think they are being persnickety. I invite you to do the following exercise as a first step in cultivating self-literacy about what you bring to love.

BUILDING BLOCK:
SENSITIVITIES, QUIRKS, AND PET PEEVES

During the next week or so, try to be aware of your own sensitivities, quirks, and pet peeves.

Feel free to make a list, ask close friends, roommates, your partner, and family members if you feel comfortable, and add to or adjust your list as new realizations occur. The purpose of this is to bring awareness to these aspects of yourself so that you can assess if they are serving you in your life and in your relational spaces or not. If you are seeing a coach, counselor, or therapist, it's a good idea to discuss these with them, too. Given their knowledge of you and your life, see what they can add to the mix. Make sure to revisit these aspects periodically, as these all have the capacity to evolve and change over time. They could also change from one individual and relational space to the other.

As these come to light for you, put words to them, and prepare for communicating them in a meaningful way with your partner and other people who are in high-stakes relationships with you. This will create a shared language and a reference point for everyone involved. You allow others to talk to you about theirs, too, which takes the awkwardness out of it.

Essences

Now I'd like you to turn your attention to those aspects of your personality that remain consistent regardless of changing circumstances. Whether you are happy or sad, excited or bored, being praised or criticized, in the bedroom, in the kitchen, or at work, in an enjoyable moment or a moment of conflict, when your dreams come true or when it feels like everything is taken from you, these are the aspects of self that stay with you. I think of these as your *essences*. Some examples that my clients have shared with me over the years include optimistic, kind, mean, competitive, impatient, compassionate, focused, graceful, gentle, opportunistic, abrasive, cowardly, over-accommodating, elegant, ambitious, people-pleasing, analytical, thoughtful, considerate, skeptical, dignified, and loving. Essences are consistent and do not fluctuate depending on the person you're with or the context you're in. For example, if grace is one of your essences, then whether you are receiving all the praise in the world or being criticized to the nails, you are still graceful and show up as that. Or if you say one of your essences is kindness, but you are only kind to the people you choose, or when the circumstances allow it, this is not your essence. Essences are who you are at your core. You can keep them or change them. Sometimes your different roles or external circumstances might have clouded them, or you might have had to mask them to survive. This is an opportunity to identify what they are and to see if what others perceive of you is aligned with how you think about yourself.

Let me give you an example. Jordan came to see me because his attempts at dating were not successful. He was thirty-eight at the time, charming and handsome, very pleasant to talk to. He was a hedge fund manager, and he was quite well off. In the first interaction he was very impressive and engaging. He'd been dating for about four years but told me that he "hadn't found the right person." He had no problem finding great candidates through the apps, and he usually went on a few dates before the woman ended up telling him some version of, "You're a great guy but I don't think we're a good match," or he got the famous "lack of chemistry" explanation. He had dated dozens of women, and all but two of them ended things first. The last time it happened the woman was forthright enough to tell him that his energy was too intense for her. "It's go, go, go all the time. It's not that I couldn't keep up, I just didn't want to feel like I had to keep up. To be perfectly honest I also felt like you weren't really paying attention to me or to what I wanted, you just assumed I'd go along with whatever you decided to do." When he came to see me, Jordan said, "I think there's something there to work with. Before that I just took women's word for it that the chemistry wasn't there. But now I'm starting to think that maybe it has something to do with me."

As we started our work together, I found him very kind, sensitive, attentive to little details, and quite thoughtful with the choice of his words and his mannerisms. At the same time, I began to notice a pattern. Whenever he sent me an email to schedule a session he expected an immediate response. If I didn't respond right away he'd send another email, then a text to make sure I got his emails. These all ended with, "Please confirm ASAP!" even when the appointment was weeks away. Mind you, all my clients know that I respond to their emails within twelve hours, and Jordan was no exception. When I brought it up in a session, he laughed uncomfortably, but it opened up a whole conversation around his need to be firmly in control of all aspects of his life because he was not able to sit with the unknown. I asked him, "What are you made of?" He said, "I am efficient, responsible, impressive; I try to be thoughtful, I like to help others grow, and I like to have a good time." I asked if he thinks others see these same qualities in him. He was hopeful that they did but shared that indecisive people drive him crazy, and he has no patience for laziness, slowpokes, or stupidity.

Jordan also told me that none of his friends and family members were setting him up for dates, which he found embarrassing and discouraging. I gave Jordan an exercise to bring to one of our sessions. I asked him to go to his circle of friends, colleagues, family, and even his stylist and his trainer at the gym, and ask them, "If I was a car, what kind of car would I be?" Here's what he came back with.

> Emily (friend): You'd be a Ferrari. I am not chic enough to ride you.
> Nikki (sister): You'd be one of those annoying cars with black-tinted windows so you can't see inside.
> Ruby (mother): A Ferrari, definitely. Exemplary and fast.
> Kirk (best friend): A sleek car, with detailed interior. Smooth, efficient, and shiny.

Anthony (boss): A Bugatti. Unforgivingly perfect and impatient.

Ramón (friend and stylist): A Lamborghini. Flashy and fast.

Jackson (brother): A Ferrari. But, like, a Ferrari that you use to pick your kids up from school. Way faster than what you need.

As we looked through his list, I asked Jordan if he saw a pattern or if there was anything surprising to him. He said, "Yes! I've really got my act together!"

"And what does that mean to a person who'd like to take a ride with you?" I asked.

"Come on board and enjoy the ride!" (Remember the model of *get in where you fit in*?)

"What's the incentive for her to go on more than a few rides?"

At that point Jordan paused and looked at me with a gaze that showed he had entered a space that was new to him. "Well, hopefully she's having a good time, the music is good, the conversation is good, I'm taking her to a fun place where we can spend some time together...Oh, I see. It's not all about the ride, I guess."

We continued this conversation until we came to an agreement about the patterns we were seeing. Jordan is impatient, he has a fear of abandonment if he doesn't impress, and he gets annoyed with people who have low energy (literally and figuratively) and force him to slow down. He has anxiety in the face of the unknown, although his work life as an investor carries a great level of risk at times. After we identified the patterns that were underlying his essence as a fast-moving race car who won't slow down for anyone, we turned our focus to how this essence was manifesting itself in his relationships. I used our relationship to explain to him how being on the other side feels in daily interactions with him. I shared with him that when he emails me multiple times I feel annoyed and uncomfortable. And I am someone who has unconditional love for him! Imagine a person who is just starting to date him and doesn't know all of his amazing qualities.

I further shared that this shows me that he does not give me the benefit of the doubt—that I might have been in sessions all day and hadn't had a chance to check my messages. And that he doesn't acknowledge he is not the only one I have to cater to all day long. While this might have served him at a fast-paced job or as the first child of the family who got a lot of attention from his mother, I shared that when he demands people's attention right away, it is disrespectful. I brought up the example of when he does not pause to ask himself how much difference it makes if I confirm immediately or I wait twelve hours, but instead writes, "Please confirm ASAP!" at the end of each message; it communicates a sense of urgency that does not match the request for a meeting in two weeks. He jumped in and said, "Yeah, like I am the Ferrari and you'd better hop on board or else. I get it."

Although he was clearly uncomfortable, he shared that what I said really resonated with him because he had heard exactly the same thing from other people, including family members, friends, and work colleagues. The most important part of our exchange was when Jordan asked me, "Where can we go from here? How do I change this?"

I invite you to do the same exercise with the people in your own life. Just tell them that you read a book that suggested a little exercise, and take it from there.

SELF-LITERACY BUILDING BLOCK: WHAT ARE MY ESSENCES?

Identify some people in your inner circle, people who you believe know you well and some who don't know you very well (outer circle) and then pose the question, "If I were a car, what would I be and why?" Be sure to let them know that you're not asking about the car they think you would *drive*, but what car you would *be*. If they are not familiar with cars, ask them "If I were a flower, what would I be and why?" Their answers might help you understand how you are being perceived and because it is with a degree of separation from you as a person, it might be easier for others to come up with more authentic answers. Then have a check-in and see if this is aligned with who you think you are and your essences. If so, why? And if not, why not?

Once you are aware of your essences, the next step is to ask yourself whether or not they are serving you in your life right now and who might be attracted to your current self. If you struggle in your relationships, or feel misunderstood or disappointed often, there is a good chance that who you think you are and what you are projecting to the world are not aligned.

BECOMING READY FOR LOVE

Understanding your sensitivities, quirks, and pet peeves, and knowing the essence of yourself as a person, will contribute to fostering a strong sense of self that will serve you in all your relationships, including romantic ones. In addition to this overall need for self-literacy (not to mention self-acceptance), there are several other individual attributes or aspects of self that had a positive correlation with satisfying relationships in our research. These are what we call individual fundamentals, and they include everything from your attachment style to childhood experiences, the tendency for having positive thoughts and emotions, the way you relate to your surroundings, how you perceive information about the world, and your thinking style (to name just a few). For example, throughout the years, I've found in my work that how you receive and interpret information from your environment, and the way you communicate that to your partner, is an often-overlooked dimension of interpersonal relating. But, as you'll see, it has a major impact on how we show up in relationships.

Ability to Connect

We all connect with the core of ourselves and to the world around us through a variety of ways. For our purposes here, I'd like to focus on three of the more important components that make up your connection style: how you think, how you attach, and how you experience the feeling of being loved.

Thinking Style

Part of your ability to connect has to do with understanding how your mind works: how you receive and perceive information about the world, how you process that information, how you plan for the future, and how you problem solve. This is an incredibly complex subject that has been studied by educators, philosophers, behavioral economists, neuroscientists, psychologists, and professionals in a host of other academic disciplines. It is relevant here because understanding the way you make meaning of the world will help you connect with others in a way that makes sense to you and others involved. This will help you give each other the benefit of the doubt, be more open to new ideas, and have more of an understanding as to what is serving you and what is not. A disclaimer here is that we can talk about how we perceive the world from so many angles, and these are in no way absolute categories, but more of a general guideline to serve our purposes here and help you navigate how you connect with the world. So, here are a few things to help you get to know your own mind. By learning about your thinking style you will learn how you think more effectively and what activities may help you think better. This is adapted from the research of Dr. Pejman Azarmina with Thinkocrats, who has shown that we use abstraction, information, organization, and facilitation in varying degrees to think effectively.

Although we have a natural ability to use a combination of the four styles, which is called a "multi-modal ability to think," most people identify with one of these more strongly than the others.

THINKING STYLES

Abstraction: Abstract thinking refers to a way of thinking that includes pattern recognition, logic, conceptualization, visualization, and fact checking. (In our research this had the highest correlation with relationship satisfaction.) Are you able to see the bigger picture, connect the dots, and see the patterns?

Information: Information-seekers need to access and process information to think more effectively. Do you ask a lot of questions and need to have detailed information before you can organize your thoughts and solve problems?

Organization: People who rely on organization may need to organize their physical or virtual surroundings or take a walk or talk to someone else in order to think more effectively.

Facilitation: Facilitation means that our thinking needs to be facilitated by doing something else, typically listening to music or looking at images, art, videos, bouncing a ball off the wall, etc., to be able to engage, concentrate, and process more clearly.

I can almost hear some of you saying, "Ummm. Okay. I think that the facilitation style is the most like me, but I'm still not sure why this matters." Well, imagine, for a moment, that you are a person who talks to think and organize your mind (organizational), so you like to process things verbally with your partner and externally. On the other side, your partner is a person who thinks to talk, and finds it difficult to be put on the spot and be expected to deliver some thoughtful remarks without taking the information away and processing it internally and alone first (informational). Knowing how you orient to the world can help you be aware of your baseline and can help avoid accusations by the other party that you are dismissive or uninterested or talking too much (or being "too much"). It also helps to plan for the most conducive context and environment for more important conversations. This is why it's important for you to understand how your mind works: Knowing how you connect to the world, and how you interpret and use information, will help you not take things personally if and when your partner perceives things differently. And this will help your coupledom by setting you up for successful interactions.

How You Attach

Understanding your attachment style has similar benefits: It helps you to understand how you relate to others, especially in high-stakes relationships. Feeling loved at the core has to do with our sense of belonging and attachment. Some of our earliest messages about who is trustworthy, and therefore could be relied upon, and who is not are formed in the first few years of life.[5] There are dozens of wonderful books on the topic if you'd like to go deeper—*Attached* by Levine and Heller[6] and *Wired for Love* by Tatkin[7] are the two that most of my clients find helpful—but for our purposes what you need to know is that your attachment style determines how much separateness and togetherness you want, and can tolerate, in your relationships. It will also determine how much reassurance you need from your partner, how attuned you are to your partner's nonverbal cues, how easily you ask for help, and even your sense of worthiness to make requests. It can explain to a great extent why some people seek or even demand attention while others are happier by themselves and might even come across as dismissive of their partners.

The three most recognized attachment styles are *anxious, avoidant,* and *secure.* If you have an anxious attachment style, relationships make you feel—you guessed it—*anxious.* You spend a great deal of emotional energy thinking about the relationship, and you are probably very attuned to even subtle changes in your partner's mood. Partnering with someone who wants to keep things casual will likely end in heartache, whereas finding someone who is reliable, consistent, and generous with reassurance is much more likely to leave you feeling secure.

Those of you with an avoidant attachment style often feel a bit uncomfortable when things get emotionally intense, especially when the other person seeks proximity all the time. You tend to dislike spending multiple days with your partner (or anyone, really), and you are wary of people who demand too much of your time and attention. Where anxiously attached individuals fear abandonment, avoidantly attached people fear being engulfed. If this sounds like you, you might want to make sure that your partner understands your need for enough alone time to recharge and replenish yourself. This way, you don't need to feel guilty while you are constantly asking for "space," which can sound punitive.

Finally, we have the secure attachment style. If you enjoy feeling close to someone and find it easy to accommodate your own needs for closeness and those of your partner, this is probably your style. You find it easy to give and receive attention, to love and be loved, and don't have too much trouble shifting between autonomy and interdependence. You don't fear being abandoned or engulfed, but instead see relationships as a natural part of life.

Your Love Blueprint

Another crucial area of self-awareness when it comes to intimate relationships involves how you conceptualize love in terms of the specific actions and behaviors that you associate with being loving or being loved. When it comes to romantic relationships, I like to think about this as your "love blueprint." Each of us, by the time we reach adulthood (and often years before that) has a unique idea of what it means to love and be loved. Our individual love blueprint is an amalgamation of everything we have ever learned or felt about love or perceived to be love. It is filled with messages we received from our infant caregivers, our families of origin, siblings and friends and extended family, as well as every romantic relationship in which we have been involved. It includes what we learned in school, in the place of worship, and from magazines, books, Instagram, TikTok, television, and other forms of media. It is also shaped by the overt and covert messages communicated by our culture and subculture, and our particular location in historical time. For some people their blueprint is filled with misinformation they've gathered throughout their lives about what love is supposed to look like and how it's supposed to feel.

All of these inputs commingle in an infinite variety of ways to inform us about how we receive, experience, and express love. We will talk about this later in the book in much greater detail, and in chapter 9 you'll have a chance to work on your own love blueprint in detail. For now, I want you to think about what makes you feel warm and cozy in someone's presence, what makes you want to be around someone, and what makes you want to keep your distance. How do you compare this with your childhood? Do you notice any similarities and/or differences? It could be intimate conversations, sex, affection, or visible signs of the other person's unwavering commitment. One woman I know told me she decided to marry her boyfriend after waking up to discover that he'd polished her shoes along with his own. "I couldn't believe it. It was just so kind and thoughtful and surprising and weird. I felt so loved. You know, my dad was a very serious guy, he didn't show much affection. He used to polish his shoes every Sunday night, and I remember how special I felt when he polished mine, too. I knew he must love me."

In the United States we have a tendency to equate meaningful connection with conversation (rather than polishing someone's shoes). You know you're loved when someone *listens* to you or tells you that they love you. In other parts of the world, connection might come through shared history, family ties, physical intimacy, intellectual debate, taking care of the other's needs, or fulfilling a mutual goal (among many other things). American culture is what researcher and author Erin Meyer calls "low context."[8] She explains that in a fairly young culture that is incredibly diverse, people need to articulate as clearly and as frequently as possible to avoid confusion. In older cultures, with more homogeneous populations, which she calls "high context," people rely heavily on the context of the communication rather than the actual words, and information is often exchanged through a look or a gesture that has meaning for members of that particular group.

Perhaps this is why so many couples seek help from a professional to work on their communication (mainly verbal) and we don't hear much about their overall sense of connection (verbal and otherwise). In fact, I see a lot of couples who talk eloquently *about* their relationship even while they struggle to actually *be* in it. They talk about it, and talk around it, as a way of demonstrating their literacy and intellectual understanding of the problem, but there is often a disconnect between what they know (literacy) and what they do (fluency).

Michele Scheinkman, who is on the faculty at the Ackerman Institute for the Family, where she teaches couples therapy, points out that many couples therapists have come to see intimacy as a primarily verbal process of sharing information about the self and having it empathically received.[9] She cautions against this narrow view, and advises professionals to expand their notion of intimacy to include a variety of ways that people connect. This is good advice for couples, too. Keep in mind that your love blueprint most likely includes a variety of ways to express and receive love that are not primarily verbal. The more ways partners can show their love, rather than simply declaring it, the more points of connection they're likely to have.

Moral and Personal Values

What matters to you? And what matters most? It's important to be honestly in touch with this, because if you don't have a grasp on what you truly value, you run the risk of adopting the values of others, at least temporarily, then feeling misunderstood or betrayed when they behave in ways that aren't in alignment with what you had in mind. Somewhere down the line you may even resent them, or accuse them of "making" you do X, Y, or Z. In reality, standing up for our values is our job, not our partner's.

In our research, we distinguished between personal values and moral values. Your moral values include the guiding principles that determine your ideas about right versus wrong, justice versus injustice, and honesty versus dishonesty. Your personal values are usually influenced by your moral values, but they are not the same thing. Personal values are more about what is most important to you, and they determine how you want to allocate your resources of time, energy, attention, and money.

In our research, individuals with a clear sense of their own *moral values* were more likely to experience satisfying relationships than those whose sense of right and wrong was less well defined. We are not talking about polarized thinking or being judgmental. We are talking about anchoring principles that help us make decisions about how to be in our intimate interactions on any given day. This is important for coupledom because your moral values provide a more consistent guide for behavior than your feelings in the moment. For now, I encourage you to think about the moral principles that you use to guide your own behavior. Our research found that the strongest predictors of a thriving coupledom included honesty, doing the right thing, being fair, and behaving with integrity.

What helps guide your decisions? This is also directly linked to your essences. If there is a discrepancy between your moral values and your essences (the person you think you are), dissatisfaction and guilt might be common visitors in your life. Let's say you humiliated your husband at a party—your moral values tell you that this was wrong and you have to mend his broken ego. But what if one component of your essence is pride? This is when should, would, and could come into play and create a jumbled mental spiral.

Once you've considered your moral values, shift your attention to your personal values. Remember, these are less about right and wrong and more about what is important to you. In our research we identified eight types of personal values, including Egoistic, Altruistic, Moral, Social, Ideological, Independence-Oriented, Utility-Oriented, and Career-Oriented. Here are a few ideas to get you thinking about your personal values: family; spending time with loved ones; building community; physical fitness and health; professional accomplishments; money; financial stability; creative pursuits; beauty and appearance; security; creating social networks, being challenged; kindness; freedom; equality; responsibility; nature; ideas; protecting my loved ones; how others see me (social status); authenticity; compassion; productivity; serenity; tradition; loving kindness; building consensus; protecting the environment; working for peace.

Once you have your list of personal values, rank them from most to least important. This is a "can I live without it?" sort of ranking. This is hard, but it matters. Shared values, or lack thereof, is a crucial factor in fulfilling relationships. If you value social justice, and your partner values social climbing, you can easily see how this could lead to trouble. A clear example of this always comes to a head during political elections. I see many couples struggling, especially in recent years, because they cannot believe that their partner voted for so-and-so. It's not only the candidate they voted for but the ideologies that candidate supports. Don't wait until Election Day to assess whether your partner's worldview and values are compatible with your own. You don't want to be on opposite ends of the spectrum. Same thing goes for deciding what to do with this year's bonus: One party wants to make a donation to a cause, and the other thinks a second car would be more of a priority. Or when the pandemic hit, many couples struggled because one didn't believe in wearing a mask and the other believed everyone must. Or one believed in being vaccinated for the good of the community, and the other person didn't see the point.

Moral values are often instilled in us as children, and they tend to remain consistent throughout life, whereas personal values are subject to change over time with shifting priorities. A person in their twenties might value social status and professional accomplishment; in their thirties and forties they might value spending time with loved ones and building a family and community; in their fifties and sixties they could shift again to valuing creative pursuits, giving back to the society, or financial security. Being able to identify what matters to you is a critical component in being able to negotiate a shared vision with your partner.

Healthy Financial Attitude

Many people don't like to talk about money, especially in a book about relationships. However, anyone who has ever been in any kind of relationship knows how critical finances are. In our research we found that having a healthy financial attitude has a direct link with the outcome of a coupledom. It involves three things. The first is *financial literacy* about the money coming in, the money going out, and for what. Next is *financial self-sufficiency*. Are you able to generate enough money to meet your basic needs on an ongoing basis? The last area, your *spending habits*, has to do with the meaning and role of money in your life. Do your spending habits reflect your financial goals, or are they a source of stress for you? People overspend for a variety of reasons: to numb themselves, to get by, to soothe their anxieties, to impress other people, or to "reward" themselves (though debt in itself is usually very stressful and feels more like a punishment than a reward). Some people go the opposite route and become restrictive about money, so focused on saving money that they deny themselves products and services that could make their lives easier or more pleasant. We associate money with power, success, love, desirability, and a host of other things. If your relationship with money is problematic, it is worth taking a deeper look.

Positive Thoughts and Emotions

The content of our thoughts and the state of our emotions determine how we show up in every interaction. Back in the 1960s Dr. Aaron Beck, a psychiatrist and professor at the University of Pennsylvania, started to research the relationship between how we think and how we feel, and concluded that the content of our thoughts has a direct impact on the quality of our mood. His research was the basis for Cognitive Behavioral Therapy (CBT), a treatment that has evolved a lot and is still widely used today.[10]

Cultivating positive thoughts and emotions isn't about being a Pollyanna who finds the silver lining in every storm cloud. Most of us have some awareness of whether we have a "glass half full" or "glass half empty" way of looking at the world. Having positive or negative emotions and thoughts, especially in relational spaces, is different from being an optimist or a pessimist. It is beyond how you approach life and how you show up in your loving relationships.

Our research indicated a strong correlation between relationship satisfaction and being oriented toward positive thoughts and emotions. Those who orient toward negative thinking tend to focus on the negative aspects of their own life, their relationships, their partner, and life in general. This often leads them to interpret the behavior of others in a negative light by imagining they are acting with harmful intentions. This leads to more negative thoughts, jumping to conclusions that have no real basis, miscommunication, hurt feelings, and resentments in loving relationships. Orienting toward the positive means that you mostly think about the good in yourself, your actions, your partner, and what your coupledom offers you. Research shows that writing a gratitude journal is one of the ways to strengthen this muscle because it brings the positive aspects of our lives and coupledom to a focus. Gratitude sustains positive thoughts and emotions. Let me just clarify that I'm not talking about some kind of toxic positivity where you pretend everything is fine when it isn't, or you avoid anything unpleasant and just sweep it under the rug.[11] Instead I'm talking about maintaining a realistic appraisal of yourself and the world that is skewed more toward the positive than toward the negative end of the spectrum. If journaling is not for you, maybe you can start by listening to some meditations around gratitude and kindness. Many of my clients, and I, have found Tara Brach's books and recordings soothing. In her book *Radical Compassion*, Brach invites the readers to follow the path of **R**ecognize, **A**llow, **I**nvestigate, and **N**urture (RAIN) to allow for forgiveness, love, and access to the wisdom within.[12]

When you find yourself building a case against someone (or something), there's a good chance you're engaged in negative thinking. People sometimes do this when they're considering leaving a job that no longer suits them. They begin to feel very irritated at work, or they find themselves annoyed by little things that never mattered before. Their thoughts escalate in a negative way; then feed off one another in a downward spiral. They find themselves thinking about, and talking about, their job in a very negative way. This happens to all of us from time to time, and it's very common. But when this happens in a high-stakes relationship and becomes chronic or intense, and you start to look for supporting evidence (while ignoring any evidence that does not support your case), your interpersonal dynamics will become stressed and may begin to crack. Relationships can rarely withstand repeated attacks of negativity. This is true for family relationships and friendships, but is especially problematic in loving relationships.

Dr. Beck referred to these as Automatic Negative Thoughts, or ANTs. To remember this, imagine that these are like actual ants, the insects. ANTs, like ants, usually don't come alone. When the first arrives and finds the context warm and cozy, because we don't take an intentional position to get rid of it, it's going to call on the other ants. Before you know it the whole colony will be there. This is actually how the brain works. The amygdala attaches emotional significance to memories, so when you are in a particular emotional state (often a negative one) your brain tends to connect other past memories that are associated with that emotion. It's harder to get out of it if you linger there for a while. That is why when you tell someone who is sad to cheer up, it does not work in the moment!

If you are someone who always assumes the worst, dwells on past mistakes with regret and remorse, and talks to yourself in a harsh and critical way, you could dig a little deeper, maybe with a professional. This will pay off both personally and in your relationships. If you want to look into something to get you started, just look up "cognitive distortions" online, or go to the *Love by Design* website at www.lovebydesignbook.com and look for the cheat sheet on cognitive distortions.

Capacity for Abstract Thinking

A person's ability to think about concepts and ideas, rather than (or in addition to) concrete facts, is a predictor of how they will experience satisfaction in their relationships. As you read earlier, among all the thinking styles that we studied, abstract thinking had the most correlation with a positive outcome in a coupledom. If concrete thinking involves how things happen, abstract thinking involves trying to understand why things happen.[13] Developmental psychologist Jean Piaget conceived of abstract thinking as the final stage of human intellectual development: "There exists an essential moment in the development of intelligence: the moment when the awareness of relationship is sufficiently advanced to permit a reasoned prevision, that is to say, an invention operating by simple mental combination."[14] In relationships, the ability to think abstractly will help you to see your situation in its full context, understand your partner's point of view, identify patterns, solve problems and negotiate creatively, and have a sense of humor.

You need a strong sense of who you are at your core so that you can bring all of yourself into your relationships. I cannot overemphasize the importance of understanding these aspects of yourself when it comes to your intimate relationships. Knowing how you see the world and connect with others will help you to ask for what you need and will set your partner and partnership up for success. Understanding what matters to you, morally and otherwise, will help you design a life, relationship, and love that feels fulfilling. Having your financial house in order will prevent some of the most common problems couples face. Orienting toward positive thoughts and emotions will not only make you feel better as a person, it will also lead you to see your partner in their most favorable light and keep generating positivity for your coupledom. And being able to see things in their context will set you up to address and put into perspective any interpersonal challenges that come your way.

Knowing who you are enables you to give generously, define and maintain healthy boundaries, advocate for yourself lovingly and firmly, and negotiate on your own behalf. And understanding the most important areas of compatibility is a realistic alternative to coming up with an endless list of what you're looking for in a partner, or you will end up kissing a lot of frogs and never finding the prince(ss)!

RECOGNIZING COMPATIBILITY WHERE IT COUNTS

Most people accept the idea that compatibility is important to thriving relationships, but this is another highly subjective idea that means different things to different people. Some people think of compatibility in terms of similarity: sharing similar backgrounds, having the same taste in music, both enjoying travel, having fun together, having the same physical abilities, working at a similar profession, or sharing the same hobbies. For others, compatibility might include wanting the same things out of life. In our research, compatibility emerged as areas of overlap between what each partner brings to the relationship—what we call dyadic fundamentals. We found that having the same hobbies or liking the same food was far less important than having shared values, compatible connection styles, and a similar vision for the future.

Like many ideas that you come across for the first time, this idea can be confusing, so let me clarify a bit: Dyadic fundamentals describe the complementarity of each partner's individual fundamentals. If you are currently single, these are the things you want to look for in a partner. If you're already in a partnership, these are the areas that might need some attention if they are visibly discordant.

For the record, there is nothing I write about, discuss in sessions, or speak about publicly that is more controversial than the idea that we should assess potential partners carefully, and in a variety of domains, before making a lifelong commitment. Whenever I talk about the elements or ingredients needed for love to have a chance to emerge, people look at me and say, "That sounds so calculating," and I respond: "Exactly! Because this decision will have a bigger impact on your future than almost any other decision that you will make in life." We spend hours researching, shopping, and preparing the food that we consume, digest, and pass on within twenty-four hours, yet we think it is cold and calculating to assess for compatibility in a potential life partner.

People really bristle at this idea, though it has existed for centuries and actually predates modern love-based marriage. For many years, all over the world, people did not choose their own partners (in some cultures, they still don't). Instead that task was given to parents, religious leaders, or matchmakers—ideally, people who knew something about long-term relationships and had the best interests of the partners in mind. Imagine that you had to choose a mate for your own child, or your brother, or your very best friend in the world. Would you want to see them with someone who had dramatically different values, was rude or disrespectful, or couldn't seem to keep themselves out of debt while living a lavish lifestyle? Of course not. So why would you choose that for yourself?

Remember, we cannot solve a problem with the same frame of mind that created it.[15] We have to see the problem anew. So, let's look at what we know based on our research and the thousands of hours I have spent with hopeful and heartbroken individuals and couples (as well as thriving ones) around the world. In our research, the essential areas of compatibility that partners shared in every relationship that was described as mutually thriving include being physically attracted to each other, having similar goals and values, having a shared vision, having a similar or compatible connection style, and sharing a healthy financial attitude. And couples who lacked even one of these fundamentals reported lower levels of overall satisfaction. The evidence on this is pretty straightforward and unambiguous.

Physical Attraction

Attraction is complicated. It is both a dyadic fundamental in the sense that it must be in place for the couple to come together and to flourish, and it is also an interpersonal dynamic because it can be cultivated over time. But there is also a slight difference in the way I use the terms. Here, mutual *physical* attraction as a *dyadic fundamental* refers to how you feel about your partner's physical person. Mutual attraction as an *interpersonal dynamic* (i.e., an ingredient of Emergent Love) is about the whole person, not just their body, and will be discussed at length in the next chapter.

Mutual physical attraction could be based on multiple facets. Many of our research participants ranked physical attraction as their primary source of initial attraction, and this was not noticeably different for men, women, or across sexual orientations, relational orientations, and gender identities. What it boils down to is this: If you both can say, "Yes, I can imagine kissing this person or wanting to have sex with this person," then you meet the criteria. You don't need to be passionately in love or filled with an unquenchable desire; you just have to find the person physically attractive. As a side note, being physically attracted to your partner is an element of Emergent Love, but there are plenty of other relationship arrangements that don't require physical attraction.

CONSTITUTIONALLY BOUND COUPLES

There are many, many people all over the world who marry for financial and/or social gain, so physical attraction is not a concern for them. They are the "Constitutionally Bound Couples" from our diagram of couple's configurations. As long as both partners are clear about the nature of the agreement these marriages can work well. For example, I once worked with a couple who had come to me initially because of stress related to infertility. Let's call them Dick and Jane. They identified as a heteronormative couple who were socially prominent in their conservative religious community because both of their fathers were respected religious leaders. They were a highly educated, kind-hearted, and beautiful couple. They wanted desperately to have a child, but they were unable to because Jane was scared of having sex, and Dick was repulsed by female genitalia. They cared about each other very much, they were the best of friends, and both knew about the other's "sexual concerns" long before they were married. Dick explained to me, "I imagine if I had grown up in a different place, surrounded by different people, I might have become gay and married a man and been happy with that."

His point, the point for both of them, was that neither wanted to change; the marriage was serving them just right. They just wanted to have a baby. They weren't asking for my opinion of what they'd done, nor were they asking me to "liberate" them from the values they'd grown up with. So I educated them about the various methods to conceive without intercourse, they had their baby, and my work with them was done. The same goes with couples who wish to open their relationships to other people in various form or shape, while keeping the constitution of their primary relationship together.

As an aside: I do not advise people to ignore or disregard their sexual or relationship orientation, nor do I have any judgment for those who choose to do so. The point is, there is no one size fits all.

Shared Values

Remember when we talked about personal values above? This is where you bring your self-literacy into the relationship. Your values don't have to match your partner's exactly, but they shouldn't be in direct conflict. If you value professional accomplishments and longer hours at work and your partner values spending quality time with his or her partner, problems are bound to arise. If one of you values social justice and activism, and the other values artistic creativity, you might be aligned, but you might also have very different ideas about how to spend your weekends. Our values determine where we want to spend our time, energy, attention, and other resources. The choices we make on a daily basis, large and small, are informed by what we think is important. When we pursue relationships with people whose values conflict with our own, hoping that with enough love we can sort things out later, we set ourselves up for extensive negotiations.

Compatible Outlook and Goals

Having similar ideas about what you want the future to look like is one of those things that is harder to change once the relationship is established. This is why it is so important for each person to have a vision about their own trajectory of life, and to understand what the other person's vision is for their life.

So, let me ask you, what do you want the trajectory of your life to be? Most of the time we are asked, "What do you want to be doing?" or "Where do you want to be living?" While these are all very important, I want to start this by asking you, "Who do you want to be in five years' time? What about ten, fifteen, or thirty years? It is okay if you don't know exactly what you want. Your wants and needs for material things, environment, etc., are continually evolving, which is why I ask you to first see who you want to be before you turn your lens externally. The next step is to see who you would like to be around. Maybe you want to live with your husband in an apartment in Chicago, walk to work, and spend your free time outside the city in a cabin on Lake Michigan. Or would you rather have a few kids and live on a farm in Vermont raising alpacas? If there are things you know about your preferences—that you don't like the cold, or you can't live in the suburbs, or you want dogs but not kids—you'll do best with a partner whose ideas about the future are compatible. You might think the above is an extreme example, but this is actually one of the couples that I worked with years ago.

This is another area that new couples hope will "work itself out" over time, as long as they love each other enough. Recently, a friend reminded me of the saying, "A bird and a fish might fall in love, but where are they going to live?" If one of you wants to be an alpaca farmer in Vermont, and the other wants to be a reputable lawyer living in an apartment in Chicago, how are you ever going to reconcile? Sometimes, "We'll work it out" actually means, "Eventually my partner will realize how important this is to me and will give up on his weird idea about alpacas and join me in Chicago," or "Eventually my partner will see how amazing alpacas really are and he will fall in love with them just as much as I did. And he will see how noisy and polluted cities are, and he will let go of his capitalistic tendency to hoard money, and we will live among the alpacas in bliss and happily ever after." In other words, "we'll work it out" rarely translates into, "I am willing to sacrifice my life's dream and all my goals and desires for the sake of being with this person." Instead, it often means, "I'll figure out a way to talk them into it."

Sacrifice is tricky, and we will talk about it more in later chapters. Compromise might be necessary, but asking your partner to abandon their vision, or abandoning your own, rarely results in relationship satisfaction.

Compatible Connection Style

Notice here that I didn't use the word "shared" when it comes to connection styles, because these areas don't depend on both partners being exactly the same. Some partners have connection styles that are complementary rather than similar, especially when it comes to how they think about the world (perceiving, processing, planning, problem-solving). People who gather information can work well with people who like to organize information. Someone who is analytical might appreciate the way her partner talks about things to help clarify the issues. And even if one person is a talker (external processor) and the other prefers to withdraw and ponder in solitude (internal processor), it is not necessarily a disaster. But the talker might want to process with someone other than the partner and then bring what is relevant to the relational space.

The same is true of how you express and receive love. If you connect primarily through verbally disclosing personal information and having it empathically received, and your partner connects through physical touch, you aren't necessarily incompatible, though you might both have to make an effort to meet the other's needs. (This, by the way, is how heteronormative couples are usually conceptualized today—with women needing to feel close in order to be physical, and men needing to be physical in order to feel close.) Trouble arises only when one person's connection style requires behaviors that the partner does not enjoy or actively dislikes. If you like to have deep conversations about your thoughts and feelings, and your partner finds this awkward or uncomfortable, or if they simply lack skills in this area, you may end up feeling like your needs are not being met or that you are too much. There are some key ways that we each connect to our environment and perceive and receive the information. Think of it as the 4P's of Connection.

THE 4 P'S OF CONNECTION

Perceiving Information: When you receive information about the world around you, do you rely primarily on sight, sound (words), touch/experience, or the energy that you feel? Do you learn best by reading a manual or by trying things out and experimenting for yourself?

Processing Information: Do you prefer to contemplate things in private in order to make sense of them, or do you think best with others, sharing ideas and making meaning together?

Planning: Do you plan ahead as much as possible and stick to a firm schedule, or do you tend to plan only what is essential and rely more on responding to situations as they arise? How important is it to you to feel organized and for things to be predictable? When you think about the future, do you like to have everything mapped out in five-year increments, or do you prefer to fantasize about a whole variety of possible futures before committing yourself to a concrete plan?

Problem-Solving: How much do you rely on intuition and gut instinct when it comes to solving problems, and how much do you rely on data? Do you approach a problem with a collaborative frame of mind and rely on consensus-building to come to a solution, or do you rely primarily on logic and facts?

Shared Healthy Financial Attitude

It is not enough for one partner to have a healthy financial attitude if the other does not (unless that person controls everything, which creates other issues within the coupledom). And most couples who fight about money include at least one person whose spending, saving, or earning is problematic. When someone's credit card is declined on the third date, pay attention. Also pay attention to requests for help with the rent, particularly if they come just after an expensive vacation to Italy. Prolonged periods of unemployment, lavish gifts, or chronic complaints about low salaries could be signs of financial instability or illiteracy. Of course, they also might be reasonable given other circumstances like illness, supporting others, or working hard at a job that does not pay a livable wage.

A healthy financial attitude has less to do with how much a person earns than with how they manage their money. Someone with a robust six-figure income might still overspend, just as someone with relatively low earnings can live comfortably within their means.

If you have made it this far with me, thank you. You've processed a lot of information about yourself and about any current or future partner(s) you may have. Being able to appraise yourself realistically is critical for all relationships, intimate or not. Knowing who you are enables you to give generously, maintain boundaries, advocate for yourself, and negotiate on your own behalf. And understanding the most important areas of compatibility is a realistic alternative to coming up with an endless list of what you're looking for in a partner. Now let's turn our attention to Part Two: The Six Ingredients of Emergent Love, where you will learn about the interpersonal dynamics that partners can cultivate to create the best possible context for love to emerge.

PART II

THE SIX INGREDIENTS OF EMERGENT LOVE

CHAPTER 4

Attraction

"Love must not entreat," she added, *"or demand. Love must have the strength to become certain within itself. Then it ceases merely to be attracted and begins to attract."*

—Hermann Hesse[1]

When couples come to me with an issue of no longer feeling attracted to each other, they're usually talking about the desire to have sex with the other person. When you saw the chapter title, I bet that's probably what came to mind for you, too: that we're going to focus on that spark and how to keep it alive or rekindle it. Well, not quite. Because even though physical connection is an important part of a committed coupledom (there is a whole chapter on this in part three) thinking of attraction *only* in terms of sexual desire is too narrow a lens—and that's coming from a sexologist! So, let's set the record straight: There is more to attraction than sexual desire. In fact, they're two different things.

Desire is that feeling of wanting something and even longing for it. It is closely associated with the neurochemicals of sex, and it is similarly short-lived, unpredictable, and often unintentional. You can desire something (or someone) for no apparent reason, and even when there are good reasons *not* to desire it—like craving fast food, or really wanting that pair of $700 heels that you can't walk in for more than fifteen minutes. Attraction is much more layered and complex, and rarely exists without a reason.

Think, for a moment, about some of the people you like in a nonsexual way. This could be a friend whom you appreciate for her candor, a colleague who always makes you laugh, a sweet barista who greets you with a smile and a perfect cup of coffee, or another parent at the playground who appreciates that socks don't always have to match. You see them, you smile automatically, and you think, "This is going to be good." Being with that person is meaningful for you in one way or another, it adds something to your experience in that moment, and you're drawn to them for a reason. We're attracted to people when we recognize certain attributes or characteristics that we value and appreciate. And the reverse is usually true as well—when people feel valued and appreciated, they are also drawn toward us.

Sy and Gabby are a good example of what long-term mutual attraction looks like. Sy and Gabby are in their sixties and have been together for thirty-five years. They adore each other (their words, not mine). Gabby explained, "Sy is always the first person I want to tell when something happens, good or bad. He's my guy. He's smart, he always has something to say, and he gets me." Sy added, "Of course I *love* Gabby, but I think we're so happy because we really *like* each other. Gabby is curious about everything, and she always has some new thing she wants to do, like learn to play pickleball or go for a helicopter ride. There's this thing at the mall where you can sign up to be a passenger in a race car and go a hundred sixty miles per hour or something. It's supposed to be a Father's Day gift, but she wants to do it, too. Gabby's fun to be around, and I love to have fun." After so many years together, they are still drawn to each other. That is mutual attraction, and it has more to do with intimacy than with sexual desire (though, for the record, that was present, too).

Each of us has our own unique set of criteria for what we find attractive in another person, whether as a friend, business partner, lover, or spouse. What makes someone seem attractive is more than a mere constellation of culturally sanctioned physical attributes, or a fleeting burst of neurochemicals that burns hot then fizzles out quickly. Attraction is multidimensional, and involves who we are, who we've been, what has happened in our lives, what we need, what we want, what we long for, and what we long to avoid. What we find attractive is partly a product of our environment, but it is also deeply personal and highly idiosyncratic. And, most important for our purposes here, it's also vulnerable to changing circumstances in our lives. We might not always be able to articulate what we find attractive in something or someone when we are drawn to them, but we know when we don't like to be around certain people or energy.

Like all the ingredients of Emergent Love, attraction has to be mutual and reciprocal. In our research it became very clear that the contribution and distribution of these ingredients cannot be one-directional: They must be both expressed and experienced. In other words, feeling attracted to your partner is good, but it's not enough. You also need to demonstrate that sense of attraction in a way that your partner can see and receive it. Remember, Emergent Love is based more on what you do than how you feel.

Mutual attraction is important early in a relationship because it pulls us toward the other person and is the first step in creating intimacy. But, like everything else, it must deepen and evolve. Rather than being a one-time deal that shapes the beginning of a relationship then takes a back seat, it is actually incredibly important to fulfilling, satisfying long-term relationships. It is the basis for intimacy. What's more, it is something couples can work on; it can be cultivated over time to improve the quality of your relationships and of your life. Where desire might be fleeting, attraction is a renewable resource.

In this chapter I invite you to think about attraction in a new way. In its broadest sense, attraction goes so much deeper than sexual chemistry, and includes everything that makes you want to be *with* and *around* your partner. The secret to sustaining attraction over time lies in cultivating the habit of paying attention to who you and your partner are right now, in this moment. When you can tune in to what is most important to you, what matters most to them, and what you each value most about yourselves, you create a pathway for connection. In the words of Dale Carnegie, one of the gurus of self-actualization, "You can make more friends in two months by becoming interested in other people than you can in two years by trying to get other people to be interested in you."[2] The same is true for couples. When you take a deep interest in your partner, and about how they are changing and evolving over time, it is like extending an invitation to bring their whole self into the relational space time and again while introducing and reintroducing yourself to them over and over again. This is how attraction, in all its forms, becomes the foundation of sustained intimacy.

WHAT IS ATTRACTION?

Attraction has been studied by clinical psychologists, social psychologists, and researchers from a variety of disciplines for years.[3] Usually the research participants of larger scale studies are college or graduate students, and they are for the most part middle-class, heterosexual, white European and American adults between the ages of eighteen and twenty-eight. The research also usually focuses mostly on the initial physical attraction between potential romantic partners and less on attraction (physical or otherwise) as it manifests in long-term coupledom where partners go through different phases of their lives together. Nevertheless, it is relevant here because it helps to dispel some of the confusion around attraction and desire.

These studies attempt to understand both the *why* and the *how* of what makes us draw closer to some people and farther away from others. Is beauty really in the eye of the beholder? Is love at first sight real? Do men always marry women who remind them of their mothers? Though there is no universal consensus among academics, there are some widely researched and generally accepted principles underscoring the notion of being attracted to someone in general: proximity, similarity, familiarity, reciprocity, and physical attractiveness.

People are more likely to feel connected, and even attracted, to people they see regularly and have things in common with. Proximity includes both the notion that you're less likely to feel attracted to someone you've never met (fandom notwithstanding) and also the notion that the more you see of someone, the more attractive they become. Proximity tends to work like a bell curve: More contact is good in the beginning and builds attraction, but in long-term relationships the opposite seems to be true, and separateness with clear boundaries that are inviting (rather than isolating) becomes necessary.[4] Proximity could be in person or online, like when you exchange messages or follow someone and read about them and their lives on social media. This is called the mere-exposure effect[5] or familiarity effect, and it refers to people's sense of preference for those individuals they are exposed to most frequently.[6] Familiarity brings affinity. Although a caveat here is that with too much exposure, one can reach a point of saturation, boredom, or fatigue because of the repeat exposure, and the impact will go away (something that happened for many couples during the pandemic).[7]

We also tend to be attracted to people who are similar to us. Similarity can be both surface level (interests and preferences) and deep (values). If you only share a love for Elvis Presley, spicy food, and horror movies, you're bound to enjoy some experiences of spending time together, but this won't necessarily lead to building a satisfying relationship. This may be why we tend to partner with people who are demographically similar to us: people who are of the same race, close in age, from similar socio-economic backgrounds, and with similar levels of education and intelligence.[8] Despite the theory that opposites attract, which can be successful in some cases, empirical research since the early 1900s in multiple disciplines suggests that similarity, rather than difference, is a better predictor of relationship satisfaction. "Sharing our values with others and having others share their values with us helps us validate the worthiness of our self-concepts."[9] write the authors of *Principles of Social Psychology*. When we are with people who are similar to us, we have a better chance of predicting their future behavior; there is also a perception that we have a better chance to be liked back. This is a "likeness begets liking" explanation.[10] Liking the same things, and having the same values, also makes daily life easier as it means there is less to negotiate.

Chances are, if you're similar to someone you're also going to feel very comfortable around them because they feel familiar to you. Evolutionary psychologists believe that we seek attributes that feel soothing to us—they evoke a sense of safety and security. Personality traits that remind us of others with whom we have a positive relationship may come into play here: The way he talks to his son reminds you of your dad's gentleness; the way she argues a point is just like your sister whom you look up to.

You're probably not surprised to hear that we tend to be interested in and even attracted to people who are interested in and attracted to us—something else we have in common! "Reciprocity of liking" is a principle that describes the importance of knowing that our interest in another person is returned and mutual. A popular notion within the idea of submergent love is the false idealization of unrequited love—we want what we can't have. Pursuing someone who remains scarce in their outward affections becomes "the thrill of the chase" rather than a waste of your valuable time. In reality, reciprocity is more often an indicator of lasting and meaningful relationships.

Finally, we come to physical attractiveness. This one might feel somewhat obvious—we are attracted to people we find attractive—but perceived beauty often plays a significant role in early relationships. The keyword here is *perceived*. Perception is what creates beauty. Most of us can bring to mind at least one person whom we think of as average in physical appearance but who is perceived by many people to be extremely attractive. Maybe it's her sense of humor, or his sense of style or confidence, or their ability to make you feel like the most fascinating person in the room. Of course, the reverse is also true: A person can conform perfectly to a culture's ideals of beauty, and everyone talks about how attractive they are, and yet no one seems to feel attracted to them. In Farsi we have two different words for someone who is beautiful (*khoshgel*) and someone who is attractive (*jazzāb*). The person who has the parameters of beauty (i.e., a symmetrical face, high forehead, large eyes) is not necessarily considered attractive (i.e., a person you want to be around).

Just a note to say that, so far, we are discussing how attraction works in general and not talking about being attracted to others based on our own personal history, especially if it includes adverse childhood experiences. For example, while we might *want* to be attracted to someone who is gentle and stable, our past experiences might lead us to see that person as boring (and therefore unattractive). Instead, we find ourselves attracted to someone who is moody, unstable, and gives us terror like what we were used to growing up. I have seen people who built a relationship with a person whom they wanted to be around and then started sabotaging their relationship because they could not stand harmony and craved chaos.

WHAT DEFINES ATTRACTIVENESS, AND WHY IT MATTERS

We tend to gravitate toward beauty, but what is beauty objectively? And who gets to decide? Generally speaking, what one person finds physically attractive in a potential mate will be highly idiosyncratic and composed of a number of variables. Some of these may be hardwired through evolution, like physical fitness, youthful looks (for female) and masculine features (for male), or facial symmetry.[11] Some research indicates that men with stubble are considered more physically attractive while men with full beards are more attractive as long-term partners, perhaps because they signal security.[12] Other studies inform us that women tend to be more physically and otherwise attracted[13] to men depending on where they are in their menstrual cycle, if they are on hormonal contraceptives, or if an individual takes certain medications for depression.[14] The brain on alcohol and drugs also tends to view a potential date or mate differently than a sober one. So whom we find physically attractive is, in part, physiological.

But there are also points of physical attraction that will be unique to you and your individual history and cultural context, like certain features or mannerisms that you associate positively with sex: beautiful hands or a goofy laugh or silver hair or a deep voice or a certain shape of nose or complexion or a certain scent.

In this way, beauty ideals are subjective and influenced by cultural and societal constructs. The related indicators often reflect the beauty standards prevalent in a particular culture or subculture at a given moment in history. Various factors, such as movies, AI-generated face constructions, commercial porn productions, and social media play a role in shaping these ideals. Consequently, they heavily impact whom we find attractive, even if those perceptions might differ from our true preferences. Cultural concepts of physical beauty are adaptable, and throughout history, different icons like Clark Gable, Marilyn Monroe, James Dean, Twiggy, Farrah Fawcett, Sofía Vergara, Harry Styles, and Idris Elba have represented diverse standards of beauty, each firmly linked to their respective era.

For example, in contemporary Western societies, there is a preference for individuals who have minimal body fat and are physically fit.[15] The concept of being thin as the beauty norm has not always been

prevalent. In Western cultures, there has been an increasing preference for women with slender, masculine, and athletic appearances
over the past five decades. This shift is evident when comparing the
body figures of female movie stars from the 1940s and 1950s to those
of present times. While certain preferences such as youth, symmetry,
and averageness appear to be relatively universal, the strong inclina-
tion toward thinness is not as prevalent in other cultures. In societies
where food has historically been scarce, for instance, a heavier body,
rather than a thinner one, is more associated with perceived attractiveness. This can contribute to the flimsiness of sexual desire—a
concept based on the whims of any given culture in an ever-changing
landscape of what is desirable and what is not.

While progress has been made toward inclusivity and appreciating
diverse body types, certain beauty ideals persist in our collective con-
sciousness and wield significant influence, often with negative implications, when assessing our own physical attractiveness. Embracing a
positive self-image can prove challenging when we do not conform to
these rigid standards, leading to potential issues. Cultivating a sense of
self-assurance is vital for nurturing mutual attraction within a relationship. Recognizing and celebrating the inherent beauty found in a variety of bodies can foster a healthier and more harmonious coupledom.

Part of initial attraction also has to do with what we think we will get
from our partner, and what kinds of opportunities an alliance with them
will provide.[16] Social exchange theory, originally introduced in the 1960s,
looks at relationships in terms of the costs and benefits associated with
a particular partnership.[17] The idea here is not that we're secretly assessing partners in order to calculate how advantageous a partnership with
them might be; instead, the theory is that a relationship continues when the
benefits outweigh the costs. Much of this happens beneath or beyond our
conscious level of awareness, and it almost always happens on both sides.

Sometimes we're attracted to a person because they can offer something we want more of, or they challenge us to overcome our own barriers, like when a shy person partners with someone who is outgoing and
can help them navigate social situations. Or we choose a partner who has

qualities we aspire to and want more of in our own lives, like discipline or confidence or a higher level of education. We might be attracted to someone's family of origin or their professional success. Remember, we are usually attracted to someone for a reason, because they have qualities or attributes that we value and admire.

Historically, and in many cultures around the world today, these points of attraction are made explicit and negotiated. For example, masculinity might be equated with strength, performance, and social power, and femininity with the opposite. What makes someone attractive as a partner will depend, in part, on what resources they each can provide. If one party perceives of themself in a "one down" position, they will find themselves drawn to a person who has greater access to resources.[18]

As you can see, there is no single "law of attraction." Instead it is more of a "puzzle of attraction." *Law of attraction* suggests a road map that many think they need to follow while a *puzzle of attraction* could be individually constructed and made sense of. We are drawn to others because of who they are, what they represent, and what we think an association with them might provide. In fact, understanding whom you find attractive can tell you a lot about yourself. Are you attracted to competence? Playfulness? Power? Intelligence? What are your reasons for valuing one characteristic or quality over another? As with all aspects of Emergent Love, if we wish to nurture mutual attraction in our coupledom we need to start with ourselves. It's good to keep in mind that what you find attractive will change over time. Basing attraction on your values would be a wise thing to do, because they are less likely to change as drastically with time.

THE EVER-CHANGING DYNAMICS OF MUTUAL ATTRACTION

The initial draw we feel toward our partners is like a little green light telling us to proceed, to find out more about this person, to see if there is the potential for something further. If we are online that green light might be a charming smile or a photo that shows the person in a context that we like, too (swimming, cooking, going out with friends, etc.). Sometimes the draw is so strong that we can't think of anything beyond making a connection happen. Sometimes we just notice *them* noticing *us*, and we become interested. For many, it is the physical attraction or specifically sexual chemistry that they feel for the other person. When we perceive someone as physically attractive, we assume that they have positive internal qualities, too.[19] This makes us feel safer and more comfortable with them, so we proceed.

As we get to know a person, and if we like what we learn, other forms of attraction kick in. Attraction has to do with the whole person. Who is she when she's not with me? What are her friends like? Is he kind, smart, funny? How is she in bed? Can I trust this person? Is she stable in her own life? Would he be a good father? Will they fit in with my family? Do they like me back? Can we hold a meaningful conversation? Could we make a go of it as a couple? We might have these questions at the top of our mind or deep in our subconscious. If we like what we find, then there will be a desire to experience more of them. If our purpose is to form a loving partnership, we start to go deeper to assess the person's potential as a partner. Part of our initial assessment usually includes monitoring the reciprocity of our mutual interest. We need to make sure that the other person is also really into this.

One of the challenges in long-term partnerships has to do with this sense of reciprocity of liking. What happens when the initial qualities that drew us toward someone, and that we found so compelling and exciting, lose some of their pulling power? Or we suspect that the reverse is true, and that our own desire is no longer reciprocated?

In long-term relationships, many of the people who tell me they don't feel attracted to their partner anymore share that they also don't feel like their partner is into *them* anymore. They refer to the particular ways their partner looked at them that made them feel special, wanted, and beloved, and report that those looks have diminished over time. For some people this happens after a few dates; for others it comes years later. And it's not only the desirous looks (i.e., I want you sexually and beyond) that tend to diminish: Verbal expressions of appreciation, admiration, validation, little acts of consideration and affirmation also tend to lessen over time in long-term relationships. The result: Partners feel "taken for granted," "invisible," even "unloved." Feeling unattractive themselves, they likewise no longer find their partners to be as attractive as they once were. Often, but not always, it's because the initial points of attraction have evolved and changed over time, and one or both of the partners hasn't kept up with these changes.

For example, Michael and Shayna, a couple in their early thirties, came to see me several years ago because they felt like they were "out of step" with each other and growing more distant. Michael and Shayna had been together for seven years and married for three. When they met in their twenties Michael was a quiet, shy guy who worked for a large company as an electrical engineer, and Shayna was working her way through college as a bartender. "He was different, more serious, and I liked that. You could tell he was super smart, and he was thoughtful about everything. Even though we're the same age, he seemed so adult!" Michael was attracted to Shayna's ease with people. He loved to sit at the bar and watch her flirt with her customers and banter back and forth. "Man, she was fun. I was spending all day every day working on projects with other engineers. I love what I do, but these guys are not exactly outgoing. Even outside of work she knew everyone—the lady that runs the bodega on the corner, the people from church, the kids she went to high school with and all their parents and cousins and even the old guys who play dominoes in the park."

Now, seven years on, Shayna is teaching high school English and working on a master's degree. When they came to see me, Shayna was feeling frustrated by Michael's constant exhortations to "Have some fun!" And Michael was confused by Shayna's frustration with him. "She works too hard," he said, "and I know she'd have a good time if she'd just let herself." Michael misses the fun they used to have. "It's like we've switched places and now I'm the one who wants to go out and she's the serious one." Shayna bristled when he said this. "I still have a lot of friends, and I like to go out and see them, but that Party Girl time of my life is over!

These days I barely have time to see my good friends, and I sure don't want to spend a Friday night in a bar with people I barely know! I get that you miss that, I really do, but sometimes I feel like you just don't understand where I'm at right now. I'm trying to build something here with you. I'm thinking about the future, and you're stuck in the past."

When I work with couples who worry about growing apart, I encourage them to think about what attracted them to each other in the first place. Most of us can list traits or qualities that we find attractive in a potential partner—handsome, grounded, educated, from a respected family, funny, interesting, mature—but we stop short of exploring *why* that particular aspect is attractive to us. Exploring what draws us toward someone helps clarify our own needs and longings as well as the expectations we had (and often continue to have) of the other.

As we saw earlier, we're usually attracted to specific qualities in the other person that are meaningful to us—they are familiar and comforting, or they enhance our lives in some way. Sometimes we focus exclusively on one particular point of attraction, usually associated with a role we hope they will play in our coupledom (earner, parent, caretaker, lover) without paying attention to the other roles they will inevitably need to fulfill. For example, I see many clients who choose a partner who they think will be a great parent, but they don't necessarily have a lot in common with them. Somewhere down the line they become discontented, and the partner often feels used. The gap between them becomes problematic. This is usually what people mean when they say things like, "I fell in love with the wrong person." Other times we focus on a few points of attraction, like sense of humor or earning potential, and expect that these will remain constant over time. When they don't, we no longer feel the same. In all of these, remember, even if the points of attraction remain the same (at least for the most part), if the other person does not see behaviors to show them this, their attraction usually fades away, too.

Through the process of our work together, Shayna and Michael both came to understand the meaning behind their initial attraction to each other. For Michael, "having fun" was not just letting your hair down, having drinks, or letting go. It was way more than that. Shayna learned that

Michael had always felt a sense of being an outsider socially. His mother, an Irish-American social worker, had married an African-American electrician who owned his own business. As their only child, Michael grew up struggling to know how to be "himself" when who he was seemed to change with his ever-changing context.

As a mixed-race boy in a majority white suburban school, he felt different. He remembered trying to talk to his mother about it, but she only reassured him, "You're just a boy like everyone else." Looking back, Michael wishes his mother had helped him to embrace his differences rather than dismissing them. The way he talked, the songs he grew up listening to, and even most of the friends he had all were aligned with the "white suburban Michael." He remembers being surprised when, in middle school, his parents had a huge fight when his father refused to let him get a paintball gun. His mother, well-meaning but oblivious, said, "But all the boys have them!" His father patiently explained, "Yes, all the *white* boys have them. But if a cop sees a Black kid with a gun in this neighborhood he's liable to get shot." Later, as a teenager just starting to drive, it was his father who gave him "the talk" about the dangers of being a Black man in America. "If you get pulled over, and you probably will at some point, *do not argue*. Even if the officer is being unreasonable, you need to be polite and keep your hands where the officer can see them. I know I'm asking a lot. But letting your pride get you killed won't help anyone." As he got older he started being more conscious about his African-American heritage, but he had never really felt embraced by either community.

Looking at Shayna, seeing how free she was in her dark skin, somehow gave him a sense of freedom, too. She was not confused at all. He loved feeling included in her enormous and diverse circle of friends and acquaintances. He felt a sense of deep belonging with her. Over time he came to love how hard she worked, and how much she cared about being of service to her community. "I was so proud of her when she graduated," he tells me. "She worked so hard for it, and she was just so proud of herself! She was happy with who she was while I still struggled to be in my own skin, literally."

Understanding Michael's experience helped Shayna to have more compassion for his longing to feel like a part of the community. Shayna, who had grown up in their Harlem neighborhood, took her sense of belonging for granted. She was raised in a tight-knit neighborhood, surrounded by extended family who all "pulled together to bring ourselves up." Her parents worked long hours at low-wage jobs and saw education as the way to an easier life for their kids. She realized that part of what had attracted her to Michael was his engineering degree, his job, and his total confidence in his ability to earn a good living as a professional. She wouldn't have to be the primary earner, wouldn't have to worry so much about money, and would have access to his family's resources (financial and otherwise), which were more considerable than her own. "I feel sort of embarrassed to say that out loud," she said, "like I'm some kind of social climber and was just using Michael. Even though I know that isn't true, it still feels bad to say it."

Just as I was about to reassure Shayna, Michael jumped in. "I don't feel that way at all. If anything, I feel like I was using you because you've always made it so easy for me to feel like I belong." I offered them a different perspective. "Rather than thinking about it as what you took from each other, why not look at it as what you each had to offer the other?" Shayna brought a large, extended family, a strong community, and a social awareness of herself as an intelligent Black woman whose ambition was part of her racial identity. Michael brought not only his financial resources but also a kind of confidence that comes with generations of financial security. "Michael had such a healthy sense of entitlement. Not like the world owed him something, but more that he expected to be compensated well for his efforts. He has always had this clarity about his own worth." This was all new ground for Shayna.

Like many couples, the qualities that brought Michael and Shayna together initially had changed in importance over time with their shifting priorities. If you want attraction to last over time, you have to realize that the person in front of you is a dynamic being (and that you are, too). As individuals we are all evolving continually. When our relationships don't acknowledge, accommodate, and even celebrate these changes, they can become stagnant and divergent.

ATTRACTION IN LONG-TERM COUPLEDOM

Nurturing mutual attraction is informed by actions that are based on a new perspective. We all grow and change, and if the ways we relate to each other do not evolve with us, we get stuck and frustrated and disconnected. While certain of your partner's "attractive" characteristics will most likely remain stable (friendliness, intelligence, optimism), others will inevitably change as priorities shift to accommodate the necessities of your real lives. For a couple who meet in college, one might be attracted to the other's social status on campus, to their passion for the subject of their dissertation, or to the way that the other was "there for me" when they were lonely and far from their family. Ten years later, off campus, with aging parents, two jobs, and a dog, those initial points of attraction may matter less. In a long-term relationship the roles we play both in the world at large and also within the relationship are constantly in flux, and we need to be prepared for that.

Life continues its journey, and we go along with it. What I observe in my couples is that, in an ironic twist of fate, the very same qualities that initially brought a couple together might become their largest sources of conflict. The person who was "spontaneous and exciting" becomes "irresponsible." The person who was "nurturing" becomes "overbearing." Sometimes one person still finds a certain quality attractive, but the other, who once possessed that quality, no longer identifies with it or expresses it in the same way anymore.

Again, the problem isn't that we, or our partners, have changed. The problem is that we expected that neither of us would. When we think our partner is going to remain a static entity, unchangeable and unchanging, forever providing us with the same benefits we have come to expect and rely upon, our ability to see our partners, and to have them see us fully in return, will be dimmed. When this happens, we limit our possibilities for connection in the present. Assuming that our own needs and wants will remain the same can also create a problem. When the initial points of attraction are not as important as before, or even nonexistent, the couple struggles to find a compass to guide them toward each other.

Attraction is a gateway to intimacy, so while it is necessary at the beginning of a relationship it is not enough on its own. Intimacy includes being seen for who we are at this moment, in these circumstances, today. We want our partners to appreciate who we have become, not who we once were (unless we have lost parts of ourselves that we want to be reminded of and rebuild again). We have to continue to assess ourselves, our partners, and our coupledom in all the years to come and across different phases of our lives in order to bring the most authentic version of our current self into the partnership. Attraction must be reasoned with, fine-tuned, and expanded to include all the roles our partner fulfills and not simply the things we liked about them in the beginning.

As you are shaping a new perspective around what attraction is and learning about what it takes to keep it alive and thriving in the long run, I want to acknowledge that this is not easy. There is a certain grief involved in letting go of *what was* in order to make room for *what can be*. Michael had come to rely on Shayna for his sense of belonging to the community, and he wasn't ready to let that go. Her position had allowed him to be social without ever having to confront his own social anxiety and delicate sense of belonging to his African-American community. The loss was twofold: He missed the old Shayna, but he also missed who he was when he was with that version of her.

Letting go of the role of social butterfly had also been difficult for Shayna. She had enjoyed those college years and had loved the attention and approval she got from customers. "It was great, it really was. I was popular, I was fun, everybody wanted to talk to me. It was a huge boost to my ego at the time, and I loved it. Sometimes I miss that girl and I'm sad about it, but there are other things that are more important to me now." When Michael pressures Shayna to go out and have fun, it's like pouring salt on the wound. In an individual session, Shayna admits, "I almost feel like he's saying that who I am now isn't enough for him, that I'm boring and dull. What's worse is that I'm also struggling to see him as attractive anymore. The way he relies on me for his social life makes me feel more like his mother than his wife."

By shifting from frustration to attentiveness and engaging in expansive conversations around the terms they had been using like "having fun" and "building something together," Shayna and Michael had a much stronger literacy about their relationship and a more salient rapport with each other. This allowed for the building of fluency between them. They started to look at the lack of mutual attraction as a joint problem, a relational dynamic issue rather than one person's problem that had to be fixed. If they were going to continue to be attracted to each other, they needed to understand how to see the other person as he or she wanted to be seen. They needed to accept that this is not a problem to resolve but a journey to embark on.

BUILDING ATTRACTION

We all connect with different parts of ourselves throughout our lives, and we offer these parts to those around us as potential areas of connection. When these aspects of self are recognized by the other, when they're well received and appreciated, we feel known and understood. We feel seen. And the more we feel seen and appreciated, the more we want to be around our partner. When we do the same for them, and make the effort to see and appreciate who they are today, the more they will feel understood and the more they will want to be around us. The more we see into each other, the closer we feel. This is how attraction helps to create intimacy. Positive interactions increase, and we find ourselves in an upward spiral of mutual appreciation and mutual attraction. When your partner supports you in feeling good about yourself, you will be drawn toward them. Remember reciprocity? We are attracted to people who are attracted to us.

When you want to build attraction in your coupledom, a good place to start is by identifying the things that matter most about you *to you* and not what matters most about you *to your partner*. The next step is to communicate that to them. And, of course, they will do the same for you.

Part of what happened to Shayna and Michael is that they each continued to relate to the roles the other had played early on in the relationship and had lost track of who the other was becoming. Shayna had expanded from being a student, friend, bartender, and lover to being a teacher, wife, and graduate student working on her professional career. Her priorities had shifted with her changing roles, and she longed for Michael to see her and appreciate her in this new capacity. Michael had changed as well, and he longed for more connection with Shayna and with his community, but he didn't know how to do it for himself because he was stuck in the past, still relying on Shayna for his sense of belonging.

In order to help this couple understand the changing nature of attraction, I asked them to reflect on their lives today in an exercise that was all about each person's main identities and the prominent roles in their life at this particular moment in time. (I have many more of these exercises you can download for free on the *Love by Design* website: www.lovebydesignbook .com.) I asked them each to make a list of what they were proud of right now in their lives. I encourage you to do this as well. You don't have to be falsely modest or worry about bragging; just focus on an accurate self-assessment. When you are both done, carve out time to get together and read your lists out loud to each other.

BUILDING BLOCK: WHO WE ARE TODAY

Make a list of all the identities, characteristics, attributes, and relationships that you are proud of and attracted to *in yourself*. Include as many things as possible. How do you nurture each of them? Are any in conflict with one another? How do you think they are serving you or not in your life and your relationship? Do you think other people, particularly your partner, know about these the way you want them to? Is there anything holding you back from having them see in you what you see in yourself?

Now, take the list to your partner and share it with them. Anything surprising about your own list or theirs? Anything that is new to you? Anything that you thought would make it to their list and didn't? Anything that does not sit well with you? Anything that is as much a source of pride as it is of shame? Remember that it is important to first let your partner share what they want to share and receive them fully before asking questions or sharing your own thoughts. I advise that you share your lists on separate days so you each have your own moment with this exercise.

This exercise is not about merging ideas or coming to an agreement about what should matter most to the other person; it's about identifying and respecting each other's diversities and multiple identities. It is usually a vulnerable exercise, and the person who is sharing is giving the other the privilege to take a look at their inside world, so please keep that in mind as you listen to your partner. Don't interrupt or offer suggestions unless they ask, and listen with interest and without judgment as you learn more about how each of you sees yourself in the present. Only ask questions when necessary for clarification, and let them finish sharing completely as best as you can.

When Michael and Shayna finished the exercise, they shared it with each other in my office. Michael went first. "I'm proud of being with Shayna, of caring for my mother and being a reliable son, helping my father with his business, being faithful to Shayna, being good at my job and being financially stable." Shayna reported, "I'm proud of being smart and determined; having a vision for my life and for our lives; being financially independent; always having a goal and working toward it; being a kind person; showing up for my extended family; being a wonderful aunt; taking good care of my health; being an African-American woman and a teacher and a role model for some of my students; my accomplishments so far and also the things I'm working on now; having good friends; being a good neighbor; and doing really well in graduate school."

When I asked them if they listed something or heard something from the other that surprised them or stood out to them, Michael said, "Her list is so much longer than mine! She has a lot of different things in there that she's proud of. Being socially connected was only one of them! I didn't even put obvious things like being Black or being a man or a homeowner or anything. It's like I'm disconnected from myself, which sort of makes sense, because that's how I feel a lot of the time." Shayna laughed and shared, "I am proud of you for all of what you shared, and I don't have anything surprising here but a realization. I feel like I sometimes cannot show my determination or ambition to you because not only do you not appreciate it but you get annoyed by it. It feels like you dim my light at times, or like you need me to keep being who I was back then and only be in that role because that's the one that serves you."

I admire couples like Michael and Shayna who are so vulnerable, brave, and honest without being cutting toward each other. This conversation took a few sittings for them to go through in its totality, and by the end of it they both felt liberated and encouraged by what they learned about each other. Most important, they didn't feel stuck as much anymore. They knew where to put their efforts to build toward the attraction they both craved.

Remember those Couple's Configurations from chapter 2? Well, Michael chose Submergent Love (1 + 1 = 1) as his ideal and Shayna chose Emergent Love (1 + 1 = 3) as hers. Michael believed that the more space and identity he shared with Shayna, the better he would feel about the relationship, and the more they would thrive. But Shayna needed her own orb to grow and thrive to be able to contribute to the growth of their coupledom.

Michael explained that it is easier to appreciate and celebrate some of Shayna's roles, for example as a member of her extended family, in their coupledom. He liked attending the large gatherings and feeling like he was a part of that kinship. But her role as a graduate student, which he fully supported, also took energy, time, money, and attention away from their coupledom, so it felt harder to celebrate as such. Shayna took this to heart and offered that maybe she could slow down the pace of her studies and take two courses per semester instead of five, realizing that she needed to start putting some of those resources back into the relationship if she wanted it to thrive.

As we continued to work together, Michael and Shayna felt the attraction between them beginning to grow. They each felt more seen by the other, and they had begun to explore how they could bring more of themselves into the relationship. They had more meaningful conversations, laughed more together, and sought each other out to create shared experiences with each other instead of avoiding or nagging at each other. At the same time, both realized that just because something was important to them as an individual, they also needed to continuously renegotiate the boundaries between their individual lives and their coupledom. This is not to pick one over the other but to create a balance.

Michael had assumed that Shayna would always be "there for him" and in charge of their social life, and Shayna had assumed that Michael would always value professional development and would not be bothered by how busy she was. By opening up the lines of communication and sharing more about what mattered to each of them right now, not seven years ago, they were able to see each other from a new, and more accurate, perspective. Knowing that Michael saw and appreciated her role as a professional, and understood how much she valued that part of herself, made it easier for Shayna to acknowledge that her individual aspirations were perhaps cutting into their shared time together. She began to set aside more time to spend with Michael to nurture the relationship. For Michael, sharing about how much he longed to feel like a part of the community helped him realize that he had perhaps relied on Shayna to do things that he could reasonably do for himself. He began to focus on his own role in the community and looked for ways to participate and contribute independent of Shayna. It wouldn't be easy, but they were happy to have a clear direction in which to move.

Attraction, at its core, thrives when both partners bring their authentic selves into the relational space. Embracing the diverse identities and roles they hold in their individual lives and within the relationship is key. This ongoing process involves negotiation and mutual efforts to foster genuine connections.

CONNECTING WHERE IT MATTERS

Having clarity about what you find attractive about yourself and your partner, and openly sharing these things with your partner, can foster intimacy and enhance attraction. However, this process isn't a one-time event; it requires revisiting and reinforcing these aspects at different phases of life. First, you go back to "in-to-me-I-see," then you invite the other to see you, too, "in-to-me-you-see." Partners who have been together a long time often assume that they know everything about the other: what he likes, what's important to her, how they think, what they value most in their lives. So they get confused when the gestures and words of support that once made the partner feel loved and appreciated no longer seem to work. This was the case with Eli and Adelina.

Adelina, a Brazilian graphic designer in her late thirties, shared with me that Eli, her husband of eleven years, was "the kindest man that has ever walked the earth." Yet she struggled with feeling attracted to him, especially since their son, Liam, was born. Eli shared that Adelina didn't make efforts to initiate conversations, touch him in any way, or engage with him much beyond the logistical conversations of everyday life. Whenever he made an effort, she seemed to feel pressured and annoyed. Eli, a journalist (also in his late thirties), was sitting beside her on the yellow couch in my office, heartbroken and confused. "I am literally doing everything I can think of, everything I can read about in all these self-help books, to make Adelina feel connected to me. But nothing seems to work."

I started to assess the state of their coupledom from the most accessible place: verbal exchanges. "When you compliment each other, what do you say *specifically*?" Adelina thought a bit and said, "You are such a good dad, so kind and attentive to Liam." Eli's common way of complimenting Adelina was to say, "Our son is so lucky to have you as a mother." The problem was immediately apparent, and I didn't need to say anything. They looked at each other and Adelina said, "Wow! We only see each other as parents, don't we?!" Eli reflected, "Well, most of the time we spend together is with Liam, so being parents takes up a huge majority of our time and mind space on any given day. Also, I know that sometimes you worry about not being a good mother, so I'm trying to make you feel better."

When I asked them what their initial attraction points were to each other, Adelina and Eli agreed that it was mostly intellectual. They shared a kind of wicked and sarcastic sense of humor and made each other laugh. Though they were from different backgrounds, they shared a view of the world and a set of values that helped them bond. They each felt seen and known by the other. The most enjoyable part of their courtship was when they would talk about something new one of them had learned or read about, then have vigorous (and often hilarious) debates. "It was like exchanging intellectual candies," Adelina explained. But when their roles expanded to include parenthood, that sense of connection faded. In the past few years, they barely had time to talk let alone read something or go somewhere to talk about it. All their exchanges became practical ones about the operations in the house.

At this point, I was just a facilitator for Adelina and Eli while they deepened their conversation. Eli said, "When you tell me that I'm a good father, I think it's what matters most to you these days. So I put more time and effort into being a good father. But then these other parts of me, as your husband and lover and partner and friend, kind of become less important. All the things that matter to you as an individual and not just as our child's father."

"Right!" Adelina added, "It seems that our focus on our roles as co-parents has overshadowed all the other things that drew us together. I genuinely appreciate your dedication to Liam, which is attractive. Thinking about it, I miss the special attraction and connection we had before becoming parents, but I am not sure if I want as much of it right now because having a like-minded and reliable co-parent is worth more to me." They both looked at me for input, so I interjected, "Exactly! So it is not that you are not attracted to Eli period. The initial points of attractions are there, but they are kind of not as relevant at this point. We don't need to keep up with everything the same way that it was before, but let's see if we can bring more balance to your roles here."

Getting to know who each partner is right now, in this phase of life, is a first step toward building intimacy, but it's not enough on its own. We also need to have some ideas how each of us wants to be seen and appreciated for all the roles we occupy. For example, I see lots of couples where one person uses the same terms of endearment for their pet, their car, their mother, and their lover. No wonder their lover doesn't feel seen by or special to their partner! As you pay attention to what each partner needs in that moment in time, you want to make sure that you're connecting with the whole person in front of you and not only to one of the roles that they perform. The next exercise, Celebrating Ourselves and Each Other, is designed to get you thinking about the specific ways each of you would like to feel connected, seen, and appreciated.

BUILDING BLOCK:
CELEBRATING OURSELVES AND EACH OTHER

Individually, you and your partner will make three lists:

- The first list, from the Who We Are Today exercise on page 90, includes everything you like and are attracted to within and about yourself in this phase of your life.
- The second one is about the ways you acknowledge, appreciate, reward, and celebrate your partner in their various roles as a parent, house manager, breadwinner, in-law to your family, social companion, adventure buddy, sex partner, community leader, soccer coach for your child's team, or any other roles that might be relevant.
- The third list (this one is the hardest!) should include how you would like to be acknowledged, appreciated, rewarded, and celebrated in all of these roles by the other.

Now, if you can, go for a walk to discuss your lists.

There is often an excited energy around this exercise, which comes with getting to know someone better. Usually when couples come together with these lists, a lot of assumptions are debunked. Many times the partners don't even know how they are perceived and received by the other. When they came back for the next session Eli shared, "Probably eighty percent of my efforts never landed with Adelina. I'm complimenting her *as a mother* when she wants me to see her *as a woman* more. Or I try to make a sarcastic joke about how everyone knows that moms are sexy and I end up hurting her feelings. She just stares at me and walks away."

Part of being intimate with your partner is knowing yourself. Adelina realized that, for her, feeling attractive meant being appreciated physically with gestures like hand-holding, kissing, and even dancing together where Eli initiated without her asking. "I feel really alive when we dance. I feel sexy and beautiful, like I'm celebrating myself. And I know Eli is attracted to that. So when he sweeps into the kitchen and salsas me around the room, it really means something to me." Some women experience motherhood as a kind of distancing from their bodies and their sexual selves, but for Adelina the opposite was true. "It's maybe a Brazilian thing. In Brazil, mamas are sexy. Walking around with a baby is sexy. Here in the US, and especially in Eli's family, motherhood is some kind of sacred, asexual thing. Like no one wants to think about what a woman had to do to get that baby in the first place! I don't like it when Eli jokes about it."

Getting clear about the specific ways you'd like to be appreciated by your partner helps couples avoid making assumptions about what each partner wants and needs from the other, and helps to create more meaningful exchanges. I have yet to see a couple that is completely aligned on this. In fact, like Eli and Adelina, most partners have some big discrepancies, even when they're well intentioned toward each other. Which is why it's so important to make sure that the messages you're sending out are aligned with your intentions. It's not about how you act, it's about how you're received.

THE GOLDEN RULE VERSUS THE PLATINUM RULE

For many people, knowing what they want and asking for it from their partners is a foreign concept. "If I have to tell him then it's not really genuine," they think, or "She should know by now what I like and what I don't like." This expectation, that our partner is a mind reader, is prevalent in submergent love, where everything is supposed to be effortless and automatic. Of course, when your partner manages to do exactly the right thing at exactly the right time, without being asked, it feels wonderful. But how will they ever keep it up if you don't let them know what you like? This is all about setting your partner up for success and setting yourself up for satisfaction. I want to also acknowledge that when you are in a long-term partnership and attuned with each other, especially around the

things that have been communicated before, there is a realistic expectation that you remember what your partner tells you and act accordingly.
These are the things that you *should* know. For example, I've worked
with couples where one of them had pretty serious allergies that the other
didn't remember; or where certain sexual practices that were uncomfortable for one partner, and had been discussed, were still being attempted
by the other. We'll talk more about this when we discuss trust and respect
in a thriving relationship.

The bottom line is, none of us opens our mouth or moves a muscle or
even breathes without intention. For our physical needs, even the involuntary ones like breath and heartbeat, the intention is to keep us alive. As
infants we cry with the intention of getting our needs met—whether it's
hunger or a dirty diaper or the need to be held. As grownups it's the same,
but often we are much less direct than the howling baby. We talk, or we
don't talk and withdraw. We use gestures or we put out a kind of energy
to let the other know we are displeased. We hint at something, or we
do something for the other person in the hope that they will reciprocate.
Often we try to get our needs met through hidden agendas, like spending time with our in-laws (who are great) then expecting our partner to
reciprocate with our own parents (who are perhaps more difficult) without
making it explicit that this is what we would like to see from them.

The Golden Rule teaches us to treat others the way we would like to
be treated: If you want people to be respectful toward you, be respectful
toward them. If you want others to be loving, then you be loving. This
is a wonderful concept, but what I have learned from my couples is that
this only works some of the time, because people don't always want the
same things you want. In light of this, I recommend that you use instead
what is known as the Platinum Rule: Treat others the way they want to
be treated.[20]

What does this have to do with attraction? A lot. Knowing yourself,
understanding what you need, and negotiating for those needs in a genuine and open way helps to minimize confusion like the kind Adelina and
Eli or Michael and Shayna experienced. We are not playing at love by
acting on our assumptions; we are building a loving relationship together.

We think if our partners love us enough, and if they are the right people for us, they should "just know" what we like, what we need, what makes us feel special and loved and appreciated. Let me save you a lot of time and heartache: They don't. You don't want them to, either, because then they fall into the trap of seeing you as you were when you first met! Michael had a hard time seeing Shayna past who she was seven years ago, what was important to her and what she needed when they first met. You have to keep making it possible to educate each other. This is not being demanding or bossy or high-maintenance. This is being generous, thoughtful, and intentional. And that's only possible if you know those things yourself, and if you make the effort to communicate them to your partner regularly. And the reverse is also true: Know your partner, see into your partner, and ask them specific questions about what is meaningful to them.

Maria, for example, just turned sixty-five years old. At this time in her life she sees herself as a powerful, sociable, wise woman who is an amazing mother and grandmother. Her husband, Ed, keeps telling her how beautiful and sexy she is because he thinks that's what she wants to hear. "Twenty-some years ago I needed to hear I was sexy because I was turning forty and I felt insecure about my aging body. But now I don't feel insecure about it at all, I'm in more of a place of acceptance, so when he tells me I'm sexy it just feels ridiculous. Sometimes it even feels like pressure, because if I respond to him then he thinks we're going to have amazing sex like we did back then." Like many women, Maria's sense of herself has changed over the years. She doesn't care so much what others think of her (physically or otherwise), but she does want her husband to acknowledge the aspects of herself that she most values and is proud of at this cross-section of time in her life: her wisdom and the healthy, happy family they created together.

When I explained the Platinum Rule to this couple, Maria turned to Ed and asked, gently and with real interest, "Do you want me to tell you you're sexy? Is that why you keep saying it to me?" It turns out he did. "Well, yeah, I guess I do. I mean, I know it's not like it was thirty years ago, but maybe I'm going through a little bit of what you went through in your forties. I can't do a lot of the things I did then. I can't play basket-ball anymore because my knees can't take it, I can't eat beef every night, and playing with the grandkids wears me out. I'm feeling my age, I guess, and sex makes me feel young."

We will talk more about sustaining a satisfying physical connection in part three, but for now I want to point out that Maria and Ed, even after almost forty years together, remained capable of being surprised by what they discovered. This is the beauty of Emergent Love: You never arrive at a place of perfection, where you can rest assured that you know everything there is to know about your partner. This is only possible if you are not living! The novelty keeps emerging. Knowing yourself, and knowing some-one else, can't be accomplished in six months or a year or even forty years. Instead, you have a set of tools to help you navigate the ever-changing landscape of your coupledom. My mother always said, being with a part-ner is like reading and re-reading a great book—you relate to it and get something out of it based on who you are in that moment in time.

Mutual attraction is what brings us together, and it is very much a two-way street. If we leave attraction as is, it might fade away, get buried in the practicalities of life, and lead to a place of disconnect and even annoy-ance and repulsion over time. When partners maintain genuine interest in each other as individual beings who are continuously evolving over time, the initial attraction of early coupledom will grow and blossom into inti-macy. The first step is to recognize the characteristics, roles, and attributes we find appealing in our partner, but that alone is not enough. We also need to learn what they like and value about themselves, and we need to celebrate who they are now in ways that are meaningful to them. We are all naturally drawn toward those who see and appreciate us as we really are. Attraction is inherently connective. You get to see your partner and be seen by them in turn; it is the very definition of intimacy.

CHAPTER 5

Respect

While we might say that a person has a disposition to act with respect, it is only in the individual acts of respect that the quality becomes actual. "Respect" as an integral aspect of life, both personal and social, is maintained by the respectful acts of individuals.

—Sara Lawrence-Lightfoot[1]

Why is it that so many of us reserve our best behavior for friends and colleagues, and even strangers on the street, yet we treat those we love with less consideration? I am often startled by the casual disrespect couples display for each other in my office and elsewhere. It truly never gets comfortable to observe, and I cannot *not* notice it! They interrupt each other, finish each other's sentences, and speak on behalf of the other because they think they know their partners "inside out." Sometimes, when I call it out, they explain, "But I was listening!" Then I have to be clearer and explain that answering a text, looking away, fidgeting in your chair, giving subtitles to what the other says, rolling your eyes, watching the clock, and making "let's wrap this up" motions are all subtle (and not-so-subtle) signs of disrespect.

You may not have thought much about respect in romantic partnerships outside of the Aretha Franklin song, but the concept permeates much of the literature on the subject. Yet in my humble opinion it is often poorly understood. We tend to think of respect primarily as a personal, internal attitude we have toward something or someone, and less as a reciprocal, interpersonal process—a way of relating to and being with someone. But mutual respect as *interpersonal* is more than something you feel for your partner, it is also something that must be embodied, *expressed to* and *received from* them. In the context of Emergent Love, respect includes holding an awareness of your partner as an autonomous human being with their own interior life, needs, and priorities, and keeping this in mind when you make choices about how you will behave. Respect underscores the value you place on your partner's sense of personal agency and self-sovereignty. And lack of respect implies the opposite: You see your partner only in terms of how they relate to you and your life, and you expect them to meld seamlessly into your agenda with little regard for theirs. This is why respect must be reciprocal.

Respect permeates every aspect of our relationships on a granular level. When couples come to me and say, "We've tried everything! We work so hard on our relationship, but nothing ever changes," that's a sign to me that we need to look at their simple daily interactions. I frequently find that there is something to explore about the quality of respect in their coupledom. There could be a fundamental disconnect between the respect partners profess to feel for each other and the reality of their daily behaviors. Most of us don't think that what we see as little things (like replacing the toilet paper roll or waiting until your partner is out of the car before you start walking toward the store) are going to have a huge impact on our relationships. But they do. There is a concept in business called the Pareto Principle, or the 80/20 rule. It asserts that 80 percent of the outcome results from 20 percent of the causes for any given event.[2] The 80/20 rule encourages businesses to identify the efforts that are potentially the most productive and make them a priority. This is good advice for couples' relationships, too, and I encourage couples to put their effort into what matters most. Well, respect is a big part of that 20 percent—an ingredient that you can embody and practice each day, each moment, and impact 80 percent of your relationship.

As you read this chapter, please consider how you experience respect for yourself, as well as how you express it to your partner, in terms of their individuality, their dreams, their will, their time, their rights, and their bodily integrity. Mutual respect is all about honoring the boundaries you draw around yourselves as individuals and also around yourselves as a couple. Each of you needs to know where you end and the other begins, otherwise all that attraction will just pull you under, right back into submergent love! Throughout this chapter I'll also ask you to reflect on how your partner embodies being respectful and expresses respect for you, and how you respond when you think their behavior is disrespectful. When respect is present, couples tend to have fewer arguments and power struggles, even when they disagree. When it is absent, unnecessary conflict and resentments tend to proliferate.

WHAT IS RESPECT?

Respect comes from the Latin word *spectare*, which means "to look," and "re," which means to "do again"—so to "respect" another is "to look again." Cultivating mutual respect means that both of you make the effort to "look again" by constantly evaluating and re-evaluating who the other person is, what their boundaries are, and how you both show up with respect in your shared space.

Most of us have at least a vague notion of what it means to treat someone with respect, and we likely learned this from parents and caregivers when we were very young. The way we think about respect is also closely linked to our culture and its values. In highly individualistic social systems (like the United States), which value hard work and personal merit, respect is often seen as deference or submission to another's superior status or accomplishments. I find that within these communities people sometimes resist the idea of respect as a fundamental ingredient of intimate relationships because they see it as a characteristic of a hierarchical relationship and therefore contrasting to equality. In this view, respect isn't something you grant to just anyone; a person has to *earn* your respect.

In more collectivistic cultures, like the one in which I was raised, respect looks somewhat different. In fact, it is completely the other way around! Rather than something that must be earned, respect is something that everyone deserves equally, simply because we share a common humanity. There are of course still hierarchies, but the way that is expressed takes different forms. For example, an elder might command more respect than a young adult or a child. In general terms, we respect others not because of who *they* are, but because of who *we* are. "Because I am a respectful and respectable person, I also treat others with respect."

As a young girl in Iran, where women were systematically denied respect, I have my parents to thank for setting the bar high for my siblings and me. I remember my father advising me, "Even when someone is not respectful toward you, that does not mean you should be disrespectful toward them. Do not lower the bar on your expectations of yourself. Just walk away and do not respond. This way you preserve your own dignity, your self-respect, and your status as a respectable person. Whether or not they are respectable people is a problem they will have to figure out by themselves. It does not concern you." When we went on car trips my father always pulled over to let people pass, especially if they were tailgating or showing signs of road rage. He never engaged. Instead, he would say, "I am with family, and it is disrespectful to do anything or say anything that is below the level of *Sha'n* of my family." (*Sha'n* is a Farsi word that is loosely translated as "worth and dignity" in English, and it signifies the value you attach to a person or relationship, and the central place they occupy in your heart.) My father's deep respect for his wife and children meant that he would not behave disrespectfully toward anyone in our presence. This has become one of the most important principles that I live by, be it in my intimate relationships with clients or in my work with the United Nations, religious leaders, or heads of corporations.

Thinking of my father makes me reflect on those of my clients who had very different experiences growing up. One woman's father demanded respect from his children, which he equated with obedience. If he thought they were being disrespectful he would beat them. But respect is not something you can demand or force. Respect is a mindful, thoughtful honoring of the other. That's not at all possible if you're making demands or trespassing their boundaries (physical or otherwise). You can never *make* someone respect you, you can only make them fear you. It is not the same thing at all.

How your family, community, and culture communicated their values around respect will shape how you experience and express respect as an adult. And, as always, what you bring to your coupledom will have an enormous impact on your relationship. As children, we seek validation and affirmation to cement our idea of self—who we are and where we belong. We also seek to avoid more negative kinds of feedback like disappointment, disapproval, or punishment. This is how values are transmitted from one generation to the next. For example, one family might censure a child who attempts to engage in political debate at the dinner table because they believe it is disrespectful to challenge your parents' beliefs. A different family might encourage the very same behavior, because they value thinking independently and challenging authority, and they believe you can disagree with someone without being disrespectful. Some families choose the names of their children with the utmost care and display respect for their children both publicly and privately. Others might call their kids demeaning names or put them down in front of others, which sends the subliminal message, "You don't matter as much as I do, and you are not worthy of respect." If these two people end up in a relationship with each other they'll have to make an effort to clarify each person's understanding of respectful behavior. Otherwise, they risk having serious disagreements about what constitutes respectful and appropriate behavior in all arenas, from their intimate spaces all the way to social situations.

This next exercise is designed to help you start thinking about the origin of your own ideas around respect. The better you know your own blueprint, the more effectively you can bring that self-literacy to your interactions with your partner.

BUILDING BLOCK: YOUR RESPECT BLUEPRINT

- What are your earliest memories of learning about respect, both as a concept and as an everyday practice or behavior toward yourself and others?
- What was considered respectful and what was disrespectful at the minimum?

- Were you praised for being respectful? What about when you were disrespectful?
- Were you shown and expected to observe social etiquette, use table manners, consider the language you used and the way you presented yourself as your practice of showing respect?
- In your childhood home, was respect accorded to everyone equally, or was it reserved only for certain people? Who was considered worthy of respect, and why?
- How did your parents (and other adults around you) express respect to each other? To their own parents? To their children? What about people from the community like friends, neighbors, or the checkout person at the grocery store? Was it different if the relationship was high-stakes versus low-stakes? How did they treat strangers, or people with different cultures, values, and rituals?
- In your primary language, are there different words to indicate different kinds of respect? What are they?
- If you migrated from one place to another, or if your family of origin belonged to a minority group in the community, how did your family's ideas about respect differ from those in the larger community? How were they the same? What did this mean in your everyday life?

As you read through your answers to these questions, did anything surprise you? For example, as a child, did you learn about respect as something that must be earned, or did you learn that respectful behaviors originate with you and not with the other person? Do you respect others because you are a respectful person, or because they have done something that you find respectable and respect-worthy? Do you feel respectable? Finally, did you notice any parallels between what you learned as a child and what you see in your relationships today? When partners enter relationships with dramatically different ideas about what constitutes respect, they inevitably run into problems, as I mentioned earlier. Though many of us admire our partners for their accomplishments, the respect that is most relevant to intimate coupledom has more to do with valuing our partners as individual, autonomous beings and feeling valued in return. This also requires that each person respect their own person, values, and autonomy as a human being.

THE RELATIONSHIP BETWEEN RESPECT, SELF-WORTH, AND BOUNDARIES

Often people have "Aha!" moments when they do the respect blueprint exercise. This happened with Imajuik, a client from Greenland whose name, in her native language, translated roughly as "silent and meek." Growing up, her family placed great value on children being "seen and not heard," and her name was a reflection of that belief. "I learned that respect was something I owed to other people, but it was not something owed to me. Respect meant never criticizing anyone else's behavior, especially not an adult, and in particular not my parents." She felt she didn't have a voice, she couldn't have a voice, and whenever she tried to, it felt false. When I asked her if she respected herself, she admitted that she didn't know. "I'm not even sure I understand what that means."

The problem that brought her to me was that she often felt disrespected in her romantic relationships, but she wasn't always sure she was actually *being* disrespected. When she first began dating someone she felt very much appreciated for being the elegant and successful woman she was, but as soon as they did something she didn't like—they weren't consistent about calling her back, or they made a joke that offended her—she started to question whether or not they really respected her. When I asked her how she responded to these "possibly disrespectful" behaviors, she replied, "That's just the problem. I don't know *what* to do. I don't want to seem harsh or critical, or too demanding, or overly sensitive. I usually try to hint that it bothered me without ever actually saying that it bothered me. If they don't take the hint, and they usually don't, I start getting resentful and annoyed at every little thing. Or I worry that I've overreacted and I start apologizing and the cycle just repeats itself. By the end it is all a mess so either I walk out or they think they have to walk on eggshells around me and they break up with me. I'm starting to think that maybe I'm the common denominator here."

Imajuik was trying hard to gain the respect that she rarely felt in her family growing up, which left her with two areas of ambivalence. The first, which had to do with feeling worthy of respect, was a bit more resolved through all the work that she had done on herself. But the second, which included being able to distinguish between the respectful and disrespectful behavior of others, was still a huge source of confusion for her. "How can I know when the lines have been crossed when I don't even know where they are?" Sometimes she could call out things that didn't feel right to her, but she didn't know how to elaborate on what specifically was disrespectful, so she couldn't make a clear ask. For a lot of our sessions, she would walk me through a scenario then ask me, "Do you think I'm overreacting?" What she was talking about was ambivalence about her boundaries.

BOUNDARIES IN CONTEXT

It is sometimes easier to maintain boundaries in one area of your life than it is in others because boundaries depend on context. Some people, like Imajuik, have no trouble assessing their worth and setting clear boundaries in their professional lives. "I know what I'm doing, I'm good at what I do, and I know how much I am worth and what I need to succeed." But when it comes to their personal lives, boundaries are less clear. Others might have clear and strong interpersonal boundaries, but they have a harder time professionally. It can be helpful to think about your boundaries in terms of different contexts and as they involve your various roles in life: at home, at work, with your parents, your in-laws, your friends, or your children. Are they easier in some arenas than others? Why might that be? How is this serving you?

Boundaries are addressed in almost every book, magazine article, podcast, and talk show that deals with relationships, and for a good reason. While the term itself is often overused, and sometimes abused, creating and maintaining healthy boundaries is essential to maintaining autonomy in relationships. Like self-worth, it is a difficult concept to define and communicate in general terms because it is so deeply personal, and we fall into the trap of either being too aggressive or being a pushover when it comes to communicating boundaries. Without boundaries, people don't know where they belong when they are in a relationship with you physically, energetically, or emotionally.

In its essence, a boundary is anything that indicates a limit and creates clarity around what is expected in that context. People operate with ease around you because they know that you are capable of holding on to your boundaries and not invading theirs. Interpersonally, having healthy boundaries means you understand where you end and another person begins. We need to be differentiated enough from the other person to be able to see them clearly and define the rules of engagement between us.

It seems important to highlight here that many people see boundaries as limits to keep people away, like a border or wall you build around you. If you google boundary, the images that come up show things like a person in the middle of a circle drawn in red or a person pushing another person away with the show of their hand. In Emergent Love, boundaries are more like guideposts that will help you and others coexist and thrive in a mutual space. You can think of them as the yellow lines on a road. They let you know where the lanes are, providing clarity around who can move where and in what ways, so we can all share the road safely. When we clarify our boundaries to others, we are helping them with how to be around us and how to engage with us. Healthy and clear boundaries do not leave room for assumptions, but instead provide information to our partner: "This is who I am and how I would like to be treated consistently, and because I equally respect you, who you are, and the way you want to be treated, we will join together to create a mutual space in which we both feel seen, respected, respect-worthy, and respectful of what matters to us individually and to us both." That is what mutual respect looks like in Emergent Love.

HOW TO IDENTIFY YOUR BOUNDARIES

For some people, like Imajuik, setting boundaries in intimate relationships can be difficult. If you weren't raised to believe you are deserving of respect, you may have an especially hard time identifying behaviors that feel disrespectful.

I once visited a day care collective in Brooklyn where the children, all of whom were between three and five years old, were taught to say, loudly and firmly, "I don't like that!" whenever a classmate did something that made the child feel sad or angry or hurt. This was the teacher's cue to check out what was happening between the kids and see if they needed help to resolve the conflict. I think it's a wonderful way to introduce children to the idea of boundaries in their simplest form: "When this particular thing happens, I get a bad feeling. And when I get a bad feeling in response to someone else's behavior, I need to tell them right away."

Part of what I love about this early lesson in boundaries is the way it supports each child's sense of self-worth. By learning to value and honor their own experience, they are being taught self-respect right alongside respect for others (no hitting, pushing, biting, etc.). Having self-respect, to me, means that you grant yourself the same attention, interest, and care that you grant to others. Of course, sometimes you need to go out of your way and serve others because the context demands it, but that is different than constantly putting yourself down (self-derogatory comments, for example) or becoming a permanent doormat. You pay attention to your own experience, you develop self-literacy about how you respond to events and circumstances around you, and you let others know (not always loudly perhaps but lovingly and firmly) how you expect to be treated.

Everyone has boundaries, but sometimes it takes a little work to be able to identify them, articulate them, and recognize when they've been crossed. These are the individual skills you need if you hope to cultivate mutual respect in committed relationships. In her insightful and humorous book, *The Book of Boundaries: Set the Limits That Will Set You Free*, Melissa Urban offers more than one hundred scripts that will help you with putting language around your boundaries. The interpersonal skills you need also include knowing your partner's boundaries and behaving in ways that show you are respecting those boundaries.

Let's begin with identifying your own boundaries. The emotions that my clients closely associate with boundary violations include feeling annoyed, uncomfortable, hurt, triggered, or offended. These are five vital sources of information—a call for our inner teacher to come over and investigate, just like at the day care. We don't think to feel; we first sense things and thoughts will follow. I developed the following exercise to help my clients identify these emotions by focusing on how they feel physically in the body—what psychologists call "felt sense." I invite you to try it, but please keep in mind that it isn't always intuitive, so be patient with yourself. Harvard psychologist Jerome Kagan gives some indication of how difficult this can be when he explains, "The task of describing our most private experiences can be likened to reaching down to a deep well to pick up small fragile crystal figures while you are wearing thick leather mittens."[3]

BUILDING BLOCK:
RECOGNIZING BREACHES OF BOUNDARIES

Find a comfortable space where you can sit, undisturbed, for at least fifteen minutes. It is best to do this exercise when you are not hungry, angry, bored, or tired so you can fully focus on your senses. This exercise doesn't need to be done in one sitting, though each segment should begin and end with a grounding exercise and enough time to take notes.

Close your eyes, get comfortable, and pay attention to your breath coming in and going out. Now begin with a body scan from the tip of your toes all the way to the top of your head. Which part of your body is most noticeably uncomfortable to you? Is it your feet, your heart, your shoulders? Take a moment to tweak your position a little bit to relieve tension or make yourself physically more comfortable. Now notice your breathing. Take a deep breath from your belly and exhale slowly. Now do another body scan. If you notice any areas of discomfort, focus on releasing the tension with each exhale. Repeat this until you no longer notice any considerable tension. Now consider your five senses as well as the energy around you and within you. How does it feel to be in this neutral state of being? What words and emotions come to the fore? It usually takes more than one attempt to be able to recognize and memorize this calm and relaxed state, and attaching words to the feeling can help you return to it.

Whether you choose to break up this exercise and engage with one emotion at a time, or you want to do them all in one go, be sure to give yourself the time you need to return to your neutral state of being after exploring each one so that you can go back to your day with energy for whatever you are doing next. Take notes if you like, or consider associating a color to each of these feelings if you are a more visual person. Your goal is to identify where in your body, and with what specific sensations, these feelings show up.

>**Uncomfortable:** Imagine that something is uncomfortable, physically or otherwise. We can feel uncomfortable around specific people, locations, or circumstances. Maybe someone said something that made you feel uncomfortable, or you felt physically uncomfortable in your body. For some of us loud noises, bright light, a sensitive topic, or certain kinds of music make us uncomfortable. Pay attention to how this discomfort feels in your body, and try to be aware of the location and intensity of the physical feeling. Do you notice any difference between the experience of discomfort and the experience of being annoyed?

>**Annoyed:** Think of a situation where you typically feel annoyed. Your train is late, or too crowded. Someone is FaceTiming in a restaurant. Your computer didn't save your work. Your partner leaves dirty dishes on the kitchen counter. Your colleague dropped the ball on something and you have to work late. Bring your attention to what is happening in your body. Maybe you clench your jaw, or roll your eyes. Which part of your body is sensing that you are annoyed and telling you that you are leaving your neutral state? Try to get beyond the cognitive process of thinking, "Ah, this person is so annoying!" Forget why you're annoyed and focus instead on the sensations in your body.

>**Hurt:** Think about a situation when you felt hurt. Hurt may be caused by the behavior of someone else, by something that was done around you, or by something that you perceived or observed. How does that feel in your body? Where do you feel it? How is it different from discomfort and feeling annoyed?

>**Offended:** Think about an occasion when you felt offended. Really offended. Maybe someone falsely accused you of something, or made assumptions about you that were incorrect, or said something insulting. Not all offensive behaviors are intentional, though the ones that are intentional usually hit the mark. Again,

notice the sensations in your body. Do you feel it in your hands or behind your eyes or throat? Some people say it's like receiving a punch to your gut. Is your breathing different? Are these sensations different than when you feel annoyed, uncomfortable, or hurt?

Triggered: When you are triggered, you go from zero to a hundred in a split second. It can come out as explosive anger, panic attacks, agitation, irritability, tears, all of these at once, or any number of other ways. It is a flood of emotion that comes on suddenly and is often experienced as overwhelming. These are the occasions when you think, "What just happened?" as if your reaction surprised even you, let alone anybody who might have been around you. What is the visceral reaction in your body when this happens? What sensations do you feel? Are these different than the sensations you noticed above?[4]

Being able to recognize these emotions when they arise is so important when it comes to creating and maintaining healthy boundaries. Remember, the goal here is to identify your boundaries so you can articulate them to others in advance, but just as important is being able to respond effectively when your boundaries have been crossed. We are working here to develop skills beyond our knee-jerk reactions. When I say respond effectively, I am referring to communicating lovingly and firmly and not in an aggressive (or passive-aggressive) way, which many of us do!

Once you're able to recognize the feelings associated with boundary violations, you can connect them to the situations that are most likely to lead to them. For example, Imajuik realized that it makes her feel very uncomfortable when people put someone down and mask it with jokes, especially when the comments are sexist or racist. (When they're rude to her she tends to feel hurt rather than uncomfortable.) She recognized discomfort, attached it to a context, and *identified* a boundary. In the "What Are My Essences?" exercise in chapter 3, she identified being kind, no-nonsense, shy, and "a pushover" as her essential characteristics. Armed with this knowledge, we talked about how she might now *articulate* her boundary to others. She decided she could use "a firm tone and a graceful smile," then proceeded to practice it with me. "I would like to be respectful to everyone; jokes about minority groups make me very uncomfortable." These all resonated with Imajuik's personality and seemed feasible for her to do. You need to think of what works for you, your personality, and your essences.

Recognizing when a boundary has been crossed, and learning to respond in a way that is most likely to be effective, ended up being a little bit harder than she had thought. Soon after Imajuik began to develop boundaries, she also discovered a temper she never knew she had. She was unpleasantly surprised by it, as were the people in her inner circle. I explained that because she had been living with such loose boundaries, and for such a long time, her first attempts to respond when her boundaries were crossed came out as harsh, rigid, and even rude—in other words, as temper. As she became more confident about being worthy of respect, she was able to soften her tone and articulate boundaries in a more loving way that was still firm. Respect is freely available. You don't need to fight for it, you just need to show up for it.

Communicating your boundaries includes communicating your feelings, and this can be scary for a lot of people. Letting someone know when you're hurt or offended feels vulnerable and takes a lot of courage. You also need to care enough about the relationship to do so. But when you tell your partner the truth of your experience you are not only respecting yourself, you are also respecting your partner by giving them the opportunity to change course and to repair any damage they may have caused.

I know a couple, Bart and Sheila, who told me a great example of how this works for them. They were at the airport waiting for a flight, and Bart went to get them some coffee. When he returned with doughnuts, Sheila joked, "Is that doughnut part of your new diet?" In that moment, Bart was deeply offended. He felt ridiculed, judged, and ashamed of himself. Later, after he calmed down, he addressed it with her directly. "Sheila, when you made that comment about the doughnut I was really insulted. It made me feel awful about myself. I've been trying really hard to stick to my diet, and I've even lost a couple of pounds. Please be more thoughtful in what you say in the future. This is a sensitive area for me." Sheila took a moment to absorb Bart's message, rejecting her first impulse to defend herself by saying it was only a joke. Then she admitted, "You know, I was joking at the time, but as soon as I said it I realized it was the wrong thing to say. I'm so sorry, honey. I would take those words back if I could. I never want to make you feel bad about yourself. I know you are trying."

Now, you should probably keep in mind that Bart and Sheila are both in their early seventies and have been married for more than forty years. At this stage of their lives they are experts in the art of repair. I'm sure some of you are thinking as you read this, "No way would my wife/husband/ partner say anything like that!" You can't know until you try. Give your partner the benefit of the doubt, like Bart did. Rather than assuming that Sheila was trying to offend him, Bart assumed that she wasn't, and kindly but firmly let her know a way to show respect for his boundaries.

MUTUAL RESPECT IS NON-NEGOTIABLE

When you have healthy boundaries, other people know how to show up for you and with you; you give them the opportunity to succeed in the relationship they have with you. If you feel like your own relationship isn't quite there yet, it might be helpful to take a closer look at what your experience of respect is like in your coupledom. The exercise below, Mutual Respect Self-Assessment, is designed to help you assess the ways respect is (or is not) actively manifesting in your primary relationship. If you have a partner, I suggest you each do this one individually, then share what you learned.

BUILDING BLOCK:
MUTUAL RESPECT SELF-ASSESSMENT

What is it that you respect most about yourself? And are you respectable?

- Reflect on your life, the person you are, the various identities associated with the roles you play, and what you have achieved and accomplished.

- Do you allow your partner to see those parts? Do you think others, especially your partner, give the same respect to what you see in yourself as respectable or respect-worthy?
- How do you show up in your dynamic? Do you hold your boundaries in a way that others, including your partner, your children, your parents, and your in-laws, see those aspects as what you value most about yourself? Are they respectful toward them as well?

Now turn your attention to your partner.

- Is your partner respectable?
- Do you respect them?
- Is there anything about your partner that you don't respect?
- How do you demonstrate your respect? Or disrespect?
- Do you think your partner feels respected by you?
- What behaviors are most meaningful to them?

You may have noticed that this exercise includes questions about feeling respectable (embodying it), feeling respected (receiving it), and also being respectful toward your partner (expressing it). All are critical.

Partners are often surprised when there is a discrepancy between the respect they express toward the other and the other's experience of receiving respect. They are also baffled when I ask them if they think they are "respectable." Sometimes also they are affirmed in what they have been feeling and yet did not have the language or the awareness to label it as such. Let me give you an example.

Sally and Charles are a couple in their forties who have been married for twenty years. They thought their marriage was "pretty good," and came to see me because they were interested in taking the Relationship Panoramic Inventory (RPI) to see if there were any areas they might improve. Sally was surprised by the results. In the RPI we use a Likert scale for some of the questions, which asks people to rank their responses from "strongly agree," "agree," to "disagree" and "strongly disagree."

Sally strongly agreed with both "I respect my partner" and "I feel respected by my partner." Charles also strongly agreed with the first statement, but he disagreed with the second. When I asked Sally why she thought Charles didn't feel respected, she looked a bit embarrassed but told me she had a good idea of the reason. "I'm not very tidy. I'm clean, and I keep the house clean, but I have a habit of leaving things around. Charles jokes that when he comes home at night he can tell what I've been doing all day by just looking around the apartment. 'You had cereal for breakfast, took a shower, worked at the dining room table, had leftover pasta for lunch, spent some time knitting, and walked the dog in the park.' You see? I left my dishes in the sink, left my computer on the dining room table, my knitting on the couch, and the dog leash on the coffee table."

Charles is a nice guy who doesn't like to argue or criticize. A few times, over the years, he has asked Sally to pick up after herself, or complained about having to tidy up after her every night, but he has never lost his temper or yelled or complained. "I always knew it was one of his pet peeves, but it never occurred to me that it was disrespectful." I suggested they both could be a part of the solution. Sally needed to be more thoughtful about how she occupied their shared space, and Charles needed to give voice to his chronic frustration about having this particular boundary crossed over and over again. By remaining silent, he implicitly allowed her to continue being disrespectful without even knowing.

If you find yourself shouting, "How many times do I have to tell you?" or if you find yourself hearing that on a regular basis, there's a good chance that the issue is less about the socks on the floor or the empty gas tank (which could be pet peeves) and more about respect. When someone has to keep repeating what bothers them about something that is created by you (e.g., your behavior), they will inevitably feel disrespected. So, please, close the cabinet door; separate the colored shirts from the white ones when you put them in the laundry; don't bring your phone to the bedroom; don't put your used tissue in the sink with all the dirty dishes; feed the dog as soon as he wakes up because he's hypoglycemic and will pass out; leave the extra key under the doormat for the housekeeper; and for heaven's sake replace the toilet paper when you use it up!

Let me clarify something: I'm not talking about making assumptions or trying to predict the other's needs—that's actually a sign of disrespect, because you are robbing them of the chance to articulate what they need and show up for themselves in doing so. What I'm referring to here is the need to be thoughtful and to hold in your mind the things that matter to your partner, especially when they have been articulated before.

To make this easier, I often tell couples to use clarifying language about how important something is to you by ranking it from one to ten. After some coaching, Charles explained to Sally, "When you leave dirty dishes on the counter, after I've just cleaned the kitchen, that's an eight out of ten for me. How much is it for you to put those in the dishwasher? Would it be difficult for you to do and to do it consistently?" It is very rare for couples to always have the same priorities for the same things, and that is often a source of tension. Putting a numerical value on your priorities communicates to your partner how much the act means to you. It's a very simple way to create healthy boundaries and communicate them. And even if it is not the same priority for both, when one steps up and does it, the other will appreciate it much more knowing that it does not come easily to them and they went out of their way to accommodate what mattered to the other person above what they would have preferred.

Dropping down to a deeper level, you also might want to ask yourself if your own behavior is respectful and respectable. For the record, few people come to me and announce, "I'm very concerned that I'm not being respectful toward my partner." Instead, respect is most often identified as something that is lacking in the other person's perception. Yet many partners who complain of not feeling respected will admit, when pressed, that they behave in ways that are not respectable even to themselves.

Mo and Julia had been together for six years on and off until they decided to live together when the pandemic hit. They shared a small apartment. They both worked from home. Julia felt disrespected because every day after work Mo played violent video games with his friends online. "He takes over the living room where the TV is, and, he uses such vulgar language it's appalling! I have to go to the bedroom, shut the door, and try to read something. But I can't read with all that noise, and I can't pretend anymore! And then, after all that, he wants to have sex. I feel like I'm just a piece of furniture in the house!" Mo on the other hand felt disrespected when Julia brought this up and gave him the cold shoulder.

He felt that he had a right to be with his friends, at least online, now that they could not see one another because of the pandemic.

One day, while both were in a session with me, Mo exploded, "She treats me like a child! She has no respect for me!" When I asked him, "Do you respect Julia?" he quickly answered, "Yes. Of course!"

"But in this specific scenario," I went on, "which happens almost every night, do you think you are respectful?"

"I wear headphones, and I never use foul language with her," he explained.

"Think of your shared space like a glass of milk. If you keep adding drops of color to it, the color inevitably changes, no?"

"I guess so."

"Let me ask you another question," I went on. "Are you respectable?" He went quiet as a confused look crossed his face.

"What do you mean?"

"I mean would you respect you in those moments when you are shouting and using the language that you do? Do you feel like a grown-up person in a relationship who is to be treated as one?" He sighed. His shoulders slumped. "I guess not. If the tables were turned I would probably respect her less, too."

When you behave in ways that aren't aligned with your values, it's hard to feel good about yourself and feel worthy of the other's respect. Mo thinks of himself as a respectful (and respectable) person, just like Sally, whom we talked about before. But there's a disconnect between how they see themselves, how they feel about their partners, and how they behave. Bringing awareness to this discrepancy is often difficult, but knowing how your behavior is received by your partner is an important part of cultivating mutual respect.

CULTIVATING FLUENCY: WHAT RESPECT LOOKS LIKE IN DAILY LIFE

Mutual respect means that you recognize your partner as a separate human being, and you keep their needs and priorities in mind. It is important in cultivating Emergent Love because it underscores the autonomy of both partners. You demonstrate mutual respect by maintaining your own boundaries and respecting your partner's boundaries. Easy, right?

There are three arenas where respect shows up in our lives that merit special consideration: interactions, communication, and respect for the other's physical body and space. If you hope to make the shift from literacy to fluency, these are all good places to start.

Respectful Interactions

Think about how many times you interact with your partner every day, whether in person or via text or phone. Whether you recognize it or not, each of these interactions has a beginning, a middle, and an end. When you walk into a room where your partner is sitting, a small acknowledgment can go a long way. Be mindful, though. If they look up and smile at you it might be an invitation to connect further, but if you enter and they continue with what they're doing, make your presence quick, sweet, and non-invasive. Catch his eye, or give her a quick kiss, or just smile and say, "Hey, you." It doesn't have to be a grand gesture, just a little something to say, "I see you." If they are engaged with something, try not to be verbal about your presence, maybe just a little kiss behind their neck or on their head will do, or leaving a glass of water or a cup of tea beside them. It is okay if they don't want it or don't even see or acknowledge it at that moment in time. Many of my couples get into a tiff just because they miss little cues like this.

> In the Middle Eastern culture, we believe that if someone brings you water when you didn't ask for it, it brings good luck! Even if you are not thirsty, if your loved one brings you water, you take a sip or two to receive the good luck. I needed years of schooling and work to see the simple wisdom behind it: It makes the receiver feel thought of and the giver feel seen and appreciated.

Do the same thing when you step away, leave for work, get up to go into another room, or open your laptop to engage with the internet or with someone else. A squeeze of the hand, a pat on the leg, anything that helps to signify that the interaction is over and you both are leaving satisfied. When we ignore these small gestures of acknowledgment we risk leaving our partners feeling unseen, which increases the likelihood that they won't respond positively the next time we extend an opportunity to connect.

When you wake in the morning, say, "Good morning." Just that simple act, acknowledging the other's presence in your space and in your life, every single morning, can express so much. "I exist, you exist, and this is another day in our lives that we are going to be in a relationship together." In Muslim and Jewish communities, they take pride in being the first to say salaam (Arabic origin) or shalom (Hebrew), thereby acknowledging the other person first. Do the same when you go to bed at night. A simple, "Good night, I'm going to bed now," with maybe a little kiss on the cheek, on the lips, or a few-second hug (a few minutes, even better!) can signify the end of another day, another brick in the love that you're designing together. There are many ways that various cultures and languages acknowledge the other person when they come together and depart from a shared space; take salut (French), ciao (Italian), aloha (Hawaiian), servus (German-Austrian), kia rra (Maori) as a few examples. Come up with your own language and way of doing this for your coupledom. These are all different forms of looking at each other, and looking again... being in a mutually respectful dynamic.

Respectful interactions include how you treat each other in private, in public, in front of your kids (if you have them), in front of your friends, and anywhere you go where you are representing each other and your coupledom. Think of it as an effort to avoid any actions that might alienate the other. Leaving your partner alone at an event where they don't know anyone, flirting with another person in an inappropriate way, getting drunk and making a fool out of yourself in front of her colleagues, teasing her in front of your parents, or making a joke at his expense when your kids are in the room all can be experienced as disrespect. Another scenario could be speaking the language that your partner is not fluent in while they are present, and your partner is in the minority. I remember that even when my father's whole enormous family got together, if my mother entered the room, they would immediately switch from Kurdish to Farsi. After a few years she picked up the language and could join in the conversations, though they would all often giggle at her accent, including my mom!

BOUNDARIES FOR YOUR COUPLEDOM

In addition to our individual boundaries, couples also need to recognize the boundary they have around their partnership. Infidelity is the most obvious violation of a couple's joint boundary and something that comes to people's minds when we talk about the subject, but there are other occurrences that are also breaches of boundaries. Sharing what you agreed to be private with others outside your coupledom or complaining to other people about your partner's behavior are common; spending your finite resources of time, energy, attention, and money outside of the relationship could be another breach. Buying your mother a new car while your wife drives around in an unsafe car that she's had since college is another example. The couple's boundary is something partners need to negotiate together, and it needn't look like anyone else's coupledom. For example, non-monogamous couples have boundaries just like monogamous couples do; they just have different agreements about where those boundaries lie. For some couples, opposite-sex relationships are forbidden (or same-sex if the couple is gay or lesbian); for others, flirting or even friendships are not permitted. It doesn't matter where you draw these lines, as long as you draw them together and renegotiate as the need arises.

Respectful Communication

Most of us recognize that it is inappropriate to raise your voice, call someone a name, criticize, insult, mock, interrupt, or otherwise demean a person verbally. Ignoring someone by distancing, stonewalling, or ghosting is equally offensive to most people. If you are enacting or experiencing any of those behaviors, there is a fundamental breach of respect that should be examined.

So what does respectful communication look like? We talked about being respectable and living by your healthy boundaries. When it comes to communicating respect, it starts with being aware of the value of your resources, especially the ones that are not infinite, such as time—both your own and your partner's. When your partner has something important to say, you can show your respect by giving them your time and paying attention. If you don't have the time or resources, lovingly and firmly communicate your boundaries and set another time to come together when you can be fully present. When you're thinking about what you want to say next, or wishing they would stop talking, you're not showing up as respectful. The same is true if you're just waiting for them to finish so you can talk about your own "stuff." If the timing is bad, let them know by saying, "I know this is important to you, and it is hard for me to listen while I'm driving. Can we pause this for now and talk about it after we're home?" Make sure to set a specific or approximate time (more on this in part three).

This also works the other way around. If you want to talk about something, beyond regular chitchat, make sure your partner is in a position to be able to listen to you. This became a huge point of contention for a lot of couples during the pandemic. If it's the middle of the workday and your partner has come into the kitchen for a fresh cup of tea, that doesn't mean they're ready to engage with you in a lengthy conversation about the dream you had last night. Some couples tell me that their partners trap them as captive listeners when they are taking a shower or even going to the bathroom! In our overscheduled lives I appreciate that there might not be enough time to connect, even over simple and mundane topics, but come on! In the *toilet*? Instead, try letting them know when you want their undivided attention, set a time, and be prepared to wait until the agreed-upon time comes.

Being respectful of your partner also includes being aware of how much you are talking, what you are talking about, when and for how long. Some couples expect to share everything and appreciate a high level of verbal exchange in their relationships. Others don't. Sharing every little detail about the fight you had with your mother that brought back unwanted memories from childhood with your partner over the phone while on the way to work, and using your partner to process what needs to be dealt with in your personal journal or with a professional might not be something your partner is willing or able to do. One of my clients put it well when she said, "I feel like my husband uses me as his dumpster and just trauma dumps on me on a daily basis about his work, his father, the jerk who cut him off on the highway, everything. When I start to tune him out, or ask him to stop because I am exhausted and had a rough day, too, he gets angry and tells me that I'm not 'there for him.'" I always tell couples that sharing is like watering: If you do it in a timely manner and in an appropriate amount it is nurturing and necessary for the blossoming of your coupledom. But if you just open the valve and let the words gush out all over the place, you risk flooding your relational space and may damage it. A quick test is to ask yourself whether sharing something right now will add to your intimacy or not, and from whose perspective. When you have an answer for this, proceed!

Matching your tone and attitude to the subject at hand and allowing your partner to complete their thought without interruption demonstrates respect. Humor, which can be a strong asset in a couple's toolbox because it can give some perspective to potentially sensitive topics, can easily feel disrespectful if you use it at the wrong moment (like Sheila, above). This is also true in situations where you offer solutions, or give advice that is unsolicited, or interrupt a person as they are trying to tell you something in order to give your commentary, corrections, or supplement or even substantiate what they are saying. This is especially problematic when you interrupt your partner to correct details in their story, or to tell them how they *should* feel about something, or assume you know what they're about to say and so finish their sentence for them. Early on in a relationship, a couple might think it's adorable to interrupt by finishing each other's sentences. "We are so in sync!" After several years together it is less cute. It is usually best not to presume you know what someone else is thinking or feeling. The same goes for presuming you understand the motives or intentions behind their behavior. It creates an enormous space for misunderstanding and miscommunication to occur. It can also be perceived by the other as a sign of disrespect for their autonomy.

All of these run the risk of being condescending and leaving your partner feeling minimized, patronized, and dismissed. Your presence is more meaningful and fulfilling for your partner when you give your partner your full attention. Listen with interest, and the relevant actions will follow (e.g., asking informed questions, giving a hug, or offering a different perspective). The way you communicate nonverbally is also something to bring to your awareness. Think about your senses as you engage with your partner. Do you look at them with tenderness or with irritation? Do you maintain eye contact and use a pleasant or neutral tone of voice? Rolling your eyes, sighing loudly, looking away when they are speaking, wandering out of the room, or scrolling down Instagram are all usually perceived as disrespectful and are best avoided.

Respect for the Physical: Space, Body, Needs

When you go out with your partner, either on a date or just to run errands, do you match your pace as you walk, or is one of you always half a block ahead? (I know many of you are laughing right now, and not because you are happy. You have either seen this, or it has happened and may still be happening in your relationship.) Do you hog the covers, go for days without showering, or sprawl on the couch so no one else can sit comfortably? Sometimes respect boils down to how we coexist as bodies in the physical space we share with each other. Our physical bodies are easy to overlook, but the ego resides in the body, and all of our experiences enter through the body. Our bodies interpret the world through our senses, and they regulate and inform our emotional responses. How we feel in our bodies (and in the presence of the body of our partner) has a huge impact on our relationships. Let me explain.

I met Margaret and Jacqueline through my telehealth platform, and I was immediately struck by how different they looked. I knew that Jacqueline was very tall at six foot two. She was also passionate about volleyball and extremely athletic. Margaret, five foot three and petite, was almost childlike in comparison (both women were in their early thirties at the time). As they were arguing one day, I realized that Margaret often felt really belittled, and it gave me an idea. I asked if they would be willing to try a little experiment. They agreed and paused their conversation for a moment. I asked them to stand up, then directed Margaret to stand on a stool so that she was just a couple of inches taller than Jacqueline. Then they began talking again. Both immediately realized that something felt very different. Margaret's tone changed: She became much more centered and assertive, and she actually stood up taller. Their whole dynamic really shifted because they were literally on each other's level. The couple took this to heart. Margaret told me later that she felt a lot more respected in their conversations in general and especially when they were having sensitive conversations.[5] I have been seeing my clients from all over the world through digital platforms since 2003 (when Skype was born), and have learned to ask about the height and weight of the partners on my intake forms. When people ask me why, this is the story I tell them. A lot can be added to the context of what people experience if we just pay attention to the way they are physically with each other.

Sometimes being respectful of physical space has to do with acknowledging that even though we would like to think that we (and our partners) are perfect, we are not. We're all human beings who live within bodies that can malfunction at any time. Taking care of yourself physically can be an important part of being respectful toward your partner. For example, I once worked with a couple in which the wife needed a hearing aid but refused to get one. She and her husband got into little fights all the time because of it. He would accuse her of not listening or not paying attention when she forgot something important, or when he called out to her and she didn't answer him, when she had never heard him in the first place. And he became so accustomed to talking loudly that sometimes his voice was too loud, and she felt offended because he was shouting at her. All people have differing levels of ability and ease. If you know your partner doesn't like to drive at night, or has a bad knee, or can't tolerate loud noises, you might want to reconsider asking them to go clubbing at midnight. If your partner doesn't like to have a dog sleeping with them all night long, try to keep the dog out of your bed. If they are trying to keep sober, stop having friends over for tequila shots (I have actually heard all these repeatedly from my couples!). One couple that was a part of our research, both widowed and in their early seventies, recently started dating. "We call it AARP dating," Ellen explained. "We meet at noon to walk our dogs in the park, then we go out to lunch, and we're both home by five o'clock. I don't like to drive at night, and he falls asleep really early, so it works for both of us."

Respecting your partner's physical needs means that you pay attention to how you share your space, and to how you interact with each other's physical self within that space. This includes things like approaching your partner for some sexy time at midnight when they've told you a few times now that the answer will always be no after nine p.m. because they have to be up at six a.m.; turning the TV on in the bedroom because you can't sleep even though you know it could wake your partner; having the cats in bed when the other person has asked multiple times not to do that. All are disrespectful of their basic physical need for sleep.

GET SOME SLEEP

While I'm on the subject of sleep, it's a good idea to take the time to listen to your partner and communicate to them the ways that each of you would like your sleeping space to be. If you have one blanket that you fight over all night, try using two blankets instead. If you like the sheets tucked in, and your partner likes to have her feet hanging over the end of the bed, you might want to consider getting two twin beds and pushing them together. I can't begin to tell you how many couples come to me complaining about a partner who snores, talks in their sleep, grinds their teeth, wakes up multiple times to go to the bathroom, likes the room to be too hot or cold, likes to have sex in the middle of the night, falls asleep watching TV, has to leave the lights on, listens to a radio on speaker, has restless leg syndrome, or wants to have the pets and/or the kids in the room or in the bed. Do yourselves a favor and get qualified help for any medical problems, and do some research on how to make your bedroom suitable and inviting for you both. Don't underestimate the importance of sleep. Healthy sleep habits improve your mood and your overall health, which in turn improves your relationship. You don't want your bodies to perceive each other as entities that disrupt your primal need for sleep.

Being respectful of your partner's physical needs includes how you touch them, and this includes sex. When one partner gives the other feedback, asking for a gentler touch, or for attention to a particular body part or a certain specific thing, and the other disregards the information and continues to do whatever comes naturally to them or brings them pleasure, it can feel dismissive and disrespectful (even when it is not intended that way). It is especially problematic when the person doing the asking has had to build up some courage to do so. On the other hand, giving constant corrective advice while having sex can also feel disrespectful to say the least (more on this later). The same goes for other types of touch that may not be sexual. I once saw a couple who shared with me that one of them really, really did not like to be tickled. But her partner thought it was very cute and didn't understand the severity of the discomfort that it created. As a child, her older siblings would tickle her until she screamed, cried, or threw up. Being tickled as an adult was actually very triggering for her. Once the partner fully comprehended this, the tickling stopped. Hopefully, we all know by now that consent is an absolute must for sexual encounters, but the idea of consent also has to apply to all forms of physical contact.

I can't overstate the importance of practicing respect in every interaction we have with our partners, large and small. I hope you have the tools now to assess the ways in which you embody, experience, and express respect. Think about how your boundaries could be set and communicated to help preserve your self-respect and guide your partner to successfully show up for you and with you. I encourage you to practice these daily acts of respect until they become habitual. Along the way, ask your partner for feedback, and give feedback yourself, to fine-tune your understanding of the other's expectations and boundaries. Make it a priority. It is worth it. Remember: Put 20 percent of your effort on what matters 80 percent of the time, and you will see the results. Respect makes the ground to build trust, which we will talk about in the next chapter.

CHAPTER 6

Trust

To be trusted is a greater compliment than to be loved.

—George MacDonald[1]

Before I even started my formal research, I knew from my work with couples that trust is a must in committed partnerships. The building of trust, the breaking of trust, and the difficulty of repairing breaches in trust are often at the core of the work I do with couples. When I talk about trust, many people immediately think of infidelity—considered to be the ultimate breach of trust in coupledom—but there are many events, both large and small, that can chip away at the belief that our partner will reliably act in ways that do not cause us harm.

I know that many of you agree that trust is important and a quintessential cornerstone of relationships. Partners need to know that when one of them says, "I'll take care of it," the other can trust that they will. Over time, this provides a kind of existential security about your life, your place in the world, where you belong, where you are going, and whom you can rely on for support. In intimate partnerships, which always include vulnerability, trust also provides safety. Trust makes it possible to be honest about how you feel, ask for what you want, and let your partner know when you're hurting without worrying that you will fall flat on the ground without a safety net.

In this chapter I'd like to help you clarify what trust means to you so that you have solid ways to define, manifest, and experience it in your relationship. We'll start by looking at the idea of trust in its broadest sense; then we'll focus in on how your experiences have influenced the way you connect with others. From there, we'll look at how the various dimensions of trust play out in our relationships, and how to repair when that trust has been damaged.

THE ELEMENTS OF TRUST: RELIABILITY AND CONSISTENCY

Though most of us have a good understanding of what trust means to us on some level, it is also something that everyone experiences differently. Trust is an idea, an ideal, an attitude, a decision, a feeling, a belief, a way of relating to the self, and a way of relating to the world. How do we decide whom to trust, why, and for what? How do we know we trust ourselves, and how do we express our trustworthiness to the world around us? Trust is complicated, which is why it's crucial to deconstruct the idea, understand what it means to each of us, then articulate that meaning to a whole other human being (who has their own ideas about it).

Dr. Jack Barbalet, who studies trust as a sociological phenomenon, explains that trust typically includes "a sense that dependence on the other's capacities or actions will not lead to a loss for the trustor."[2] In other words, we have to believe that we can count on our partners not to let us down, to hurt us, or to let their own self-interest override our needs or the needs of our coupledom. Baked into that kind of trust is deep vulnerability: We open ourselves to the possibility of disappointment, loss, or heartache. When we believe that a person will show up for us by acting in ways that support our well-being, and will avoid causing us harm, we trust them. And that trust is a privilege.

In fact, trust is the only element of Emergent Love that must be earned, and it is built slowly, over time. Trust may be a belief, but it is grounded in evidence of consistency and reliability. For instance, I believe that if I hold an apple three feet off the ground, then let go, it will fall to the floor. Why do I believe this? Because this has been my experience 100 percent of the time. Consistency and reliability are essential elements of trust, and one cannot suffice alone. *Reliability* means we do what we say we are going to do, and *consistency* refers to how predictable we are both in terms of our actual behavior (what we do) and in terms of the quality of our behavior (how we do it). Of course, as human beings we are sure to make mistakes, but our own trustworthiness is directly proportional to our ability to be reliable and consistent.

Being trustworthy might not be sexy, glamorous, or exciting, and doesn't involve two people merging to become one, or professing undying love, or making grand gestures to demonstrate one's passion, or any of the things that make submergent love so enticing. But, like gravity, it is what roots us in our coupledom. It is an underlying current, a foundational force that provides the safety love needs to thrive.

WHAT TRUST MEANS TO YOU

"He has trust issues," Jaclyn said matter-of-factly the first time she and Ahmed came to see me. Jaclyn is a vivacious blonde from southern California, very friendly and expressive when she speaks. She was raised in a middle-class American family and works as a marketing director part-time. Ahmed is more subdued. As he listened to Jaclyn in my office, he sat forward, forearms resting on his knees, looking at the floor. She continued, "I accidentally forgot to pay the rent for a couple of months, and he totally freaked out. I mean, I was wrong, and I know that. I thought I had set it up for autopay. I told him I'd take care of it and I didn't, so my bad. I totally acknowledge that and I apologized profusely. I've already dealt with it, all good now, everything's okay. But he actually started talking about divorce. Divorce! Who divorces over rent? Something else is going on."

At this point Ahmed, visibly trying to keep his cool, spoke up. "I asked her multiple times to take care of it. When the first notice came in, I said, 'Will you please take care of this?' I was very busy with work at the time. She said she would, I thought she did, then we got a second notice. Again, I asked, 'Will you please take care of this?' Again, she said she would. Then, two weeks ago, police showed up at our door! This is the little detail she left out. Our landlord actually called the police to complain about us, saying we were making noise. We weren't, but he's fed up and I guess he wanted us to know it. Sure, it's just the rent, but last week it was just that she forgot to stop at the store for pasta on the way home, so dinner was late because she had to go back out. We had a whole chaotic situation with our son, who's three years old and starts to seriously melt down if he hasn't eaten by six o'clock. It's always small stuff, but it is a *lot* of small stuff. She's irresponsible, and I'm so tired of dealing with the consequences. She can't seem to understand that her actions affect me, *my* plans, *my* life, *my* reputation, and our child for god's sake. We've talked about it and talked about it. She's always sorry, she always says, 'I own my part and take responsibility.' I guess she learned that from all the podcasts and self-help books she reads, but nothing actually changes."

Sensing that there was more to the story, I asked, "What was that like for you, when the police showed up at the door?" Ahmed became very still, then burst into sobs. Jaclyn looked shocked. As his tears slowed, he explained, "My whole life I have never been in trouble. I did well in school, went to medical school, became a doctor like my immigrant mother wanted. My parents moved here from Afghanistan before I was born, and let me tell you that being from Afghanistan was not easy for them in the 1990s. Still it isn't easy. When the officer saw my face, *his* face changed. He immediately put a hand on his gun. I knew he thought I was a terrorist. I'm a doctor! You have no idea how humiliating that was."

"Oh, I have some idea," I replied. He smiled sheepishly. "I hoped you might," he admitted. "I can't seem to find the words to explain it to Jaclyn. She thinks I'm overreacting." Jaclyn sees the police as benevolent, or at least neutral. For Ahmed it's different. It was only after she saw him break down in our session that she began to appreciate his perspective.

Trust can be bruised, or even ruptured altogether, in so many different ways. When breaches of trust happen with those who were supposed to care for you, the wound goes a bit deeper, and the impact may be more ingrained in the way you operate in your everyday life. For example, if you grew up in a family system where your parents or other adult caregivers were not present for you on a consistent basis, or where your requests for help or support were not met, you may have developed a level of self-sufficiency and independence to protect you from relying too much on other people, emotionally or otherwise. This is what plenty of couples I see call "trust issues," and they can make it a little harder for you to be in an interdependent relationship in which you trust that you can ask for help and support from your partner and they will show up for you to the best of their ability, and they trust you to do the same.

Ahmed's "trust issues" had less to do with his family of origin and more to do with his experience of being treated as a suspect by authority figures, something so common among people whose physical appearance puts them in a so-called minority category. Jaclyn's unreliability went way beyond being an inconvenience; it was potentially life-threatening for him. People sometimes talk about having "trust issues" as though they're superficial or problematic—something we can and should turn off in an instant. But often they're grounded in very real concerns and past experiences, and in those cases a different kind of trust has to be built and earned. For example, Ahmed needs to be able to trust that Jaclyn's actions (or inactions) won't put him in danger like that again.

The way each of us identifies and receives signals of trustworthiness is shaped by our experiences in childhood and throughout our lives. In fact, *how* you trust is sometimes even more important than *whom* you trust. The way you learned about trust includes whom you were taught to trust, whom you were warned never to trust, and any breaches of trust (large or small) that you've experienced. It also includes what you were taught about privacy (who is entitled to it and who is not), secrecy (the difference between a "good" secret and a "bad" secret), and dishonesty (when, if ever, it is acceptable). Your experience of trust is also hugely impacted by the behavior of authority figures in your life, from parents to politicians, and whether or not you believed they would act in your best interest. Understanding how your own experiences have shaped how you think about trust is essential if you want to be able to cultivate trust in your relationship. With that in mind, let's try a self-literacy exercise to help you decode your own blueprint for trusting and being trusted by others.

BUILDING BLOCK: YOUR TRUST BLUEPRINT

- When you were growing up, what kinds of messages did you receive about trusting people? Was there a specific person or a specific type of person who was trustworthy or not trustworthy? Could you or your family trust authority figures like teachers, coaches, religious leaders, elected officials, or the police or military?
- Have you ever felt deeply betrayed? Have you ever been lied to by a person who you did not expect would lie to you? How did that feel? Did an adult ever ask you to keep a secret? How did it feel to be asked that?
- Did you have a life-altering event because someone broke someone else's trust (like one parent betraying the other in some way)? What were the stories told around that? Who agreed? Who disagreed? What were the lessons you were told you should learn from it?
- When you needed help, advice, guidance, or emotional comfort, did you have people who could provide it consistently? Did you provide this for others?
- Did the people around you have a sense of trust toward you? How did you know either way? Could they leave you with a task and know that you would get the job done, or tell you a secret and know that it would be safe?
- Do you feel like you were able to consistently show up in your relational spaces in the role that you acquired or that was assigned to you? How did that serve you? Was it rewarding or taxing?
- Have you ever betrayed someone else's trust?

Maybe you experienced an event that was beyond your control or level of comprehension, such as a parent dying when you were young, bankruptcy, divorce, or violence in your home or community. Each of these will have its own legacy, depending on how you experienced it at the time. You might carry a sense of being betrayed or abandoned by the parent who "left you," or a sense of deep regret that you could not control the situation. This fear of potential loss could make it difficult for you to bond with others at a deep level. Experiences in which a person feels unsafe or threatened, or their life is in danger, can lead them to develop a level of hypervigilance around others' behaviors, always looking for signs that it's about to happen again. Adam Phillips, a British psychologist who wrote the book *Terrors and Experts*, explains, "In fear the imagined future joins up with the unpleasure of the past. Tell me what you fear and I will tell you what has happened to you."[3]

TRAUMA

People who have physically survived war, hunger, displacement, forced migration, sexual assault, physical assault, imprisonment, torture, or any other experience of physical danger can develop post-traumatic stress disorder (PTSD) as a result, especially if they didn't have an opportunity to process the impact of the event at the time. These experiences are distinct, extreme forms of what happens when situational or relational safety is not available and our nervous systems become hyper-attuned to potential danger. Serious trauma is stored in the body and has a tendency to become reactivated in times of stress, or when situations in the present remind us of events from the past. Dr. Bessel van der Kolk, a psychiatrist and leader in the field of trauma, explains, "Nobody can 'treat' a war, or abuse, rape, molestation, or any other horrendous event, for that matter; what has happened cannot be undone. But what can be dealt with are the imprints of the trauma on the body, mind, and soul."[4] If any of this resonates with your own experience, you may benefit from additional support—both for yourself and as a couple navigating the legacy of trauma. Van der Kolk's book *The Body Keeps the Score: Brain, Mind and Body in the Healing of Trauma*[5] is a wonderful starting place if you'd like to learn more. You can find additional resources at www.lovebydesignbook.com.

Your experiences of trust and/or betrayal do not have to be physically or psychologically traumatic to have an impact on your sense of safety in intimate relationships. Even in lesser transgressions there is usually a level of anger that accompanies the hurt. You probably have heard that *sad* and *mad* are two sides of the same coin. If these emotions don't have a healthy channel to be experienced and expressed, they can turn into rage directed at the self or at others who may not have been involved. All of these feelings must be acknowledged, validated, and addressed. Otherwise the betrayal ends up traveling from one relationship into the next, like an unwanted hitchhiker, in the form of hypervigilance and suspicion. The old betrayal is projected onto the new partner.

Remember when we talked about knowing the sensitivities you bring with you into your relationships back in chapter 3? This is somewhat similar—both are past experiences that shape your current perspective—but experiences of betrayal go much deeper and can result in significant injuries to your sense of safety in all of your relationships. When a social contract is breached, there are a lot of personal and social consequences that go with it. In the series *Gutsy*, former first lady Hillary Clinton talks about how keeping her marriage together after the public humiliation of her husband's transgression was one of the hardest challenges in her life. Something that she also wrote about in her book *Living History*: "The most difficult decisions I have made in my life were to stay married to Bill and to run for the Senate from New York."[6] As you can see, from what we might consider small to big, from a person next door to the most powerful people in the world, these so-called trust issues are among the most common injuries all people carry with them.

THE IMPORTANCE OF SELF-TRUST

How you trust others is also influenced by how, and whether, you trust yourself. Think about it: Placing your trust in someone involves a certain level of confidence in your own ability to accurately assess the trustworthiness of others. If you trust people that break your trust time after time, eventually you might lose trust in yourself to make decisions that are in your own best interest. This damage to self-trust is one of the reasons betrayal hurts so much: It leads people to question their judgment. Betrayed partners often lament, "How could I be so *stupid*?!"

Most of the ingredients of Emergent Love are socially constructed. Our ideas about attraction, respect, commitment, compassion, and being loving are largely the product of our upbringing, experience, and the sociocultural context within which we live and shape our relationships. Though they're somewhat influenced by innate personality traits, genetics, and gender, they are not as directly linked to our basic biophysiological and bioneurological conditions. Trust is different in this regard, since our past experiences often have an impact on how we physically respond to threat in the present moment.

For the purpose of our journey here it might be helpful to think of self-trust as having two dimensions: our judgment and our gut. When you trust your judgment you are trusting yourself at an intellectual level in terms of your ability to assess a situation and respond appropriately. Trust in your own judgment is developed over time, and is based on the outcomes of your past decisions. It's also influenced by the voices we carry in our heads of the people around us who didn't trust us, or who warned us that one bad decision could lead to disastrous consequences.

We have a sense of agency over this part of our decision-making, so if we fail to get the outcome we want, we might feel ashamed or blame ourselves. If this happens a lot, we could end up losing trust in ourselves and instead let someone else make decisions for us so we can avoid feeling the shame and blame that are associated with the potential failure later.

At the other end of the spectrum, people who have suffered the consequences of someone else's bad decisions (like growing up with a parent who is incarcerated) might have a hard time trusting anyone else with any decision that might remotely impact them. Instead they believe that if they are in charge they can control the situation and avoid mistakes. Neither extreme is healthy in a partnership.

In addition to our judgment, we also make decisions from our gut-brain. Like our judgment, our gut-brain is informed by events from the past. Significant experiences of safety and danger are stored in the body as physical memories that inform our *felt sense* about a person or situation. When we receive certain signals from the environment, the body begins to decode the input and scan the physical memory bank to determine if that stimulus means safety or danger.

Whether or not your gut-brain is a reliable source of information will depend on your past experiences, particularly if there was trauma involved. For example, Nada, who is forty-three, is terrified of dogs because she was bitten by a boxer when she was four years old. When she sees a dog approaching, her gut-brain tells her to run even though her judgment tells her she's probably okay. People with a high level of vigilance might experience more things as dangerous than as safe. When this is the case, their responses tend to be more impulsive and reactionary. Remember: The body's purpose is to signal the brain that the situation is not safe, and the fight-or-flight response kicks in. Part of trusting others includes trusting yourself to identify events that trigger intense emotions in your gut and knowing how to manage them so that your judgment can step in. I call this having a polished gut!

THE IMPORTANCE OF BEING TRUSTWORTHY

Trust might be built slowly over time, but it can be destroyed in an instant—as in cases of infidelity, financial betrayal, or the discovery of other hurtful secrets. The French film *Force Majeure* is a moving example.[7] In the film, a couple and their young children are having lunch on the terrace of a ski resort in France when an avalanche comes crashing down the mountain toward them. They don't know at the time that the ski resort regularly implements controlled avalanches as a safety precaution. They genuinely think they're going to die. As the woman moves to shield her children, the man grabs his smartphone and runs inside. When the wall of snow stops at a safe distance from the terrace, he returns to the table and continues eating his breakfast as if nothing has happened. The woman is not only traumatized by the near-death experience, she's also horrified that her husband ran away. But when she asks him about it later, he denies doing any such thing. The more she presses him, the more he denies what happened. Her trust that he would protect his family is shattered; his trust in himself and his judgment are equally destroyed. (I won't spoil the ending, but if you haven't seen the film I highly recommend it.)

This is what most people think of when I talk about a breach of trust. It is sudden, dramatic, and life-changing. But trust can also erode slowly, through countless acts of disrespect or disappointment, or when one partner does not show up in the way that the other had complete faith they would. The majority of the couples I see are more like Ahmed and Jaclyn than the couple in *Force Majeure*. They haven't gone through a major betrayal but instead have experienced these kinds of micro-transgressions that, over time, lead to distrust of themselves or their partner or both.

Trust as an interpersonal dynamic is twofold: Partners need to *receive trust from* their partner and they need to *express trust to* their partner. Because trust must be earned, this dynamic looks a little bit different here than elsewhere. We receive trust (or earn trust) by demonstrating our own trustworthiness, and we express trust in our partner by exhibiting trusting behaviors that acknowledge that they have earned our trust. This sounds more complicated than it is, so let me clarify it a bit. We demonstrate that we are trustworthy when we respect boundaries, are reliable and consistent, and behave with integrity. We express trust in our partners when we are willing to be emotionally vulnerable, are honest about our needs, respect their privacy, and give them the benefit of the doubt in any situation. Let's take a closer look at how this works.

Boundaries that we discussed in the previous chapter are also important to trust for a few reasons. First, they are important because you need to respect your partner's boundaries in order to build trust. This is especially true when it comes to the boundaries you draw around yourself as a couple. If you share information about your partner or partnership to a third party (she lost her job, we've hired a surrogate, they have irritable bowel syndrome), it could constitute a breach of trust if it wasn't agreed upon in advance. Part of being trustworthy is respecting your partner's privacy. It's also part of expressing trust, and we'll get to that in a minute.

Somewhat less obvious, but equally important, is demonstrating your trustworthiness by maintaining your own boundaries. When one partner repeatedly ignores their own personal boundaries, it creates confusion and distrust in the other. People-pleasing behavior—doing things for others that one does not wish to do or cannot reasonably manage to do—usually ends in resentment, disappointment, and loss of trust for both partners.

Individuals who were praised as children for what they did, rather than for who they were, often feel the need to prove their worth in relationships by over-functioning and taking on more than they can reasonably expect to accomplish: "Look how worthwhile it is for you to be in a relationship with me. Look at all I can do for you. I will take care of you." In the beginning of a relationship, both partners might be pleased with this arrangement. But as the years go by, the over-functioning partner begins to feel overwhelmed by the burden of taking care of everything. Resentments build up. By the time these couples come to my office, the issue is way beyond pleasing each other.

For example, when Natalie wanted to join a local running group to train for a marathon, Joshua immediately worried that taking care of their three kids every Saturday for four hours would be too much for him. But when he said, "Sounds great, Natalie," she believed him (she trusted him) and joined the group. Three weeks into the training, Natalie called to check in on Joshua and the kids; he said that they are great, homeworks are done, and everything is in order. When she came home from her run, she found the house in shambles, and all three kids were still in their pajamas in front of the television. A huge fight ensued. Natalie explained to me later, "He does this a lot. He says something is fine when it isn't. I don't know what to believe, so I feel like I'm always walking on eggshells around him, trying to guess how he really feels. If he had just told me the truth we could have hired a babysitter. Instead we had a huge fight and now I feel guilty and really angry that he lied." When we communicate our own healthy boundaries, we demonstrate to our partner that they can trust what we say because we know we can deliver (unless something unpredictable happens).

This brings us to *reliability*. Promising more than you can deliver will eventually lead to your partner seeing you as unreliable and therefore untrustworthy. Reliability simply means that when you say you will do something, you do it and to the level that is expected and agreed upon. If we think of a partnership as a long-term investment with a vision to build something together, we need to know we can rely on the other person.

Lack of reliability is so common that honestly it could affect 95 percent of the couples that I know socially, professionally, and within the community. Partners have to chase each other down to ask, "Did you pay the bill? Did you make the appointment? Did you call so-and-so back?" Lack of reliability not only leads to distrust, it can also lead to a larger trouble. I remember Marilyn and Taylor, a couple I saw several years ago. Taylor was responsible for submitting their income tax returns but had let the ball drop. He didn't tell Marilyn about it, either. She didn't find out until they received a letter that they were being audited by the IRS because they had not paid taxes in four years. They were faced with enormous fines and owed tens of thousands of dollars. Because they filed as a married couple, the responsibility fell on both of them, as did the damage to their credit. After filing their taxes, Marilyn filed for divorce. "I just don't see a way back from this," she explained. "This is becoming dangerous. I can't trust him."

It is very difficult to repair trust when reliability is so gravely damaged. Remember, trust in a relationship includes a belief about the future behavior of a person based on their past behavior. If you can't do something, just say so. Will it be uncomfortable? Yes. But it is not as damaging as when the balls start to drop. If you have a healthy relationship, stating your capacity clearly will open the door for a longer conversation in which you can negotiate an arrangement that works for both of you, and that maintains the trust in your coupledom. This is also true for professional relationships. When people take on tasks that are beyond their capabilities, then fail to deliver, they end up disappointing their colleagues, feeling terrible about themselves, and reinforcing the idea that they are "not good enough."

Finally, we demonstrate trustworthiness when we exhibit consistency in how we show up for others, and this has everything to do with integrity. If reliability means doing what you said you would do, then I would like to think of integrity as being who you said you would be. Having integrity means that you know what you value and you behave in ways that are consistent with those values, even when it is difficult. In our research, we found that individuals who have a less developed sense of their own moral values, and who have a low level of commitment to those values, also tend to have low levels of trust in their relationships. These couples usually present in my office with trust issues stemming from a lack of integrity. "You said that family is the most important thing in your life, and you took a work call when I was in the delivery room giving birth to our child; how are these aligned?"

Behaving with integrity means that you are able to look inward, understand your own values, and behave in ways that are in accordance with those values. There is a difference between someone who doesn't cross a line because of what might happen (they don't want to risk what's at stake if they get caught) and someone who doesn't cross that line because it is not who they are or what they do. You need to know what motivates you to be able to have a North Star, so to speak, when the situations become challenging, tempting, or tricky.

Dr. Brené Brown, an insightful researcher who studies vulnerability and trust, explains that when you behave with integrity, "You choose courage over comfort. You choose what is right over what is fun, fast, or easy. And you choose to practice your values rather than simply professing them."[8] In her work, Dr. Brown developed an anatomy of trust, which she describes through the acronym BRAVING as a way to assess whether all the necessary elements that build trust are present in a relationship. The initials stand for: Boundaries, Reliability, Accountability, Vault (keeping confidences), Integrity, Nonjudgment, and Generosity.[9]

Remember, moral values provide a more consistent guide for behavior than your feelings in the moment. This is why it's so important to know yourself and understand your values before you can bring that into your relationship. It's hard to behave with integrity when you don't know what matters to you. Some of my clients have a hard time because they had a nude dream about someone besides their partner and are not sure if they are breaching their trust by not telling them about it. The event that caused a breach of trust itself could be real, perceived, or imagined.

DEMONSTRATING TRUST IN YOUR PARTNER

Now let's take a look at what it means to express trust to your partner by exhibiting behaviors that let them know when they have earned your trust. Exposing what is precious and personal to you is a good place to begin. In popular culture this is known as vulnerability. Practicing real vulnerability is hard for a lot of people. It takes courage to bring all of yourself, your identities and your fragility, into your relational space. We are not always proud of everything that has shaped us. When you consistently have an experience in which your partner listens without judgment, holds the space with compassion and gentleness, and offers a sense of safety and protection, it becomes easier.

Being honest about your needs, and letting your partner know when your needs aren't being met (or when your boundaries have been crossed), is another expression of trust in your partner and in your coupledom. It can be embarrassing or even scary to ask someone for help, or for a hug, or for some encouragement and support. It's also sometimes difficult to let them know when they have hurt your feelings, disappointed you, or behaved in a way that left you feeling diminished, unseen, or unappreciated. But when you speak the truth of your experience, you demonstrate to your partner that you trust them to listen, to care, to show up for you, and to help you if and as they can. You trust that they are a capable adult and not a fragile child to be protected.

As a side note, the value of asking for help as an expression of trust is seriously undermined if you don't also exhibit trust that your partner is competent enough to complete the task at hand. Asking your partner to do the dishes, then standing behind them and micromanaging where they place each item in the dishwasher is not an expression of trust. The same goes for critiquing their efforts after the fact. Tension over dishwashing habits of couples might sound arbitrary, but it is more common than you think!

Respecting your partner's privacy, as I mentioned above, is both a demonstration of your own trustworthiness and also an expression of trust in your partner. Partners often disagree on the level of transparency they would like to have. For some, reading each other's emails or texts, using apps to determine a partner's location, or asking them what they talked about in their therapy sessions is seen as closeness. For others, it is experienced as an expression of distrust—not to mention intrusive and disrespectful. When you respect your partner's privacy, you are expressing your trust that they will tell you anything you need to know.

This is closely associated with giving your partner the benefit of the doubt in any situation by being generous and positive in the way you interpret their behavior. When your partner is late coming home, or forgets to put the clothes in the dryer, you don't automatically go to, "They are so inconsiderate and disrespectful!" Instead, you consider other possible explanations, like, "He's been working so hard lately. I'm sure he hates staying late as much as I do." Being generous in this way should not be confused with avoiding difficult conversations, or with people-pleasing, or with disregarding your own boundaries. If someone's behavior crosses your boundaries, you owe it to them, to your relationship, and to yourself to address the issue. But you can express your trust in these situations by giving them the benefit of the doubt rather than ascribing harmful intentions to their behavior from the get-go.

These are all general parameters for understanding how trust manifests in everyday life. There are many other ways of expressing and receiving trust, and you might have different ones that work for you. Now I'd like to turn your attention to some of the domains of trust that are likely to be more or less important in your coupledom, depending on your stage of life and the stage of your relationship.

DOMAINS OF TRUST

Every couple is unique, and there are no hard-and-fast rules about what trust should look like between two people. What's important is that there is enough trust to support each partner's sense of safety, stability, and security. What that looks like and how it is expressed and received are subject to change with changing circumstances and roles. Our research participants described themselves as lovers and roommates, co-parents, friends, best friends, financial partners, emotional supports, and social representatives. Because of this, relational trust is not limited to emotional trust and the level of vulnerability you can have with your partner, or honoring your agreements about sexual exclusivity (whatever they may be). Trust also includes a sense of physical safety, confidence in how they will present themselves and represent you in social situations, intellectual trust that your partner will "get" you, trust that they will not betray you financially, and trustworthiness in any other domains in your life that are significant for partners at any given moment. Let's take a closer look.

Emotional Trust

Most people, when they think of trust in intimate relationships, are thinking of emotional trust. Are you going to handle my feelings with care, or am I going to fall flat when I'm sharing my vulnerabilities with you? When one person seeks the other out for attention, compassion, or connection, and the other does not appreciate or recognize the gesture for what it is—a moment of vulnerability—emotional trust can be damaged. This is especially true when partners subscribe to a hugely idealized version of intimacy that includes prioritizing your relationship to the extent that you will drop everything at a moment's notice to "show up" for your partner. As a real person who is in a real relationship in the midst of a very dynamic life, I can tell you that this is not possible for most people.

Mutual trust and mutual respect intersect in many areas, and emotional intimacy is one of them. Respecting your partner's time and respecting your own need for undivided attention are valuable guidelines for building and sustaining emotional trust. As we discussed in the last chapter, if your partner reaches out to you for support, and you're in the middle of a crisis at work (or have other competing demands on your attention), let them know that you want to be able to listen and suggest another time that could work better. It's important to follow through with this, which means knowing your own limitations around your availability. One of the most disrespectful things you can do in a relationship is to leave your loved ones hanging by telling them, "Let's talk later," and then never bring the topic back up again.

I keep these squishy, heart-shaped balls in my office that I give to clients. I want you to imagine that you have one as well. When you're getting ready to start a conversation (on any topic) or to talk about something that is especially difficult for you, I ask you to consider whether or not your partner is in a position to catch that squishy heart, let alone give it their full attention. If they aren't, and you toss it anyway and it just rolls on the floor, then you need to ask yourself, "Who dropped the ball here?" Not your partner; they didn't even see it coming.

VULNERABILITY AND TRANSPARENCY

There is an important distinction I need to make here, and that is between vulnerability and transparency. Practicing vulnerability is a relational process. Here, both the speaker and the listener *matter* to each other. If the expectations are not met, it could lead to hurt. Transparency, disclosing all of one's secrets and personal history, is not necessarily relational. When you share *everything* just for the sake of getting it out there and on the table, it doesn't matter how it lands. There's not much emotional investment or stake in it, and the receiver is less important than the broadcaster. This is not necessarily a bad thing, but it doesn't build emotional trust. At best, transparency is neutral; at worst it is experienced as overload.

Physical Trust

Neurochemically speaking, oxytocin is known to be the main hormone in building trust and bonding. It plays an important role in labor and delivery, and also during breastfeeding. It is closely related to proximity, touch, and also sex. That warm glow afterward? That's because of the activation of dopamine and oxytocin receptors. Shared laughter is a sign of relationship well-being[10] and stimulates production of oxytocin,[11] and playing together[12] can have the same impact. In general, any signal that tells your brain and your body that this person is going to be predictably safe (though not necessarily predictable in everything) will build physical trust.

But what about when we don't feel physically safe? I'm not talking about *knowing* you're safe—you can know in your rational mind that you are safe from physical harm yet still *feel* unsafe in your body. When your gut-brain senses danger (with or without your judgment corroborating the evidence) the sympathetic nervous system is activated and the fight-or-flight instinct kicks in. If, for example, your partner has an explosive argument with his father over the telephone, and you are only hearing half of the conversation, your body might process that as a danger signal. Someone who rattles your emotions constantly (by criticizing, shouting, throwing things, touching you in unwelcome ways) will do the same thing. Let me give you an example.

Melody and Ashton came to see me because Melody had lost all interest in sex. Ashton was desperate; he couldn't bear the lack of physical contact. "Forget about sex," he explained, "I just want to cuddle in front of the TV or curl up with her in bed." Melody, a radiant woman in her early fifties, was trying to figure out if this was related to menopause. "Or maybe I'm depressed? Maybe I need some sort of medication?" In our first meeting I asked about their style of conflict—a mellow version of a disagreement as well as a scenario that got out of hand. For the mellow version they talked about bickering, or passing snarky comments to each other, and let me know that this was a common practice in their everyday life and often done with humor. When things got out of hand it was usually because of Ashton's temper—he had a low tolerance for frustration and could "get really nasty, really fast." I asked them to describe to me what "get nasty" means, and Ashton explained, "I feel my heart start to pound, and I get really frustrated. Then I start shouting and I'm so sorry, Melody. I know it scares you. So I usually leave the room until I can calm down." Melody added, "Well, you also usually bang on the table, or you break something, and you swear. A lot."

Incredibly, as they were describing this scenario to me, it came to life. We were having a telehealth session, and Ashton accidentally knocked his cup of tea onto the computer. In a fraction of a second he went from being calm and engaged to being in a state of frenzy. His chair toppled as he jumped up, shouting, "Oh no! NO NO NO NO NO! JESUS! WHAT THE F***!"

After the situation was managed, I asked them to take a deep breath and walk me through what happened. Ashton was extremely embarrassed and apologetic. Melody had a concerned look on her face when she said, "I'm glad you got to see that. We have these episodes at least once a week, and even when it isn't directed at me—and in fairness it usually isn't—it still shakes me up every time." I asked Melody if she felt like she could touch Ashton in any way in that moment, and she replied, "Honestly? If you weren't here I would have gone for a drive. That's what I usually do because I don't even want to be in the same building as him. It took me years to learn not to freeze and find a way to get myself literally out of the situation."

Many of us aspire to deal with conflict using our intellect and reason to talk about everything until there is an agreement or resolution. And while that is certainly helpful, it's also important to remember that the body is designed to process input directly, draw its own conclusions, and hold on to those memories *physiologically*. Melody's judgment tells her she is safe with Ashton, but *her body* recognizes *his body* as unsafe. No wonder she didn't want to have a sexually intimate experience with him.

Of course, not every relationship has such dramatic outbursts. But what happens when your partner drives in a way that makes you uncomfortable, or forgets that you don't like to be surprised from behind (not even for a kiss), or takes out her frustrations by yelling at the dog? It is easy to think that these incidents in everyday life don't really matter in the long run, but they do. Each of them can act as a danger signal that sets off a burst of adrenaline that you now have to regulate. This is the "felt sense" of the boundaries we talked about in the last chapter. When our boundaries are repeatedly crossed, it damages both respect and trust.

Trust always builds slowly. Remember, trust is a belief, a prediction that we can anticipate how our partner will behave in the future. But it is a belief that is firmly grounded in reality. If you have a hard time regulating your emotions, or your partner does, I urge you to make this a priority. Meditation, exercise, and psychotherapy can be beneficial. And there are many self-help books that offer concrete skills in emotional self-regulation. If you feel physically threatened by your partner, you may need some additional support getting into a safe situation. You can find additional resources for all of these on the *Love by Design* website at www .lovebydesignbook.com.

Social Trust

We care what people think of us. Many of my clients bristle when I say this, but humans are social mammals, like all primates, and we evolved this way. When you go out in public with your partner, you represent both each other and your partnership. Whenever I talk with them about social trust, I always invite my couples to think about the message they're putting into the world. When people see the two of you together, you probably don't want them to think, "She's the one who hates her husband," or "That's the couple who fights in public," or "He's married to that guy who drinks too much." Think of it as your couple brand. If you're like most people, you'd probably prefer something more like, "They are so good together," or "They really seem to enjoy each other's company," or "They're such a fun couple."

One tool many couples find really helpful is an exercise I call Couple's Branding. As part of my ongoing research in Emergent Love, I have annual check-ins with many former clients, and this is regularly mentioned as a fundamental item in their toolkit that they use for years afterward. It's very simple. Basically, whenever you anticipate a social setting where you will be presenting yourselves *as a couple*, make sure to check in with each other beforehand about which part of your brand you will be highlighting and what each of you hopes to achieve. This could be a family gathering, a concert, a holiday party, drinks with friends, a religious gathering, or anything at all. I've known couples who got into really bad fights whenever they went out socially because they had not clarified expectations before they arrived. One partner didn't mingle enough, or mingled too much and failed to check in with the other, or had just a little too much fun, drank too much, and embarrassed the other. Whatever the reason, partners ended up feeling distanced and dissatisfied.

COUPLE'S TOOLKIT:
WHAT IS YOUR COUPLE BRAND?

Before attending a social function, come to an agreement about the following (a casual conversation will do):

- What is the purpose of this event?
- What kind of experience do each of you hope to have?
- Is there anything in particular your partner wants you to be aware of?
- How much will you drink, eat, or imbibe?
- How late will you stay?
- How will you signal to the other that you need rescuing?
- How will you signal when *they* need rescuing?

It is so important to be in alignment about the purpose of the gathering and the expectations you have from each other. This is especially important if you are entering a situation where one partner has more of a connection than the other, like staying with in-laws or attending a work event with your partner. If you want your partner to make you look good, tell them. Don't be shy here, either. Be specific by saying something like, "Can you please just compliment me in front of so-and-so in such-and-such a way?" It can also be helpful to agree on some nonverbal cues to signify things like, "Come rescue me, this person is talking too much!" or "This is someone you should really meet," or "I'm in an uncomfortable situation." One intercultural couple I know even has a signal for "Please stop doing what you're doing right now because it has a different cultural meaning in this group and you're making people uncomfortable." (They actually inspired me to include the last item on the list: *How will you signal when* they *need rescuing?*)

After the event, maybe on the drive home, check in with each other by asking, "How was it for you?" Make sure to turn the lens on yourself first by asking, "Was there anything I could have done differently?" The more you do this, the less awkward and rigid it will feel. This is especially important at the very beginning of a relationship when you are just getting to know each other. It is a vulnerable spot to put yourself in, but it will pay off later. This gives each of you the opportunity to address any problems, resolve them, and devise a plan for the next occasion so you don't dread going to parties together in the future.

A few words of caution: If you have a huge amount of feedback for your partner after every single event, then it will be very legitimate for them not to want to go anywhere with you ever again! So be gentle, loving, and firm with this (as with everything else we discuss in this book). You are doing this to benefit your couple's brand, and it should be presented that way, and not as a personal demand or petty annoyance. Also, do your coupledom a favor and come to an agreement about what substances you might ingest (and in what quantities) before you go. All of the above agreements and alignments are much more likely to go out the window if you overindulge, and you will be left with a lot more than just a headache the next day.

Of course, trusting your partner socially means more than just avoiding public humiliation and embarrassment when they are present. It also includes trusting that they will not speak badly about you in front of other people (and will not allow others to do so), they will let the cute new colleague at the office know they are in a committed relationship instead of saying, "I'm married but it is complicated," and they will avoid doing things that might negatively impact your social or professional reputation. Ideally, we all want to feel proud of our partner, proud to be with them, and proud of ourselves for choosing them.

Ethical Trust

Ethical trust is all about shared values. If you have extremely divergent views ideologically, politically, socially, morally, or in terms of anything that is really important and existential, it is harder to trust that your partner is going to grasp where you're coming from and be able to engage with you around that topic. This is often easy to overlook in the beginning of a relationship, when you're more focused on all the ways you are similar to the other, but it grows in importance the longer you are together.

For example, Kathy is a CEO for a cosmetics manufacturer who has spent her whole life working hard to get where she is today. Her wife, Stacey, is a fine artist, a weaver, who sells her custom work online. When they first met, Stacey's minuscule income was not a factor for Kathy, who earns more than enough for their family. But as the years go by, the fact that Stacey has no interest in being disciplined about her work and growing her business has been a major source of conflict. Kathy says, "I can't understand your lack of discipline and ambition." Stacey counters, somewhat defensively, "I am ambitious! I'm just not ambitious about making money. I'm happy making custom pieces for people who really value what I do. I'm ambitious to be a better artist and to have a balanced life doing what I love. Just because I don't want to advertise, or outsource labor, or try to get a contract with a major clothing designer and really make a name for myself doesn't mean I'm not ambitious. That's who *you* are, it's not who *I* am."

Ethical trust includes the belief that your partner will continue to hold the same basic values they had when you met and will continue to behave in accordance with those values. If your values become misaligned, like they were for Stacey and Kathy, you will most likely have to spend considerable time explaining yourself to each other.

Financial Trust

When it comes to finances, our research speaks for itself. When both partners have a healthy attitude toward money, they are much more likely to experience satisfaction in their relationship. This is another factor that might not seem important in the beginning of a relationship but plays an increasingly important role over time, particularly for couples who pool their resources. It is harder to experience a sense of thriving in your life, and satisfaction in your relationship, if you fear your partner will be irresponsible with your resources. This has less to do with how much or little you each earn, and more to do with making and honoring agreements about the role of money in your coupledom. If one of you wants to save aggressively for the future, and the other wants to seize the day and values experiences more than financial security and stability, you are likely to run into conflict. In countries like the United States—with a high cost of living, a weak social safety net, expensive healthcare, and a lack of afford-able housing—financial insecurity is a very real stressor for many people. Trusting your partner financially means holding the belief (based on their past behavior) that they will not act in ways that result in a loss of secu-rity for you. Some of the tangible examples that would impact a couple's financial trust are agreements about who pays for what in the coupledom, creating transparency around individual and shared accounts, having pre- and post-nuptial agreements, keeping your will or trust up to date, and having a secure retirement plan.

This list is by no means exhaustive, and every couple will have their own nuanced version of it. Partners who are also parents will need to trust each other with the safety and well-being of their children; partners who are aging will want to have conversations about what they can and can't rely on the other to provide in the event of physical or cognitive decline; partners who work together or are co-owners of a business will have their own ideas about the domains where reliability and consistency matter most for them. No matter what domains your coupledom encompasses, make time to assess what areas require absolute trust for you and/or your partner, and to develop the skills to redefine and renegotiate those areas as the need arises.

REPAIRING BREACHES OF TRUST

Trust builds slowly but can be undone in an instant. Serious ruptures, if not repaired, can lead to suspicion, hypervigilance, covert (or overt) sur-veillance of the partner, and a whole range of other undesirable conse-quences. Infidelity is, of course, one of the worst breaches of trust that can happen in a coupledom, but it is not the only one that qualifies as major. For example, when substance or alcohol abuse is left untreated, it can destroy the trust between partners and within the entire family system. And large financial betrayals—lying about significant debt, refinancing property without the other's consent, making major purchases unilaterally, or forging the partner's signature to withdraw from retirement savings—can have equally devastating results. Withholding important information that has a direct impact on your partner can be experienced as an enormous betrayal—like not telling them that you lost your job, or keeping a diagnosis private because you don't want them to worry, or engaging in careless, illicit, or illegal behaviors that risk their future well-being. If any of these have happened or are currently happening in your relationship, you might want to seek help from a qualified professional to see what the first step is to change the trajectory of your relationship and lives.

Minor breaches of trust happen in most relationships at one time or another and also require repair, but they are sometimes more difficult to identify. When we spoke above about respect as an interpersonal dynamic, I highlighted three areas where we demonstrate trustworthiness to our partner:

- We respect their boundaries and maintain our own,
- We are reliable and consistent in our behavior, and
- We maintain our integrity by living in accordance with the values we profess.

These also provide a helpful framework when it comes to repairing breaches of trust, because they give couples a way to think about which area of trust was damaged. For example, John comes to me and says, "I have a hard time trusting my partner (in a general sense) because he doesn't take care of himself." Using the framework above, I can then describe the different components of trust and ask which ones he thinks were most damaged and which still seem to be holding (in this case, living according to the values we profess). Then we can use the intact components to build and rebuild the components that were damaged. A majority of couples find this very helpful. This model is also useful when a client says, "I can't point to anything specific, but I'm not at ease with this person." It gives us a way to identify the source of their discomfort and lack of a general sense of trust.

One of the most important components of repairing trust has to do with your willingness to be responsible and accountable when you make a mistake. Becoming defensive, justifying your behavior, making excuses, or deflecting blame onto your partner (or someone else) is not likely to repair damaged trust, and will probably damage it further (this is portrayed so well in the movie *Force Majeure*). These behaviors have the effect of invalidating your partner's experience. They imply that your partner is not allowed to feel betrayed or angry or hurt because *it wasn't my fault* or *the situation as I see it was different*. Being able to recognize and admit your own contribution to any conflict is an important part of establishing and maintaining trust in all of your relationships. But it is only a beginning.

One of the tools I give to couples to make sure they fully resolve and repair their conflicts is something I call A-ARM. It goes like this.

COUPLE'S TOOLKIT: A-ARM FOR REPAIR

Acknowledge what happened by reciting the facts as best you can remember. Keep it concise and precise.

Appreciate the impact it had on the other person and also on yourself.

Reassure the other person that you are committed to your relationship, to your own growth, and to resolving the issue at hand.

Mend: Offer a solution to mend (or amend) the problem going forward. Follow through on any promises made.

When you acknowledge what happened, you show that you care and are aware when things don't go as expected (shared values and vision). The next step is to appreciate the impact it had on your partner and yourself. You validate both your partner's experience and their response to that experience. This is a good time to dig a little deeper with your partner to comprehend exactly which component of trust was damaged from each of your perspectives. Did you violate a boundary? Were you unreliable? Did you behave in a way that isn't aligned with your values? Ask them what that experience was like for them, and how it made them feel. This can be very hard to do, because you open yourself up to hearing about the impact of your behavior on another person. None of us likes to hear that we made someone else feel embarrassed or ashamed, or that we hurt the person we love. But repairing trust truly requires that you show up in this way and set aside your own guilt to attend to the damage you caused. It demonstrates your partner's importance and value to you.

Reassuring your partner that you are committed to the relationship, to your own growth, and to resolving the issue at hand also underscores their central importance in your life. Offering a solution to mend the problem going forward, and then following through by making the changes you agree to make, is the final step in repair and also the most important. This could be as simple as, "Let's put time aside Sunday after lunch to talk about this." I hear a lot of people use the language of accountability when they say things like, "I own this part of it. I accept responsibility. I'm working on it. I'm sorry. I know this upset you." These are all a great beginning, but they run the risk of being received by the other as superficial if they are not followed up by action. (Remember Ahmed and Jaclyn?) Though apology is often a necessary component of repair as a way to demonstrate remorse to your partner, many people go to apology first and then fail to demonstrate real change. After a while "I'm sorry" loses all meaning and does not help to repair the trust that was damaged. A survey of 9,594 Americans in April 2023 reported that "One quarter (24%) of Americans say they apologize for things outside of their control at least daily, including 11% who say they do this several times per day. On the opposite end of the spectrum, 16% of US adults say they never apologize for things outside of their control."[13] How often do you reflect on when, how, and for what you apologize? Is this the same way in different contexts? How about with your partner? Next time you apologize, take the time to get clear about exactly what you are apologizing for. Better still, do the full A-ARM repair!

It's important to point out here that sometimes this process has to be preceded by a period of physical separation from each other in order to regulate your emotions. Trying to resolve a breach of trust and repair the damage is almost impossible when you are still physically very upset. Usually, this takes about twenty minutes of active calming techniques, but it can take longer for some people. When the rational part of the brain is short-circuited by the fight-or-flight response, it is hard to be objective and reasonable. Taking the time to calm down before you say something damaging is crucial. If you want to take time out for this reason, you need to make sure to articulate it and offer an alternative and exact time to come back to check in with each other.

It's also important to connect with each other physically afterward. And, no, I'm not just talking about makeup sex. It could be as simple as a hug or a little kiss or just sitting side by side and letting your bodies experience each other in peace and harmony. I cannot emphasize this last part enough: Part of the repair must be physical, so that your partner's gut-brain is able to recognize you and your body as a place of safety.

For many of my clients, just having this model to work with helps them to articulate the areas of trust that need to be strengthened in their relationship. And while this is very useful for current relationship conflicts, sometimes we have to dig a little bit deeper. Many couples never develop the skills necessary to make repairs to damaged trust in the moment. Over time, these injuries scar over, but they rarely disappear, and it may be necessary to do some excavating of past hurts and transgressions so that a new foundation can be built. In these cases, I like to use an exercise I call Pebbles and Shells. Of course, you don't have to do this with pebbles and shells—any small items will do as long as they represent duality by being two distinct types of objects. You can even choose to list these on papers with different colored pens. Pebbles and shells are simply what I use in my office.

A word of caution: If you find yourself facing a heaping pile of pebbles with very few shells, this is not a good exercise for you. In fact, it's a signal that you would benefit from some professional help for yourself, your partner, or both. This exercise is not an opportunity to overwhelm your partner by venting a lifetime of resentments; it is an opportunity to receive and accept healing from your partner, and to offer that to them in return. I recommend taking a break if the exercise lasts for more than an hour, with a plan to resume in the future. You can take one pebble and shell at a time, for example.

COUPLE'S TOOLKIT: PEBBLES AND SHELLS

Sitting comfortably at a table, put two piles in front of you, one of pebbles and one of shells (or something that resembles them). Reflect back over the course of your relationship and choose one pebble to represent each event or situation from the past that still hangs heavy on your chest. These are things you can't quite let go of until you feel seen and heard, and you are reassured and satisfied that your partner has witnessed the pain you felt and will share the load so that you no longer have to carry it alone. Being as accurate as you can, write down the date, a brief description of what happened, how it made you feel at that moment in time, and how it made you think about your partner, yourself, and the relationship. You can use individual note cards, or write it down in columns, or put it in a document on your computer. Whatever works for you.

Then go to the other pile, the shells, and choose one item to represent those events or situations that still bring a smile to your lips. Maybe your first date, or the birth of a child, or a small moment when you felt especially close and intimate with your partner. Going back to your notes, do the same thing for the shells that you did for the pebbles. Afterward, take turns going through each item on your list with your partner, giving them the chance to receive your experience and doing the same for them. I recommend you each share one shell and one pebble each time you connect over this exercise. Start with pebbles and end with shells. I usually say start with five of each.

Any items that are still present in your relationship, or that still cause you pain, represent areas that may need more focused attention. You may find some remedies and solutions throughout this book, though you may also want to discuss them with your therapist or relationship coach. I have found that doing this exercise helps couples to remedy the open wounds they are carrying from the past. Ideally, the injuries will be seen in a different light once you know that you no longer have to carry the burden alone, in your own private space and with your own private feelings, having monologues with yourself. There is enormous power and healing in having your partner witness your pain and know that in spite of that pain you still have space for the joy you've created and cultivated in your lives, too.

When you adhere to the ideals of submergent love, you enter into a relationship believing that there is someone "out there" who will fulfill all of your needs and whom you can trust immediately and completely. Whomever you are with will need to exhibit extraordinary characteristics of trustworthiness and reliability so that you can feel safe losing yourself in the relationship. And when they fall short, which they will inevitably do, because humans are fallible creatures, you will be heartbroken and maybe even discard them.

In Emergent Love, partners appreciate that trust cannot be demanded; it must be earned. Trust always builds slowly because it is based on tangible experiences. We demonstrate trustworthiness by being reliable and consistent, and by behaving in accordance with our values. This is how we create safety in our coupledom. When we make mistakes, and we absolutely will, we know how to acknowledge the damage and repair our bond, which strengthens trust and ensures that the overall sense of safety in the relationship remains intact.

CHAPTER 7

Shared Vision

In the garden of the heart, plant the seed of devotion, water it with sincerity and watch it bloom. Commit to love like the moon commits to the night sky, radiating its gentle light to all who gaze upon it.

—Rumi[1]

Clients often come to see me when their lives are in transition: They've moved in with a partner or moved out, become engaged, are newly married or newly divorced. They come when a baby is born, an older child leaves the nest, or an aging parent comes to live with them. Or they seek help when a major breach of trust has occurred. And while transitions are a common stressor for couples, they aren't the only thing that brings people into my office. Sometimes the biggest problem isn't too much change, it's a lack of change.

Individuals come in because of persistent anxiety, low-grade depression they can't seem to shake, feeling hopeless about ever finding a partner, or the fear that they are with the wrong person. We usually end up exploring issues from their family of origin that seem to be interfering with how they operate in the world today—old patterns or beliefs that are no longer serving them. For couples, the presenting problem can include change—moving to a new house or a new city, adopting a toddler, or a disruption in their professional lives—but *lack of change* is more frequently the incentive to seek help from a professional. This could be anything from mismatched sexual desire to feeling taken for granted in the relationship to one partner behaving in ways that the other did not anticipate and does not like. Often, at least one partner expresses disappointment that their needs are not being met, or the division of labor is not equitable, or their arrangements are unfair in some other way. They've tried everything, and nothing changes.

The common refrain that underlies these presenting problems is, "This is not what I expected." I often ask my couples who are married to bring their marriage license into a session. Then I ask them to turn it over and read the fine print on the other side (the seemingly blank page) for me. These are the unwritten expectations that they had at the time of the wedding. I am met with a range of reactions from confused looks to chuckles to uncomfortable silence. Our expectations might not have been spoken out loud, or we might not even have been fully conscious of them, but that doesn't mean they didn't exist. And couples inevitably run into problems when what the partners *thought* their lives would be like ends up being different from their current reality.

Creating a shared vision with your partner means coming to a consensus about what you want your life, and your relationship, to look like going forward. It's a way of aligning your separate visions for the future into one unified vision that you can both commit to and feel fulfilled by. You start this process by having a clear idea of what matters to you, and how much: What is an absolute requirement, what is open to persuasion, and what can you live without? Who will you be in a partnership, and how will your partner need to be compatible with you in the critical areas of the life that you are envisioning for yourself? The next steps are communicating and negotiating with your partner so your visions are aligned, committing to your shared vision, and demonstrating that commitment through your daily behaviors by prioritizing the distribution of your resources. Having a shared vision without committing to shared priorities will not go very far.

As I write these words I realize they sound very businesslike and pragmatic, and that's partly because they are. Bringing your separate visions into alignment does take work, but if you know where to put your attention and efforts, the task is going to be smoother than you think. Building a shared vision is the catalyst to intentionally create a relationship that supports you in the fullest expression of your being. Partners who share a vision of the future know what is important to each of them and to their coupledom, they have a clear focus and a sense of perspective about what matters, and they are mutually committed to realizing this vision.

KNOWING WHAT YOU WANT

You cannot create a shared vision if you don't have an individual vision. When you think about your future, what images come to mind? Do you see yourself living in a high-rise apartment in the city, going to museums and cultural events? Are you a snowboarder who dreams of living in the mountains of Utah one day? Or an engineer who wants to continue to travel the world building hydroelectric power plants for rural communities? Do your career ambitions require long hours of work? Do you want to stay at home to raise children? Some readers may still be actively trying to work these things out for themselves; others will have made these decisions years or even decades ago. But regardless of a person's age or stage in life, everyone has a future to consider.

Creating a shared vision requires that each of you have a clear idea of what you want your individual future to look like, and this can take a little work. Sometimes we have to dig deep to understand the interplay between what we've learned from the past (experience), the current circumstances that define our lives (reality), and what we hope to attain in the future (desire). Let me give you an example. I once worked as a consultant for a company that needed expertise in customer behavior. One of my tasks was to help them understand why people purchase one item over another. We asked a focus group what they look for in a blush. Their answers included color, texture, ease of application, ease of removal, and their individual preference for a powder, gel, liquid, or cream. Then we gave each person a wide variety of products to test. The very first thing they did was to open each product and *smell it!* No one had listed scent as a criteria, but almost every single person smelled the product before they touched it. Scent turned out to be a very important factor.

I like to tell this story to clients who are trying to come up with a personal vision for their future, because sometimes what we *think* we want is not the same as what we actually *do* want, or it is not aligned with other things we envision for ourselves in the future.

For instance, when I asked my client Xavier why he became a lawyer, he answered, "I just sort of fell into it." Four years of college, then three years of law school, then interning as a clerk didn't sound like happenstance to me, so I pressed a little harder. He explained, "I wanted to be a lawyer because my mother wanted me to be a lawyer and have a better future. This served me when I was in Argentina, but when I moved to the US that law degree was useless. I would have to work full-time doing something else while I educated myself about a whole new legal system. This was my chance to do something new. I decided to become a financial analyst, which was a much faster route to the lifestyle I wanted in New York and would also help me secure my immigration status. But now here I am, six years later, and even though I have everything I wanted and I'm making good money, I don't feel satisfied. I always wanted to start a family, but how can I do that when I don't even have enough free time to go on a date?"

Xavier is a great example of someone who was clear about the vision he had up until the point his context changed. Although he had made the right decision for himself at the time, he is finding himself at a crossroads again. Our vision for the future changes based on many different factors, and even being in a position to make a plan at all is a privilege that some people don't have. If you're dealing with an illness, or your economic or sociopolitical context is not safe or stable, or there are other factors impacting your future that are beyond your control, just dealing with your current situation is the only tangible priority.

Even those of us who are fortunate enough to be able to plan for the future can't predict with 100 percent accuracy what will happen. Like Xavier, your priorities might change over time. I advise my clients to anchor themselves in their values when they think about the future, rather than their circumstances or priorities at any given moment. Your values rarely change at a fundamental level.

Though everyone's vision for the future will be unique, there are some consistent categories in which people have a lot of strong opinions about the direction they want their lives to go in. As you read through the sections below, try to keep in mind your core values in life and the importance of each. This is crucial when it comes to communicating in good faith with your partner. Also make a note of areas that remain unclear or nonspecific for you. Resources like the research and tools developed by Dr. Pejman Azarmina of Thinkocrats[2] and the book *Designing Your Life* by Drs. Bill Barnett and Dale Evans[3] can help you clarify your goals and ambitions. You can find these references and other resources on the *Love by Design* website at www.lovebydesignbook.com.

Geographic

Where on earth do you want to live? This has to do with both the geographic location (continent, country, province, state, city, or town) as well as the setting within that location (urban, rural, or suburban) and the type of home you envision for yourself (penthouse, farmhouse, cozy and tiny house). Do you long to live somewhere warm and tropical? Do you hate winter, humidity, or rain? Who are the people that you would like to be living among? How do you feel about moving, and how far would you be willing to move? Is the proximity of extended family a concern for you? Some of these might be preferences, and others might be serious likes or dislikes rooted in your values (for example, going back to your hometown or country to care for your elders).

Physical

It might seem odd to think about your vision for the future when it comes to your physical body, but there are several reasons why this is important. If you plan to continue running marathons until your eightieth birthday, and your partner wants you to give up training on the weekends so you can spend more time together, you're going to need to consider a level of compromise. For example, being able to explain that weekend training is important to you, but you're willing to shift it from late afternoon to early morning, will help those communications run more smoothly. If you're a professional athlete, model, actor, or influencer, or you have a job that's physically demanding, taking care of yourself physically might be a greater time commitment than it is for the average person out there. Do you have any ongoing physical or psychological health issues that are likely to impact future decisions you make as a couple? Are you committed to a plant-based diet or do you someday hope to be? Do you plan to hike the Pacific Crest Trail when you retire?

All of these fall under the umbrella of your vision for the future in terms of your physical body. Other considerations might include access to healthcare, the role of sex in your life, the importance of sexual exclusivity, physical expressions of affection, daily practices of hygiene, compliance with a healthy lifestyle, and your general level of activity. In the United States we tend to value being highly physically active for as long as possible, perhaps because physical activity is often associated with productivity. If you are someone who often likes to do things with your partner that involve physical activity ("Let's go for a hike!" or "Put on your dancing shoes!") and your partner's idea of a day together is more like snuggling on the couch watching movies, you might need to spend more time in negotiation than couples who have similar physical activity levels.

Levels of energy and ability, as well as the capacity for physical activities, are different for different people. This is a very common issue that I hear from my clients. I have seen many people who chose a partner who inspired them by being active and fit, but now that they're in a relationship together they feel pressure to keep up. Sometimes circumstances change, like when a baby enters the home and one partner is too physically drained to do much more than survive. People who like to be active, and who thought their partner did, too, can feel let down when their partner isn't really up for those kinds of experiences or their commitment starts to wane. If you are in a similar situation, you might need to be more intentional about your resources to make sure that the time you do spend together is as fulfilling for you both as possible.

Financial

This has to do with the role of finances in your life and in your partnership, and the value and importance of money to each of you. Conversations about money are as hard as conversations about sex, and sometimes harder. (Notably, in cultures where love is not the sole criteria for marriage, conversations about finances are considered respectful and mature rather than dubious.) In the book *Eight Dates: Essential Conversations for a Lifetime of Love*, Dr. John Gottman encourages partners to consider the question, "What is enough money?"[4] The answer is different for everyone. Money often is associated with feelings of power, freedom, responsibility, security, and success. For some people, "enough money" means being able to pay their bills on time, take a vacation every year, and save for retirement. For others, there is no such thing as "enough money." Again, what matters here is knowing your own vision for the future, and accepting that this might change over the course of your life.

The amount of money you earn (or could earn, would like to earn, or would like your partner to earn) also falls into this category. Some other things you might consider include:

- What does "enough money" mean to you?
- What is the role of money in creating and continuing the lifestyle you desire?
- How do you want to arrange your finances (e.g., with joint or separate accounts)?
- What do you want to do with extra income (save it, spend it, go on vacations, or use it to support an individual project or hobby)?
- Would you bring your family's money, if any, into the mix?
- How would you like to divide the labor (paid and unpaid)?
- What kind of debt is acceptable to you, if any (e.g., student loans, a mortgage, credit card debt, personal debt)?

If you are in an intercultural relationship, you might want to take an even closer look into all these. Keep in mind that financial arrangements typically need to be renegotiated periodically and when there is a big life or financial event (moving to a new house, being laid off, immigrating, planning for a major renovation, and so on). And decisions about when or whether to work are not always a matter of finances. Some partners who might not *have* to work for financial reasons will still want to work as a way to pursue their interests, develop their professional skills, be socially active and involved, or have something of their own besides the family life and the coupledom.

Social

The Harvard Study of Adult Development, a research project that has been active since 1938, informs us that the single most important factor in an adult's self-perception of happiness is having meaningful social connections.[5] Your social life includes friends, parents, in-laws, colleagues, people in your religious community, neighbors, extended family, and anyone else who is a central or peripheral part of your life (the number of followers you have online does not necessarily qualify here). Are you satisfied with your personal social life, or would you like it to be larger, smaller, or otherwise different? Do you prefer to socialize separately or together or both? Do you like your partner's friends, and do you think you need to? Do you enjoy planning social activities, or would you prefer if your partner shared that role or took it over completely? Do you expect your extended family to be part of your daily life in some way? What about your partner's extended family? In the last chapter of this book, regarding check-ins, I provide an exercise to help you create the social life (and social capital) you desire.

Values

You may remember from earlier chapters that our moral and personal values are a fundamental aspect of who we are, and we bring them into all of our relationships. Sometimes, when I mention moral values, people give me a funny look like they're expecting me to start preaching about good and evil. I am not. Moral values are usually universally considered as the right thing. In our research having high moral values was associated with a more successful relationship outcome. Qualities such as honesty, doing the right thing in any given situation, being fair, and having integrity are some examples. These tend to be instilled in childhood, and they remain relatively fixed over time.

Your personal values, on the other hand, reflect the importance you grant to various areas of your life. Concepts like creativity, family, financial success, community, or self-sufficiency are some examples of personal values that are morally neutral, though they might be impacted by your moral values as well. Your personal values are fluid and will change with changing circumstances. You might place a higher value on adventure in your teens, stability in your forties, and family relationships in your eighties (or stability in your teens, family in your forties, and adventure in your eighties!). It is not as clear-cut, but you get the point.

Your personal values don't have to align 100 percent with your partner's values, and in my experience with couples they rarely do. But you do need to commit to a vision that respects what each of you holds as most important. For example, if you value being a full-time parent and you want to quit working full-time to raise your children, your partner will need to be on board with that. If they aren't, you may need to engage in extensive negotiations to reach a compromise that feels equitable to both of you. You need to know what's important to you, and how important it is, and why it is so, when you communicate about it.

Religion and Spirituality

Your religious and/or spiritual beliefs shape your beliefs and conduct in general, as well as the rituals and the community that you affiliate with. These have to do either with the faith tradition of your family of origin during the critical developmental years when you were learning about who you are or with the path that you have chosen along the way for yourself. The norms and laws of that context shape what you consider to be appropriate today, and also what you consider inappropriate, right, wrong, fair, unfair, embarrassing, humiliating, or beyond the pale.

The beliefs you learned as a child trickle down to influence how you identify and define your religious or spiritual beliefs today. They might not be exactly as you have been taught, but your level of observance (daily conduct) and your expectations around rituals and practices could be still impacted by those teachings. This is especially relevant if you and your partner come from different faith traditions, and you are both carrying on with all or some of what was associated with your faith. Even differences within traditions can cause conflict if expectations aren't clarified. For example, if you were raised in an observant Jewish or Muslim household and plan to keep kosher or halal but your partner is more "culturally" Jewish or Muslim, you'll likely have some clear conversations about your needs and expectations. You need to have these conversations early on and ideally before you move in together so that the particulars don't have to be negotiated afterward. What are the specific holidays you celebrate? Who would you like to include? How much involvement do you want your partner to have? How will you raise your children? If two holidays collide, which one would take priority? What are the expectations of the other party, from wearing long sleeves at the church to converting to the other person's religion or getting circumcised?

You don't necessarily have to share a faith tradition to be in alignment. My own parents were from two different spiritual paths. My father was not observant, though he was a highly virtuous and principled man. My mother was observant and engaged in daily practices and rituals around certain holy days that reflected her beliefs. They respected each other enough to work out compromises so that neither had to behave in ways that felt disingenuous. My father was not required at certain ceremonies while we as children could choose to go. He always participated in events that involved social engagements, though, such as Eid, because they were important to my mother and their shared community. They also didn't ask my siblings and me to commit to a certain way of being or doing, though they did find ways to demonstrate to us their shared vision of faith and the values they each took from it. It's worth noting that one's affinity to a spiritual path could change over time. Some people grow closer to it for a sense of guidance and comfort with age or during troubling times. Others build on it, or move away from it and evolve toward a whole new path altogether.

Lifestyle

This category includes elements from many of the areas mentioned above, like where you live, what you do for fun, your sense of style, how you travel, how you socialize, and how you spend money. Maybe you have a hobby you're especially passionate about that requires large commitments of time, energy, attention, or finances—skiing, boating, surfing, and travel all come to mind. Or maybe you're a city kid, born and raised, who never learned to drive because you never intend to move somewhere that doesn't have reliable public transit.

I remember one client, Hunter, who told me, "I knew Rory liked to ski, but I thought it was going to be a couple of trips a year and not every single weekend. For the past six years we've put the kids in ski school every winter, which is Saturday and Sunday from nine to four for ten weeks. Ten weeks! For the first few years I went with them, but I'm not much of a skier so now I stay home. I don't love it, but I'm here with the kids all week while she's at work, so having a little time to myself is nice. We make it work, and it definitely has its pluses for me, but it's not what I expected my weekends to look like."

If you love to sail, or your dream job requires long hours (or overnight hours, frequent travel, frequent relocations, or sporadic visits to war zones), or you plan to go to your mother's house for dinner every Wednesday night and you expect your partner to accompany you, this might all have to be negotiated if your partner has different ideas. You and your partner will need to negotiate if your personal vision of the future includes elements that will have a significant impact on their lifestyle. Also consider each partner's ability to shift their lifestyle if and when the situation demands it. It is all good if one of you travels a lot and the other is also busy doing their own thing, or your relationship is sometimes long-distance because you work seasonal shifts. But will that work when you have children? Will it be okay for one of you to miss some significant milestones and just see the pictures?

Having a shared vision doesn't mean that you have a lot of shared interests; for example, you don't have to like all the same foods, have all the same hobbies, or want all the same things out of life. This is not submergent love, where any divergence is seen as a threat! But you do need to be reasonably aligned about the things that are most important to you, and the everyday priorities that you establish around how you will spend your time, energy, attention, and money. Your partner's joy cannot be your pet peeve—their music your torture, their unique style of clothing your embarrassment, their devouring meat your nightmare, or their ideal vacation your disaster scenario. I am exaggerating here, but you get the point. In these cases, you need to clarify how much these matter to you (e.g., on a scale of one to ten). If they still don't think it's worth a try, then the two of you have a different level of negotiation to get into.

NEGOTIATION, COMPROMISE, AND SACRIFICE

We usually do a good job clarifying our expectations in short-term, low-stakes, transactional relationships, especially if money is involved. When you pay someone to paint your house, both parties know what is expected. But when it comes to social relationships, and especially romantic ones, our expectations are often much less clear.

When I described our research in part one, you may recall that one of the important areas of overlap in terms of what you bring into a relationship has to do with having a life outlook that is compatible with that of your partner. These are where the deal-breakers come into play: Janey wants to see other people, John does not; Tracy doesn't want children, Wendy does; Shannon is a cattle rancher who raises organic beef, Patricia is a vegan who believes all life is sacred and is repulsed by the idea of slaughtering animals for money; Jamil wants to run for office and is not sure where he will end up living, and Carine is a medical student who is bound to her location for many more years to come. When these romances end, few people are surprised.

But in long-term commitments, maintaining a shared vision involves more than a one-time agreement about what you want out of life. It might start there, but it will have to evolve. Creating a shared vision is an interpersonal dynamic that must be communicated, negotiated, and renegotiated as circumstances change and each of you evolves. Remember, change is a given. Knowing what's important to you, being able to communicate in a spirit of collaboration and respect, and being willing to compromise when compromise is called for are all essential elements of creating a shared vision that both of you can commit to.

The tools we have to do that are negotiation, compromise, and building consensus. All of these require a level of intentionality. When you fail to communicate proactively and consistently about what you want, or don't have a clear vision for your own future, it's easy to take on a passive role and adapt yourself to someone else's vision. Sometimes this works out, but in many cases individuals find themselves unfulfilled, trapped in a life they did not actively choose. They might then feel victimized and blame the other person for not giving them what they needed.

This is why it's so important to have clarity about your own vision for the future before you begin to create a shared vision with your partner. You might even want to process your thoughts with someone else before bringing the conversation to your partner. This will help you avoid saying things, agreeing to things, or even promising things that you cannot see through to the end. Your family members, a close friend, your coach or therapist, or anyone who knows your capacities and ambitions in life would be a good choice. You need to have a benchmark for yourself to know how to navigate a conversation that could potentially change the trajectory of your life or any important aspects of it.

Once both of you have some clarity about what you value, what you want, what is non-negotiable and what is open to persuasion, you can come together in a spirit of collaboration and get to work. A healthy negotiation almost always includes compromise on the part of each partner. According to our research, compromise has a level of intentionality for all parties involved. A person is usually willing to compromise on something that is important to them if it means a significant gain in another area, or for the relationship as a whole. Compromises are not exactly equal, or even similar, but in thriving relationships they usually are perceived as equitable overall in terms of their worth.

Let me give you an example. When Margarita moved from her hometown of Rio de Janeiro because her husband got a great job in Los Angeles, she experienced that as a compromise on her part. She and Casper negotiated and agreed that she would take two years off from her own work in order to explore the city, make social connections, and try to envision a way that she could build a future for herself in Los Angeles. "Casper is happier this way, which means he's in a good mood most of the time. I'll miss my family in Rio, of course, but I think he wants to move to LA more than I want to be around my family. I might change my mind later, but I'm committed to two years." For his part, Casper compromised by agreeing to be the sole earner while they lived overseas, to budget for Margarita to visit her family several times a year, and to travel with her for Carnaval. "When I told Margarita what I would be earning, and explained that we could afford for her to take a sabbatical, she started to see this as something that might work for her."

To give you another example, let's go back to Hunter and Rory for a moment. When Hunter realized that Rory intended to spend every weekend in the winter skiing with the kids, all he could see was the sacrifice it would mean for him. In the first year of ski school, he and Rory were waking up at six in the morning to pack lunches, get the kids and all their gear into the car, and drive eighty miles to the mountain. Rory and the kids loved it, but Hunter was miserable. He felt like he had no viable options. He tried staying home, but since they had only one car, it wasn't especially enjoyable for him. Entering into the second year, they started to negotiate in earnest.

Rory explained, "I grew up skiing, it's my passion, and it's really important to me to pass that on to the kids. And they love it! I know it's a lot of work, but it's worth it to me to make it happen. I hardly get to see them during the week, and bonding with them over skiing feels really important. I don't want to give this up, but I also don't like feeling guilty all the time, and I know this isn't working for you. Is there any way we could do this that would feel okay for you?"

After many conversations and some creative problem-solving, they decided that Rory would take over 90 percent of the labor involved with ski school (which was considerable). Hunter would pack the lunches and have dinner ready when they got home. He might join them a few times a season for the shared family experience, but otherwise he was free to plan other things for himself. They prioritized their finances and bought a second car. Hunter came to really enjoy having some totally unstructured time to himself, which was rare and valuable to him as a stay-at-home dad. And Rory was able to share something she loved with her children, which was incredibly meaningful for her.

You see how healthy compromises work? He gives a little and gets a little, she gives a little and gets a little, and they come to a consensus about their vision for the future that feels equitable, and both can commit to it with confidence.

COMPROMISE VERSUS SACRIFICE

I want to make a very important distinction here between compromise and sacrifice. When couples talk about sacrifice, there's usually an undertone of resentment; one partner gives up something important, and they don't receive something equitable (or anything at all) in return. You're probably wondering, "Why would anyone do that?" I'm afraid there's no simple answer. Sometimes people make sacrifices as a kind of covert contract, believing that they will be entitled to ask their partner to do the same at some undisclosed time in the future. "I didn't want to buy this house, but I did it because you wanted it so much. Well, now I want to buy a car and you owe me." Other times people make sacrifices to please the partner, to keep the peace, or because they don't believe they deserve to be treated fairly. If something really matters to you, it deserves a proper conversation. If you cannot ask for what you need or air your concerns in your relationship because you lack the skills, a therapist or a coach can help you. But if there is a reason within your relationship that you cannot do this, like being intimidated or bullied by your partner, or fearing violence, then we are talking about a very different issue. I highly recommend you seek help from a reliable, qualified, and informed professional if this is your context.

Creating a shared vision is an ongoing process. While certain aspects of your vision will remain stable for long periods—like finishing your PhD, raising a family, having an active social life, or buying your own home—others will require frequent readjustments. This is especially true when it comes to division of labor in the household, financial arrangements, professional development, and caregiving obligations. You need to have both a long-term vision about where you're going and a short-term vision about how you will get there. And your arrangements must be made explicit so that you can commit to them with integrity.

IRRECONCILABLE DIFFERENCES

This book is for individuals and couples who want to strengthen their bond. It is my sincerest hope that none of you ever has the experience of being unable to negotiate a fair and equitable vision for the future of your relationship, but sometimes this does happen. When it does, it is very painful for everyone involved.

Alec and Sebastian are a good example. They first contacted me right after Alec learned that Sebastian had slept with one of his coworkers. Again. This was the last straw for Alec. "I feel stupid, humiliated, and so hurt that I cannot even put words to it." Alec had set a boundary, and Sebastian had crossed it multiple times. He always apologized, but his apologies were meaningless at this point. "I don't want to hear you say you're sorry one more time. I want you to stop doing it. What kind of fool do you think I am?" Alec asked. When you do something that you know hurts your partner, and you do it repeatedly, you dismantle the ingredients of Emergent Love one by one. Trust is destroyed, along with respect, and the rest soon follow.

"I just don't think I can do monogamy," Sebastian admitted. "I know it's important to you, but it isn't important to me. To me, what's important is having autonomy over my own sex life. I feel really trapped. I love you, and I don't want to lose you, but I also don't want to keep having this conversation where I feel pressured to agree to something I don't want." While Alec could respect Sebastian's desire for non-monogamy, he knew he couldn't live with it. "You knew, when we met, that monogamy was non-negotiable for me. I know other couples are open, I know it's socially acceptable by some people, but I won't live with it. I love you so much, but I don't want to go through this with you again, not ever. And I don't want our son to grow up thinking that it's okay to make commitments that you can't honor."

When each partner's individual vision contains non-negotiable elements that are in direct conflict, compromise is not possible. In the words of John Gottman, these will cause *perpetual conflicts*, which happen when you have fundamental differences in your life-style needs.[6] At some point in your relationship, you will invariably find yourself in heavy negotiations, contending with heartaches and tension. The only option then is sacrifice. If being in a particular relationship means you have to abandon your life's dreams or put them on hold for a while, grow a thick skin, master the art of negotiation or conflict resolution, or accept behaviors that are unacceptable to you, take some time to really think about how this is going to make you feel toward your partner (and yourself and your life) over time. It doesn't necessarily mean the relationship has to end, but Emergent Love will no longer be a possibility. Sacrifice is not a viable option when you know that you are going against your moral values. Even when you are sacrificing around your personal values for the sake of your relationship or to accommodate your partner's desires or circumstances, if you feel the outcome was not what you expected or promised, or you feel your sacrifice has been overlooked, unappreciated, or that the sense of fairness in the relationship is fragmented, you may develop a deep sense of resentment, which could make contributing to Emergent Love impossible.

WHAT IS COMMITMENT?

We all know that satisfying relationships require commitment, but what does commitment require? When we commit ourselves to a particular course of action, what exactly are we promising? Commitment means different things to different people, and sometimes it even means different things to the same person over time, in different roles and different contexts, or with different people. For many couples, particularly heteronormative couples, commitment begins with a promise to be sexually exclusive and ends with living together and/or the institution of marriage as the visible marker of their commitment (and the institution of divorce or moving out as the visible marker of the end of that commitment). Commitment is seen as something that you do once, at the beginning of a relationship, and then you check it off your list. But real, lifelong commitment is an ongoing process.

In its simplest form, a commitment is a conscious decision to abide by a certain course of action. It is an agreement, a decision, and a promise about one's future behavior, particularly with regard to the object of the commitment—whether it is yourself, another person, an institution, a project, a moral value, an ideology, or any number of other things. Regardless of the object, the subject is always the self; in all cases a commitment is a decision you make about how *you* will show up. It is a commitment, first and foremost, to yourself.

In our research, commitment is closely correlated with moral values, integrity, and reliability. Individuals with strong moral values around concepts like respect, forgiveness, fairness, honesty, or collaboration also experience a strong sense of commitment both toward and from their partners. And this is true even when those values are more individualistic in nature, like ambition, independence, or competence. This makes sense when you consider that both integrity and commitment reflect the ability to align your behavior and your values, even when it is hard, or you don't feel like it, or there is something else you would much rather be doing in that moment. Commitment is linked to reliability—doing as you say you will do—but commitment attaches itself to the future in a much more significant way because it demands consistency and determination over time. In working with couples, the analogies of rowing in a boat and ballroom dancing are used a lot because they both require the people involved to move in the same direction and ally with the same beats. Imagine that you and your partner are in the same boat; if one of you decides to give up and stop rowing, or rows in the other direction, what will happen to the other person and where will your boat end up? A commitment is a decision to stand on solid ground as individuals and to go somewhere *together*.

Every time you communicate or renegotiate a shared vision for your coupledom, you also need to commit to working toward that vision individually and together. In this way commitment is closely related to consent. We cannot, or at least should not, consent to something that is vague or unclear. Make your expectations explicit—first for yourself, then for your partner. We need to know what we are committing to, what expectations are attached, and what positive and negative sanctions await us if we fail to abide by the agreed-upon rules of engagement. I am not talking about laying down a long list of rules and taking all the joy and relational closeness out of your coupledom. I'm talking about discussing arrangements with your partner and being specific about what those arrangements entail so that you and your partner can both know what you are committing to and can work together to build together. Leaving things loose, hoping that the other person will go along with your vision, or leaving it to chance usually doesn't end well.

Some couples tell me that they were not clear about everything they wanted at the beginning for their relationship so they didn't want to put any rigid parameters around it (for example, whether they wanted to have kids). So they compromised by agreeing that if one of them ever wanted a kid, the other would be on board.

When you commit to a new shared vision, it's a good idea to state your intentions out loud to the other, so they know what they can expect and rely on going forward. Rory went about it by asking Hunter, "What is it that bothers you most about ski school?" When he told her that all the work leading up to the ski trips and being trapped at home without a car were the biggest challenges, she offered what she could realistically. She stated her intention by saying, "I commit to doing ninety percent of the labor around skiing, and to help with the budgeting for a second car." Hunter then stated his intention and replied, "I commit to not giving you grief about ski school, to be available to take the kids if there are extenuating circumstances, and to make sure that there's something good to eat when you get home. I'll also do bedtime on the nights that you ski, because I'll want to spend time with the kids and you're going to be really tired." If either of them fails to honor the commitment, the other can remind them (gently, gently) that this is the vision they agreed to. If they want to change the parameters, that will require another conversation.

AGENCY AND CONSENT

The premise of *Love by Design* is that we have *agency* over creating the love that we desire and deserve. Both the feeling that our own actions have an impact (i.e. "I did this which led to that") and the process of thinking about and evaluating whether you or someone else is responsible for an action or outcome give us a strong sense of authorship in our partnerships.

One crucial way our agency shows up in relationships is consent, which is the voluntary and mutual agreement among all parties involved in any given situation. Like the Emergent Love itself, consent is a dynamic entity and not a once-given-and-live-forever kind of thing. It is an ongoing process and can be withdrawn or given at any time. Consent is also a highly nuanced concept (for example, one might want to be in a dominant role financially as a breadwinner but still want be conquered in the bedroom).[7]

We explore what we want to consent to through self-reflection, implement it through clear communication, and act on it when we commit to mutual respect for each other's boundaries. It is less important what the rules of engagement are in your coupledom, than that you actively and thoughtfully consent to them. As you consider the vision you have for your coupledom, take some time to think about these critical areas of consent: sexual and physical engagements, financial decisions, privacy and personal boundaries, child-rearing choices, household responsibilities, and social commitments.

WHAT COMMITMENT MEANS TO YOU

Because Emergent Love is rooted in behaviors, creating a shared vision is less about how you *feel* and more about who you *are* and what you *do*. Dr. Robert Sternberg, an American psychologist, developed a triangular theory of love with passion, intimacy, and commitment as the three vertices.

His theory has been a catalyst for many other scholarly works in the past few decades. Sternberg explains that while commitment may lack the emotional impact of passion and intimacy, it is the element that we have the most control over.[8] Feelings and emotions are, by their very nature, transitory. You can no more promise to feel love forever than you can promise to feel happiness, frustration, contentment, anger, excitement, or disappointment forever. But you can promise how you will show up in your relational space, and how you will behave (repeating myself here) *whether you feel like it or not*. All healthy relationships have their highs and lows; commitment is what keeps us together when times are hardest.

Each of us has our own ideas about what commitment means to us. How you learned about commitment, and how commitment was honored (or not), will influence whether you see commitment as consistent or conditional. These reflections will help you realize what the words "promise" and "commitment" mean deep down for you, and whether you see commitment as a privilege or a burden.

BUILDING BLOCK:
YOUR COMMITMENT BLUEPRINT

- When you were growing up, how was commitment expressed by the adults around you? How did you know that as a child?
- Were your parents or caregivers married or otherwise committed to a life with each other? Did they have a shared vision?
- When a promise was made to you as a child, was it kept? What about when a promise was made to someone else?
- When a promise was broken, how was that explained or justified? Was there a scarcity of resources (not enough money, time, or energy)? Was an adult's reliability dependent on their mood (they were angry, overwhelmed, depressed, or sad)? Or was the broken promise deflected onto another person ("Mom didn't get home in time" or "You were misbehaving")?
- Did you often discuss how to get out of things when you could not deliver (good excuses for being late or not delivering homework on time)?

- Was honoring your commitments a critical part of your family values? Did adults insist that you "see things through" to the end? If you played sports, or took lessons outside of school, were you expected to play for the whole season or show up for the lessons even if you didn't want to?
- Were you allowed *not* to promise something that you knew you could not deliver, or that was not aligned with what you thought was right?
- Did the people closest to you see commitment as a privilege that demonstrated adulthood and responsibility, or were commitments more likely to be seen as obligations or burdens?

We all carry learned behaviors around the meaning and importance of commitment at micro and macro levels. Many come from our family of origin, but the idea of commitment itself is also a social construct. In more collectivistic cultures, having ties to the community through marriage, kinship, or other forms of commitment is often considered an asset in terms of the benefits it can provide, like free babysitting, or finding a job through word of mouth, or knowing someone who knows someone who can fix your car. Commitments provide social stability and a sense of belonging. In more individualistic cultures, particularly market-driven capitalist economies, commitment is often seen in a negative light, as something that includes cost and obligation. The idea here is that every commitment represents a "sacrifice," since when you commit to something, whether it's a job or an apartment or a vision for the future, you close off other potential choices. Because we value freedom and seek self-fulfillment, our primary commitment is often to ourselves. This does not inherently make us commitment-phobic, but when *commitment to self* precludes *commitment to others* we are at a disadvantage when it comes to partnerships of any sort.

Regardless of which social system we are coming from or living in, being a part of the online world has given commitment a new meaning (as is true for many other things in our lives). Many people today make their commitments public by announcing the promises to the world online. "I joined this new company and I am going to make my mark in the world!" "We are in love and here is an image of happiness and commitment." "We are going through a horrible divorce, but I am being strong because I know I'm better off without her." "He cheated and I am heartbroken." What I see offline, in my office, are individuals attempting to retract their widely publicized commitments to give their marriage a second chance, leave their job, or not move forward with their fiancé. In their inner circles it is relatively easy to explain a change of heart; online it is more difficult. Sometimes people put off making the decision they need to make because they fear being judged by hundreds of people who have been supporting them along the way.

LOOKING OUT FOR NUMBER ONE

When COVID-19 hit the United States and Europe in early 2020, many people who were living alone found themselves completely isolated. Some of my clients shared with me that keeping their options open by going with the flow, keeping things casual, and looking out for number one really failed as a lifestyle choice and relational orientation during a global pandemic. In order to have a support network, you need to be part of a support network for others. Commitment tends to be reciprocal in this way, and people who didn't have these structures in place at the start of the pandemic really suffered. Many people who lived through COVID-19 came out on the other side with a desire to reevaluate their lives in a way that prioritizes human connection, which includes making and keeping promises and committing to building a deep bond with another person.

THE JOY OF MISSING OUT

It probably doesn't surprise you to learn that our research also indicated that individuals who avoid relational commitments tend to be indecisive in other areas of their lives as well. They lack trust in their ability to choose what is "right" and fear regret, so they don't commit to much in life. Instead they wait until the last minute to make a plan, fearing or hoping that something better might come along. Fear of missing out

(FOMO) is the plague of our times. My observation is that in larger cities where there's a lot going on this is more common. See if this aligns with your observations about where you live. Even when people are invited to events, they wait until the last minute to RSVP just in case something else that is better comes along.

Avery and Eric, a couple in their early thirties who had been living together since college, admitted during our first session that they both suffered from FOMO. They came to see me because they wanted to know if they were truly compatible. They took the Relationship Panoramic Inventory and wanted me to help them review it. They had just put down a deposit on a house and were thinking of starting their family. They were very sweet together, exchanging compliments and joking with each other in an easy way. The short version: Their individual and interpersonal dynamics were strong. We could tweak a little bit around their conflict management styles and financial arrangements, but overall, their partnership was solid. However, I also realized that both of them leaned toward an avoidant attachment style when it came to their intimate bond.

As is sometimes the case with couples, the presenting problem (*Are we compatible?*) masked a different problem (*Why can't either of us make a commitment?*). In this case, the coupledom was not under question, but being able to achieve a tangible milestone together was. "We've been together eleven years," Avery groaned. "How can I not be sure? Some of our friends have had marriages that didn't last half as long." I brought up their attachment styles and explained how this might be showing up in their lives. Eric chimed in, "That sounds about right. We're that couple who confirms at the last minute and cancels at the last minute!" I gave them a joint diagnosis: "You have a case of FOMO! The cure is to give JOMO a try for a change." I explained how to practice the joy of missing out, pronounced them engaged, and asked them to live accordingly for two weeks. Their assignment was to make firm plans in advance, even when they knew it might mean missing out on something else. They were fine with the diagnosis and the engagement announcement, but their laughter turned into a bit of an uncomfortable chuckle at this point. Their task was to make the decision work in a way that left them both satisfied.

I had only one rule: Whatever decision you make, give it a fair shot. Don't be like the person who is walking in one direction while they look back in the other. Two weeks later they reported back to me.

"At first it was really hard," Avery admitted. "I booked a window table at a restaurant but when we arrived, and I saw the patio, I felt so bad I couldn't enjoy my meal. I know it sounds silly, but I really could not." Eric jumped in. "We got tickets to this play and then got invited to a party on the same night. We went to the play, but when people started to post pictures of the party I was constantly checking my phone to see what I was missing. We stayed until the end of the play, but it was hard. Thankfully, money was involved or I think it would have been even harder." We were all smiling, and even laughing, but I knew we were hitting a nerve here. Avery was the first to report, "It was really hard, but sometimes it was kind of relaxing, too, though. We went to see a friend who just had a baby, and we had to be scheduled around the baby's nap. I think not having an option helped." Eric added, "We made plans with friends for the weekend three days in advance, which went well, too. It felt good to know exactly what we'd be doing Saturday night. I was actually looking forward to it, which isn't something you get to feel when all your plans are last-minute. I think I experienced JOMO firsthand!"

They were surprised to learn that making a plan and committing to it actually made them feel less stressed rather than more stressed. They just needed a bit of practice with it.

Fear of commitment is based on the idea that commitment comes at a cost: It entails obligation, closes off other options, and signifies the end of freedom. And, to some extent, this is true. But commitments also come with benefits that are unavailable otherwise. Francis, a client who married during the course of our work together, explained it this way: "Yeah, maybe it's less freedom, but freedom for what? Do I really need to be free to go on six thousand more mediocre dates with men who only want to talk about carbs? I actually feel *more* free with Jacob, not less. It's like I'm finally free to stop looking, to stop focusing on finding The One and focus instead on being with This One and doing all I can to make it succeed. I get to move on with the rest of my life. I'm free to be myself, free to act really goofy and know that he's not going to roll his eyes or tell me to act my age. Jacob is the best! He really knows all of me, and we're both exactly where we want to be. What could be more liberating than that?"

When I talk to couples about creating a shared vision and committing to it together, this is the outcome I have in mind. When you know where you are, and you know where you're trying to go individually and together, it gives you focus and perspective. You get to stop worrying about the "what ifs" and the "maybe I should haves" and focus on what is.

Today, many people question and challenge our normative ideas about marriage by committing to the relationship itself rather than the institution of marriage, or by locating their commitment outside the arena of sexual exclusivity in non-monogamous or polyamorous relationships. It is noteworthy that people in these groups often have more complex, nuanced, and specific ideas about negotiating a shared vision than those who opt for the more conventional model of marriage. Everyone assumes they know what commitment looks like in monogamous marriage, right? Based on this assumption, many people conclude that commitment *in general* only has to be discussed if you *aren't* getting married, or you *aren't* being sexually exclusive.

In Emergent Love it is completely different, and partners are careful to avoid making any assumptions or presumptions about the future. This model of negotiated commitment has definite advantages over the kind of Commitment-with-a-capital-C that partners make once, at the beginning of their relationship, then never discuss again. Creating a shared vision starts by looking inward and developing clarity about what you want your own future to look like, what you value, what is non-negotiable, and what is fluid and open to persuasion. Then you are ready to bring the conversation to your partner, always in a spirit of collaboration. You'll probably need to negotiate, and one or both of you may need to accept a compromise in order to build consensus. Sometimes this will be simple and straightforward; other times it won't. When the stakes are especially high, and they were for Margarita and Casper in their move from Rio to LA, it will probably take more than one session.

Couples who regularly renegotiate their shared vision have far fewer misunderstandings, because expectations are clear and nothing is assumed. It's not so much about being on the same page, but more about using the same map to navigate. It is a map that you create together so you know where you are, where you want to go, and how you want to get there. Your map doesn't have to look like anyone else's map; it will be unique to your coupledom. Remember, relationships are subjective spaces. You and your partner are the only ones who get to decide what, and how, you will prioritize what matters to you individually and as a couple.

CHAPTER 8

Compassion

I have found that the greatest degree of inner tranquility comes from the development of love and compassion. The more we care for the happiness of others, the greater is our own sense of well-being.

—Tenzin Gyatso, His Holiness the Dalai Lama[1]

Each of us will experience times of extreme distress over the course of our lives. We have major losses and minor setbacks; illness, disability, and death; financial downturns and financial disasters; disappointments both large and small. Suffering, like change, is inevitable. Human beings are moved by suffering, and we feel compelled to help, and this is especially true when it comes to those we love. As social creatures we're wired to respond to others, and we need others to respond to us. This is why, in our most significant relationships, we place a premium on showing up for each other. Yet so often our attempts fall short of the mark. Most of us have had the experience of seeking comfort from our partner and receiving something very different than what we had in mind. And the reverse is also true: We have offered what we thought was comfort, but instead it was received as pity or condescension. Sometimes our attempt to comfort by identifying is experienced by the other as a kind of one-upmanship; their suffering is minimized or eclipsed entirely by our own. Or we feel their pain as intensely as they feel it themselves, we fall apart, and they end up having to take care of us. In all these cases our partner ends up feeling worse than they did before we intervened.

Our research found that couples who practice mutual compassion exhibit the highest levels of overall relationship satisfaction and general well-being, so clearly this is important. But what exactly is compassion? Though most of us begin to feel and express concern for others while we are still very young children, the words we use to talk about it are largely seen as interchangeable. We care about people, we care for them, and we take care of them. We are concerned for their well-being, we empathize with them, feel sympathy for them, and we worry about them. Even the prepositions can't seem to agree on who is doing what to whom.

In Emergent Love, compassion is both an attitude and a skill. We practice compassion by developing the capacity to respond to our partner with tenderness, support, and caring while still knowing the boundaries between our own emotional reality and that of our partner. We take care of ourselves so we can take care of them. When we're able to show up for our partner consistently, and they do the same for us, we know and feel in our bodies that we are in the right place and with the right person. We are home. Mutual compassion allows us to co-create a sense of safety and belonging in our relational space. Even when we lose our cool, fall apart, overreact or underreact, say the wrong thing, do the wrong thing (or otherwise make one of the many mistakes we are bound to make over the course of our coupledom), our relational space remains safe when we know we'll be treated with compassion.

In this chapter we'll begin by clarifying what we mean when we talk about compassion, and why it's more important in relationships than empathy. Then we'll work on your self-literacy around compassion by examining some of your earliest lessons about what it means to treat others, and yourself, with care. Finally we'll talk about strategies and tools for manifesting compassion in our daily behaviors.

FROM EMPATHY TO COMPASSION

"If you're a bird, I'm a bird." Noah's famous words to Allie in *The Notebook* are the epitome of submergent love: Whatever you are, whatever you feel, I also am. And for many of us this is the gold standard of how we relate to each other in romantic relationships. The promise of True Love is often an expectation of the same unity. Our partner will know us better than we know ourselves, they will anticipate our needs, they can regulate us, they will intuit how to provide exactly the kind of comfort and reassurance we need at exactly the right time, in exactly the right way, *and we won't even have to ask.*

Empathy—be it emotional, cognitive, or physical—involves entering into another person's experience and feeling their feelings as if they were our own. It fulfills a primal longing to return to our very first experience of closeness—the blissful state of union between parent and child. Think about it: The infant *in utero* is literally sharing the body of the mother and is aware of her movements, the cadence of her speech, and even her emotional states. The moment of birth brings about a physical separation between mother and infant, but the infant does not recognize that separation until weeks after birth. This heightened empathy is also what enables an infant to be soothed. When a caregiver picks up a screaming infant, holds him close, and whispers reassurances, she helps the infant regulate his distress with her own body. Over time, co-regulation teaches the infant self-regulation. When she is calm, he becomes calm, so much so that researchers Judith Schore and Allan Schore propose that attachment theory is in fact a *regulation theory.*[2]

Our capacity for empathy evolved to ensure our survival, and it is a foundation of human social behavior.[3] Robert Katz, who wrote about empathy in the early 1960s, describes it as "a somewhat odd and elusive skill, a divinatory art, a sixth sense, an instinctive and primitive form of penetrating to the core of another person."[4] When we are in an empathic state we lose awareness of our existential separateness and become absorbed in the other's experience. If they are joyful, we will be joyful; if they are sad, we will be sad.

In some circumstances, this can be a positive thing. For one, it plays a role in the physical connection you share, coming into full bloom when a couple has an empathic sexual interaction, which we'll talk about more in chapter 11 when we delve into physical connection. Empathy can also be helpful when you are grieving a loss, or you've suffered a deep frustration or disappointment that affected you both. Nobody needs to be the stronger one; you both fall apart, grieve, and come back to life together. These moments of commiseration are priceless and contribute to the overall level of trust and closeness that you have with each other. If you are a parent of a strong-minded toddler or a tough-to-handle teenager, for example, you might have these moments pretty frequently.

But what happens when the emotional contagion is rage, or frustration, or despair? What if your partner is in a state of shock or extreme emotional distress? Even if they're only experiencing typical daily stress and anxiety, taking on their feelings is not likely to help. When we empathize, sometimes we feel even more strongly than the person we're empathizing with because we are owning their emotion without having experienced the context or buildup for it. Neuroscientists refer to this as "neuro-resonance," by borrowing a concept from physics. Resonance occurs when an object vibrates in response to sound waves of a certain frequency. Most musical instruments use resonance to amplify the sound waves and make the sounds louder. Neuro-resonance is a similar process. We perceive the other's emotional state, we amplify it, and the result is that everyone is flooded and out of sync with their own harmonious state (dysregulated). As much as we ache to have someone inhabit our internal emotional reality, taking on someone else's emotions as your own can be exhausting and destabilizing for everyone involved.

For this reason, empathy can make it harder to show up in a way that is helpful or meaningful to your partner, because it doesn't allow for any distance or space between the two of you (you literally feel what the other person feels). There's nothing to build on and nowhere to go when $1 + 1 = 1$. So although empathy has its place in a coupledom, it will not help you to create the shared but separate relational space that is the hallmark of Emergent Love.

Maintaining a separate sense of self, and a separate emotional reality, is the key distinguishing feature between compassion and empathy. If empathy is feeling *with* someone, compassion is feeling *for* someone.

For our purposes, I define compassion as an expression of deep care and concern for the well-being of others. It requires maintaining enough separateness to be able to show up for the other person without making it about ourself. We express our compassion by remaining present and focused on the other in a way that is meaningful to them. Earlier in the book I talked about the difference between the Golden Rule (treat others the way you'd like to be treated) and the Platinum Rule (treat others the way they'd like to be treated).[5] This is especially relevant when it comes to practicing compassion in intimate relationships. You keep the focus on what your partner needs at that moment in time while keeping yourself grounded, and not on what you think they need, or what you might need in a similar situation (which is a very intuitive thing to do). It is not about you!

Paul Bloom, a psychologist who studies the role of empathy and compassion in moral development (among many other things), explains the distinction this way: "Compassion means I give your concern weight, I value it. I care about you, but I don't necessarily pick up your feelings."[6]

Let me give you an example. Professionals whose work brings them in close contact with the suffering of others (for example, nurses, police officers, and paramedics) often suffer from something known as "compassion fatigue."[7] This term describes the physical, emotional, and psychological impact of helping others, often through experiences of stress or trauma. In recent years, with modern advances in neuroimaging techniques, compassion fatigue is being reconceptualized as "empathic distress fatigue."[8] It is not compassion that causes burnout, it's empathy.

Several years ago, a group of researchers studied the neurobiological differences between compassion and empathy, and concluded that empathy "not only induced a stronger sharing of painful and distressing experiences, but also increased the susceptibility to feel negative affect in response to everyday life situations."[9] The study subjects were trained to respond with empathy to a variety of situations; most felt overwhelmed as a result. Those same subjects were later given compassion training, which focused on strengthening their capacity to feel warmth and care in the face of suffering, including their own suffering, but without taking on the feelings of the person suffering.[10] Incredibly, researchers found that the compassion training actually reversed the effects of empathy overload. Responding with compassion decreased negative emotions and increased positive ones.[11] Compassion heals both the receiver and the giver.

When we mistake empathy for compassion, our partner is often left feeling unseen and unsupported. The same is sometimes true when we try to express our support for our partner by identifying with them. I explain it to my couples this way: When one person says, "I'm bleeding," and the other person comes and says, "I'm bleeding, too!" what problem are we solving? Now we have two people who are bleeding at the same time.

Melanie and Samuel got into an intense fight that left Samuel completely baffled. Melanie, after having an argument with her mother, came home wanting to tell Samuel all about it. Samuel thought he showed up fully for her, but Melanie didn't seem to appreciate his efforts and got mad at him, which to him made no sense. From Melanie's perspective, she came home exhausted and beaten down from the harsh conversation with her mother, but before she even finished telling Samuel the story and giving a full account of what happened, Samuel got extremely angry on Melanie's behalf. She explained, "It's like he was getting angry for me, but to the point that he started hyperventilating. I ended up having to calm him down." Samuel thought he was responding appropriately because he "truly and deeply felt Melanie's pain and anger." But for Melanie, these incidents leave her feeling like Samuel has hijacked her emotions. "I start to wonder if he lacks the maturity to show up for me, because I always end up taking care of him, even when I desperately need the reverse."

One of the earliest lessons I received about responding to another person's pain was from my wise parents, whose thinking shaped my own so much that their words appear throughout this book. I was about eleven at the time, and my brother was seven. We were having a disagreement, and we took it to our mother. I said, "I'm going to be late because he's so disorganized with his things in the mornings!" My brother replied, "And I'm always late coming home because you take forever to say goodbye to your friends!" My mother responded, "Look. If you come to me and tell me, 'I had a bad fall and now I am hurt. I am limping,' and I turn around and say, 'Okay, but look at that other person down the street. He is limping, too. Look to your left, that person is limping, too. And, by the way, did you notice that I am also limping?' If I say that to you, does it take away any of your pain?" We both said, "No! I'm still hurting and limping." She said, "Yes, that is right. And if you pay close attention you will see that you two are doing exactly the same thing here. Instead of listening to the other person and seeing where his pain is, you are just trying to show him that you are limping, too. Therefore, in this scenario, we have two people limping and nobody is being helped."

Too often, identification devolves into a kind of competition to see whose suffering is worse, like a "traumalympic" sprint to the top of the heap of pain. Of course, self-disclosure can help to build trust, and most of us offer our own stories in a genuine attempt to communicate compassion for someone else's suffering. When we say, "Yes, I *understand*, because I have been there, too," our intention is for the other to feel less alone. Mutual support organizations like Alcoholics Anonymous, as well as therapeutic groups convened to process grief and trauma, are built around members' common experiences. It is encouraging to know that someone who was once in your shoes has been able to heal, and telling our stories to each other helps to reduce secrecy and shame.

But our efforts to demonstrate our concern by relating to the other's experience end up backfiring when we inadvertently hijack the conversation. I always declare to my clients that "my love and regard for you is unconditional and I will be there for you fully, but I will never truly *understand* what you have gone through." Reality is perceived to be subjective. We call this *subjective constructivism* in social psychology. There is no way that anyone can claim otherwise, because even if two people have gone through exactly the same experience, their interpretation of the event and their level of emotional arousal resulting from it will be different. So now that you know, please don't use that language as a part of being there for anyone who is suffering.

Robert Katz warns us about the consequence of such identifications: "When we see the slightest indication of a similarity of feeling between the other person and ourselves, we may imagine that the correspondence between him and ourselves is complete. We are then no longer curious about his feelings because we take for granted that they are identical with our own."[12] (There is a joke within the Iranian community that goes something like this: Mothers always say, "It's cold outside, put on your jacket." A Persian mother says, "I'm cold, put on your jacket!") Partners who frequently rely on identification often get accused of making every conversation about themselves. When it comes to you and your significant other, it's best to use this tactic sparingly, if at all.

The same goes for sympathy, which is also a go-to response when someone else is suffering in one way or another. The problem with sympathy is that it's inherently unequal, and puts the other person in a one-down position. When we witness another's suffering, and we feel bad for them, *we* feel sympathy for *their* misfortune. For me, sympathy comes with a certain amount of pity or feeling sorry for the other person, and often a bit of hidden gratitude that the misfortune is theirs and not mine. Sympathy can also be offered from a distance, and doesn't require a lot of emotional investment or engagement on our part. *Let me know if you need anything. I'm so sorry for your loss.* Sympathy is what happens when you watch the news, feel awful for those poor people whose lives are upended, then turn off the TV and make dinner.

In humanitarian settings, sympathy is seen as patronizing or condescending and is strongly discouraged. Sebastian Rich is a photojournalist who mostly covers conflict zones, and our paths crossed through our work with the United Nations. He shared with me that before he tries to capture anything on his camera, he always takes a moment to pause, check in with himself, and make sure that he is going to capture the dignity of his subject and not only the sorrow, the pain, or the fact that they are debilitated because of their current circumstances.[13]

Feeling sympathy for your partner is not categorically harmful, and there are times when sympathy is the response that is most needed. If your partner has the flu and is achy and whiny, sympathy could be a good choice. In this case, you really *are* in a better position in that moment, and you actually *do* feel sorry for them. Your circumstances are, in fact, unequal, but it's also a temporary state. And, let's face it, we all go through times when we just want our partner to acknowledge our suffering, see how miserable we are, and take pity on us. But we don't want them to stop there. We want them to actually do something about it and take care of us. So sympathy could be the starting point in this case, but if it does not lead to an act of compassion, then it is just that and nothing more.

Sympathy quickly becomes problematic if it is the default dynamic in an intimate relationship. I have seen so many couples who came together because one partner felt sympathy for the other and wanted to be there for them, rescue them, or change their lives for the better. Consciously or unconsciously, alleviating the partner's misery became their main purpose in life. For example, when Petros met Harper, she was working long hours to support herself and her five-year-old daughter. He explained, "We got married because we love each other, but I also knew I could give them both a better life." Now, seven years later, Harper experiences Petros's sympathy as patronizing. "Yes, the money is nice, and I'm definitely more financially secure. And I'm grateful, I really am, but it's not like I was some desperate woman when we met. I was working as an emergency room nurse, supporting myself and my daughter, and I took a lot of pride in that. I didn't need to be rescued, and it makes me really angry when Petros acts like he knows what's best for me."

Joseph Bailey, the author of *Slowing Down to the Speed of Love*, captures the distinction between sympathy and compassion well when he explains, "Compassion is what happens when our heart is open while being with another person but *without trying to change, fix, or otherwise rescue him or her*. It also allows us to care for another person without bringing us down or taking on his problems as our own."[14]

Empathy, identification, and sympathy all have a role to play in committed coupledom, but they are not the same thing as compassion. When we confuse these concepts, our attempts to show up for our partner often fall flat. When we feel too much and become flooded, we are unable to show up for either our partner or ourselves. When we identify by sharing our own stories, it has a way of taking the focus off the partner and often leaves them feeling unseen. And when we feel sorry for them and offer them our solace from a distance or try to fix their problems, we undermine the equitability and trust in our relationship.

Compassion means that you show up *for* someone, you feel *for* them rather than *with* them, and you do so without making it about yourself or your own experience. Now let's turn our attention to what compassion means to you, and how you learned to express it in your close relationships.

YOUR COMPASSION BLUEPRINT

When you say, "I'm there for you," what do you mean by that specifically, and how do you act on your intentions? When someone you care about is going through a hard time, how do you typically respond? What if you, also, are going through a hard time? Does compassion look different when your partner's suffering has something to do with you?

Our blueprint for compassion is a composite of our culture, upbringing, and positive and negative experiences. Our ability to cultivate compassion is deeply rooted in how we were taught to view vulnerability, and how we were treated in the past in moments when we were perhaps vulnerable or didn't feel our best. Those lessons are often deeply ingrained in us and are sometimes attached to emotional states that we try to avoid as adults. Below is an exercise to help you increase your self-literacy by understanding the role compassion has played in your own life and the various meanings you might attach to that word.

BUILDING BLOCK: COMPASSION AND SELF-COMPASSION BLUEPRINT

Think of a memory from your childhood where you thought you had failed at something and felt embarrassed, humiliated, ashamed, or exposed. It could be anything from failing a test to falling off your bicycle, breaking a vase, or not being able to accomplish something even though you tried your very best. Now think about any adults who were there. What was their reaction? How did they express it with a touch, a word, a gesture, or a look? Were they comforting and reassuring? Did they scold or mock you by saying, "You're so clumsy!" or "You should have tried harder!" or "Can't you do anything right?"

Were your experiences minimized? Were you told to "toughen up," "shake it off," or "stop making such a big deal out of it"? Were you ever called a crybaby? Or a long face? Who is the person that comes to mind? How old were you? How old were they? What was their relationship with you, their power and influence over you? How did you feel? What did you think? Is there still a sensation attached to that memory for you? Was there a correlation between the gender of these people who were reacting (men and women around you) or did you notice a gendered expectation being conveyed to you (e.g., boys should toughen up but it's okay for girls to cry)?

How did the adults in your life value compassion? Were you rewarded for being kind and compassionate to others, or was that considered weak? Was care extended to anyone who needed it, or was it reserved only for family, close friends, or people who otherwise looked like you? How much responsibility was shown for the well-being of others, and which others? Did your family make fun of people or otherwise criticize and diminish them?

Now take a moment to think about all the significant, high-stakes relationships you've had since then with these questions in mind. Do you notice any of these four main patterns?

1. You look for your blueprint in other relationships by attracting (or being attracted to) partners who provide a response that is similar to that of your early caregivers.
2. You perform your blueprint in current relationships by becoming the person who was comforting, scolding, or mocking in your relationships.
3. You cannot accept other forms of behavior beyond your blueprint. For example, if you were mocked when down as a child and your partner tries to comfort you, you cannot accept this.
4. Do you see yourself losing patience when someone is not at their best or shows vulnerability of some sort (such as when someone is sick or not able to perform at their usual level)?

How was this for you? If you grew up in a household where compassion and vulnerability were seen as signs of weakness, there's a good chance this was difficult, or at least uncomfortable. This exercise brings up painful memories for many of my clients. Your earliest experiences with compassion (or lack thereof) shape how you express compassion to others, how comfortable you are receiving it, and—just as importantly—how easily you offer it to yourself.

THE ROLE OF SELF-COMPASSION

You probably noticed that "self-compassion" was part of the exercise, and for good reason: Compassion begins with yourself. It is the deep care and concern for our own well-being—though not in a narcissistic way, which often shows up as shutting other people out, or prioritizing yourself at their expense. To me it seems that self-care is something we do, self-love is a state of being, and self-compassion is an expression of care and concern for our own well-being.

Sometimes, when I encourage my clients to practice self-compassion, they get confused. "I'm not going to sit around feeling sorry for myself!" Just as compassion and pity are not the same thing, self-compassion and self-pity are also not the same thing. The main difference, as I see it, is that feeling sorry for yourself doesn't require any action on your part to resolve or correct the situation. There's not much sense of agency. Your problems continue to exist, and you continue to dwell on them in a self-centered spiral of despair that leaves little room for anything (or anyone) else. Self-compassion, however, gives you the power to acknowledge what happened, appreciate the impact it had on you without self-recrimination, reassure yourself that you are committed to finding a better way the next time, and search for a solution. You may recognize this as the A-ARM tool I offered in the chapter on trust. It is the same process, only here you're applying it to yourself.

Practicing self-compassion can also help you to avoid burnout. In relationships where one person keeps giving and giving without paying attention to their own feelings of depletion, they might begin to feel resentment, anger, contempt, or empathic distress fatigue. This is especially true when their cup is not being filled by the other person equally. Some of the signs include a decline in feelings of sympathy and empathy, a decline in caring behaviors (which are replaced with more task-oriented behaviors), an impassive and detached manner that leads to social isolation, and profound physical and emotional exhaustion.[15]

Let me give you an example of what this looks like in real life. Adriana and Lucas are a couple from Portugal whom I saw virtually from New York. They came to me because Adriana was madly in love with someone else, and Lucas was devastated. From the moment they joined the session he was sobbing. My heart ached for him, but Adriana did not seem bothered by it at all. I pointed out that she seemed dissociated, almost as if she was disgusted by his tears. She said, "Yes, I am. Because he is very weak. This is the problem; this is why I'm so attracted to Raul. He is a real man. He is like my father. He's not as successful as Lucas because he has a bit of a temper, but honestly I don't care. I need a man in my life, someone who is not talking about his feelings and his suffering. I don't need a poet, I need a man."

Lucas grew up with a single mother who was devoted to him, and they spent hours together. His mother was interested, attentive, and comforting. She sat with him through disappointments and heartaches, and even when he just wanted her presence. They were (and are still) very close, and Lucas thought that Adriana was like his mother. Shortly after they met he broke his leg, and Adriana came to his house every day for a whole week. "I thought she was so caring, but now I can remember that she became really irritated when I couldn't go out with her that weekend." Looking back, he realized that every time he was sick, or had trouble at work, or needed some comfort, Adriana would distance herself, and then the mockery would start. One time, when he had to call a tow truck because his car broke down and he wasn't able to fix it himself, she said, "I guess that's what happens when you grow up without a father. What kind of man can't fix his own car?" Of course, she always said this in a joking way, so Lucas didn't really take it to heart until we started to talk about it.

Adriana told me that she was attracted to Lucas initially because he was so helpful and attentive. He always had ideas for how to grow her business, and he helped her by stepping up to cook or run errands. He even helped her family. Adriana had grown up with a very domineering father who did not accept anything less than his ideal for perfection. She and her two sisters played in a band, took ballet lessons, and played soccer. She went to a great university with a full scholarship. Her father was very harsh, and she knew she wanted someone more compassionate. The problem was that Adriana didn't have the capacity to receive Lucas's compassion, or even be around it, let alone reciprocate it. Adriana was a woman who was proud of the fact that she hadn't cried since she was eight years old, and she couldn't tolerate crying in anyone else, and especially not in Lucas.

The reason that a practice of self-compassion is so essential in relationships is that people who lack compassion for themselves often lack compassion for others. Dr. Kristin Neff, a researcher who studies self-compassion, explains that when we treat ourselves with kindness rather than judgment, we stop over-identifying with our failures and inadequacies and begin to appreciate our common humanity, which leaves us feeling more connected to others as well.[16] Those who lack self-compassion tend to have unrealistic benchmarks (for both themselves and others) that most people can't achieve. Then they react with frustration and anger when those standards aren't met. Like Adriana, they express their disappointment with sarcasm, criticism, mockery, insults, and harsh judgments of both the self and others. What you can't tolerate in yourself, you won't be able to tolerate in others.

Cultivating self-compassion is sometimes a long journey, especially for those who received little compassion or understanding as children. Though it is essential in Emergent Love, it's a bit outside the scope of this book to deal with this subject in the fullness it deserves. If you are someone who lacks compassion for yourself or for others, please know that there are many resources out there to help overcome the old stories and unforgiving voices you might carry within you. If you'd like to learn more, you can find other resources on the *Love by Design* website: www .lovebydesignbook.com.

COMPASSION IN PRACTICE

Compassion comes easily to some people because it is what they grew up seeing, but most of us have to work at it. Modern lives are busy and complicated, and we spend a great deal of time focusing inward—our work, our plans, our goals, our to-do list. Being compassionate in your significant relationships requires that you set aside your own concerns and focus exclusively on the other person. It can be surprisingly difficult.

Genuine compassion manifests itself when people are hurting, and that's not always convenient for us. Compassion is easy when the other person is not in an exposed or vulnerable position, or when their needs don't conflict with our own. It also requires us to have more than the roles of *utility* for each other.

In the chapter on trust I talked about the heart-shaped squishy balls I keep in my office, and how you need to make sure your partner can catch that ball before you toss it. I still stand by that recommendation, but when someone is really experiencing deep emotional pain you might need to dig a little deeper, because asking them to wait could injure the sense of safety in your relationship. Remember, compassion provides relational safety. This means being able to show up for your partner when they need you, and the way they need you, and not just when it is easy or convenient for you. Being compassionate is one of the ways that you set yourself apart from all the other people in your partner's life.

There is no denying that compassion requires energy. If you really aren't in a position to catch that squishy ball, please make sure you communicate that to your partner as lovingly as you can. In the moments that you don't have anything to offer beyond a few moments of your time, don't underestimate the power of just being present. It could go a long way to show your partner that you see their suffering and can be there with them. Having someone witness your pain even silently—holding your hand or giving you a hug—has great healing power.

Now, it would be wonderful if there were a universal law that says that partners will never both need support and compassion at the same exact time. Unfortunately, this is not the case. When this happens, there is time to have a commiseration moment. I tell my couples, "Soak together so you don't sink together." Let me explain.

Marta and Tim were married for eight years with a four-year-old son, Jason, who had special needs. Marta quit her job to stay home in part because all the doctor appointments and therapies took a lot of time. This was after more than fifteen years in an executive role, so it was a huge adjustment for her. Tim, now the sole financial provider, picked up extra clients to make ends meet. When COVID hit, he was laid off. They were stuck in their house, with Jason going to school on Zoom every single day while Tim looked for work. Marta was barely keeping her head above water. It was a very stressful time in their relationship and in their life in general. One day, after hours of prep and three rounds of interviews, Tim learned that he didn't get the job he thought was a sure thing. "I felt like I was buried under an avalanche and had to find my way out to gasp some air again." He went to Marta to vent and seek comfort, but Marta had nothing left to give. She'd spent a very challenging day on her own with Jason and was spent.

When they got into an argument in my office about who was suffering more and who needed to be the stronger one, I stopped them. "Look, the way you're doing this isn't going to work. You'll sink before you know it. Why don't you try soaking together instead?" Depending on the couple, and the size of their bathtub, I either tell them to take a fifteen-minute bath together or just sit or lie down together. They don't need to talk or do anything at all. Just be in each other's presence, share a plate of strawberries, have an apple and some cheese, maybe a cup of tea and a little light music in the background, and see what happens. It did work, I have to say. Now Marta and Tim have a language between them. When they know that they have nothing more to give, but they need comfort and compassion from each other, they say, "Do you want to soak?"

MEETING ANGER WITH COMPASSION

Compassion is easiest when the events or circumstances causing your partner's suffering don't affect you in the same way—like when they have a disappointment at work or an argument with a parent. It's harder when you're also suffering, or when you feel like you have nothing left to give. But compassion is most challenging when your partner's pain has something, anything, to do with you (or when they think it does). If he's ready to explode because he thinks you were flirting with the bartender, or she "can't believe" that you would use that tone of voice with her, the urge to defend yourself is powerful. It can be hard to respond with genuine care and compassion when your partner is upset with you or is attacking you. I never promised that compassion would be easy, and this is one situation where it might take a Herculean effort to pause, emotionally separate yourself from the situation, calm down, and really try to hear about your partner's pain. We'll talk a lot more about emotional self-regulation in the chapter on navigating conflict, since conflict is the area where this skill is the most necessary.

Meeting anger with compassion doesn't mean that you have to agree with what your partner is saying. Instead, it allows you to be there for them without being impacted by their anger to the point that you fuel the tension at hand. Being able to regulate your emotions enough to really listen when your partner is upset with you is an important part of compassion, and also one of the hardest. Often partners need to step away from each other for a few moments, sometimes longer, to be able to manage their defensiveness so they can really show up for the conversation.

When I see couples in conflict, it generally starts when one partner says some version of "You hurt me because of X, Y, or Z." The other partner immediately goes on the defensive and starts to justify, or they deflect it back to the partner, or they bring up their own hurt feelings. The situation escalates quickly to the point where not only is compassion completely absent, but the partners aren't even listening to each other. It looks something like this.

Kelsey: You said you'd be home by nine o'clock and it's ten-thirty.

Taylor: I did not say I'd be home by nine, I said I'd *try* to be home by nine. I didn't even leave work until eight-thirty, then the train was late and I was so exhausted I slept through my stop. I tried to call you to come pick me up, but you didn't answer your phone, so I had to wait for another train in the opposite direction. Why didn't you answer your phone?

Kelsey: I didn't pick up because I'm tired of your excuses, and I knew it would be more of the same.

Taylor: I can't believe this! I've been working twelve-hour days for weeks, I'm completely exhausted, and all you can say is, "You're late." Give me a break!

Kelsey: I work twelve-hour days all the time! Just because I like my job doesn't mean that I'm at a spa every day. You don't see me getting any breaks around here, do you?

The interesting part about this is that both parties are right! But it's easy to see that this is going nowhere. I often have to stop couples at this point and ask them to slow down, take turns speaking, and really listen to what the other person is saying. I also remind them of who they are talking with and what the problem is that they are trying to solve. Taking turns helps, but only if you're actually listening to what the other person is saying and not thinking about why they're wrong or what you're going to say when it's your turn to talk. Sometimes, depending on how unregulated each person is in that moment, this ends up being very difficult for all parties involved. Learning how to receive what the other person is sharing is an important part of practicing mutual compassion.

In these moments, because we're often expressing these feelings verbally, listening attentively and with genuine interest is vital. The idea of being a good listener has evolved since psychologists Carl Rogers and Richard Farson first introduced the term *active listening* in 1957.[17] They explained that listening has to be done in an active manner with sensitivity and attention; you need to show the other person you're listening with verbal and nonverbal cues, and actively make an effort to grasp the meaning behind their words. Active listening was later joined by ideas like *empathic listening*,[18] *deep listening*,[19] and *compassionate listening*.[20] Each of these models builds on the idea that listening requires more than the passive absorption of what the other person is saying.

Over the years, I have developed my own model of listening, which I use in my work with couples and beyond. I call it "engaged listening." It's based on the idea that effective listening requires that we be fully present in the moment and focused on the other person. We listen with tenderness and freedom from judgment, and without making assumptions about how the person might be feeling or what they might need. It invites you to see your role in co-creating the interaction in terms of what is shared with you and how you show up in and for it. There is one major element that gives listening an engaged quality, and that is framing the conversation before you have the conversation. Here's what it looks like.

COUPLE'S TOOLKIT:
FRAMING THE CONVERSATION

Before you begin a conversation, make sure that both participants know what is expected by framing the conversation. In your role as listener:

- Ask the other person, "How do you want me to show up for you right now? Do you want me just to listen so you can get something off your chest? Do you want to know my thoughts or opinions? Do you want my advice? Do you want reassurance and comfort?"
- Constantly self-check to see where you are and how you are showing up for the other based on the framing they offered.
- Sometimes it changes over the course of conversation. Feel free to offer your guess (for example, "Can I give you a hug?").
- Also be open for your partner to accept what you are offering or not.
- Maintain awareness that this is not about you, even if the whole issue was created by something you said or did.
- Do not interrupt (even if you know that the thoughts will not come back to you later!).
- Listen with an attitude of openness and interest about the meaning the other is trying to convey. Listen to the needs not the exact words.

Framing the conversation significantly reduces the risk of miscommunication or misunderstandings by making expectations explicit rather than assumed. Our partners show up in the best way they know how, but sometimes it is not what we need from them in that moment. Leaving it to them to figure out what our needs are is just going to set them up for failure. This is not a place to test how attuned they are with you. Engaged listening is what comes after you frame the conversation, and it is specific to the role of the listener. Often the person who shares might not be aware of what they want, or they are so emotionally charged that they forget to use this tool. Either the person who shares or the one who receives can use framing. Engaged listening makes the interaction reciprocal in that the parties walk away feeling fulfilled, useful, and connected.

COMPASSION TRAPS

Compassion in Emergent Love is something we *express to* and *receive from* our partner, and treating your partner with compassion carries an expectation of reciprocity. But it's not a commodity that you can barter for something else. Real compassion doesn't have a price tag attached to it. It has to be freely given. When you attach expectations, you create a trap for both yourself and your partner.

It can be helpful to think of the distinction between being kind (compassionate) and being nice. The way I see it, being nice is something that we do on the surface; it's superficial, and there is often an expectation of a certain outcome—the other person will like us, be nice back to us, express appreciation, or do something for us at a later time. Let me give you an example. Eva learned that a family in her neighborhood had a fire in their house and would not be able to use their kitchen for at least a month. She didn't know the family personally, but a mutual friend, Alison, organized people in the neighborhood to cook meals and leave them on their front porch. When Eva rang the doorbell to drop off her meal it took a few minutes before the dad came to the door, holding a crying infant, and said, "Thanks. You didn't have to ring the bell; usually people just leave it here."

Later, recounting the story to Alison, Eva explained, "I went to a lot of trouble to make that lasagna. He could have shown a little gratitude." Eva felt like her act was not received or reciprocated properly. Alison explained, "They've had a lot of people coming by to ask how they can help. They also have a six-month-old baby who wakes up every time the doorbell rings. If he seemed abrupt, that's probably why." Eva was not mollified. She wanted to be recognized for doing something nice for someone else. Being nice usually includes an expectation about how the other person will respond.

Compassion doesn't include these kinds of expectations. When Alison realized that her friends needed help, she didn't sympathize by saying, "Oh, I'm so sorry. Let me know if there's anything I can do for you." Instead, she offered, "I'd like to organize people to cook dinner for you and drop it off on the porch, so you won't have to manage cooking without a kitchen. Would that be okay?" Acts of compassion are performed with the intention of being of service to others. The satisfaction experienced by the giver is internal: She feels good because she behaved in a way that is aligned with her values. The spirit in which her act is received is secondary to the spirit in which it was given.

I would like to be very clear here: We all have expectations; it's how we make sense of the world. If you go to work every day for two weeks, you expect to get a paycheck at the end of it. If we treat our partner with compassion, we expect it in return. But problems arise when we mistake "being nice" for compassion. Whenever I hear someone say, "My problem is I'm just too nice!" I immediately start to dig deeper to find out what they really mean. Michael Cavanagh, a pastoral counselor and writer, describes this as "pseudo-compassion." He explains that when we act nice because we want to be liked, or we want to avoid confrontation, we are not being truly compassionate. Nor is it compassionate to protect people from the consequences of their bad behavior. Instead, these so-called nice behaviors tend to be destructive because you end up hindering the growth of the other person. People who are "too nice" are sometimes not compassionate at all. They just have weak boundaries. Rather than asking for what they want directly, they tend to prefer passive-aggressive strategies to hide bad intentions behind good ones. "There's no gas in the car!" "Well, honey, you're the one who said I spend too much money, so I didn't get it filled."

Your ability to express and receive compassion is highly susceptible to problems when other relationship dynamics are not aligned. Partners need to trust that the other will show up reliably and consistently when compassion is needed. It is also harder to have compassion when partners fail to respect each other's boundaries or fail to maintain their own.

The second compassion trap has to do with the intersection of respect and compassion. I think of it as the difference between hurting someone, which is usually unintentional, and acting intentionally to cause harm.

Have you ever done something that you know your partner doesn't like but you did it anyway? Most people have. Compassion requires not only being aware of how your partner is going to interpret or respond to your actions, but also using that awareness to guide your behavior. In this way it is closely linked to respect. If you leave the wet towels on the bathroom floor, you're being disrespectful toward the person you live with, especially if he's asked you not to do that, but you're not necessarily lacking compassion. Maybe the phone started ringing when you got out of the shower, or your toddler needed something, or you were preoccupied and you got distracted. You won't get any Spouse of the Year awards, and you'll probably hear about it later, but chances are you haven't caused any lasting harm. But if you and your husband are having an argument, and you shout, "You're just like your father!" when you know he has a very difficult relationship with his father that has caused him a lot of pain, then you're being both disrespectful and cruel.

There's a difference between hurting someone and harming them. We all get hurt based on our vulnerabilities, even by people who love us the most. Harm, on the other hand, has a level of intentionality to it. It's the difference between doing something *even though* it might hurt the partner and doing something *because* it hurts the partner. Let's say, for example, that you and your wife are having a Very Loud Discussion about whose turn it is to mop the kitchen floor, and you stop and say, "I need a timeout. I know you hate when I do this, but I am not my best self right now and I need to calm down." That might hurt your wife (who loves a good argument and never needs a break) but it isn't going to harm her. In fact, it will probably prevent harm. But if you're still not talking to her three days later, beyond providing one-word answers to questions that require a response, then you're causing harm. You're punishing her by stonewalling *because you know it drives her crazy.*

Hopefully, you're thinking as you read this, "That's awful. I would never do something like that." No one likes to think of themself as a person who intentionally causes harm. Some of you might also think of incidents in which you have been either the doer or the one done to in these situations. Yet I see this every day in my practice, as do many of my colleagues. The late Dr. David Schnarch, a respected couples therapist, even had a name for it. He called it "Normal Marital Sadism." In my experience, these intentionally harmful behaviors usually happen because one of the partners, if not both, has a very hard time recognizing and articulating their needs in a way that the other can understand. Frustration builds quickly into rage. Lacking compassion for their own suffering, they lose compassion for the partner and lash out.

This is one of the reasons I tell my couples it is so important to let your partner know when they've hurt you. Whether it's pride that prevents you from sharing what is bothering you, or embarrassment about bringing something up because you think you're being a jerk for even being bothered by something as minor as a wet towel on the floor, it is still important to talk about it. Little annoyances and minor hurts can turn into harm over time if they're not dealt with right away. It's like being poked in the same spot over and over again. You can ignore it the first time, maybe even the first hundred times, but eventually that spot will get so sensitive and so sore that even the slightest touch will cause unbearable pain.

───

When mutual compassion is fully present in a coupledom, both partners feel seen. There is a sense of safety in the relational space, which allows both partners to bring all of themselves—the good and the not-so-good—into that space without fear of judgment or criticism or that the other person will turn it around and make it about themselves. When a situation requires a compassionate response from you, be sure to frame the conversation by checking in with your partner so you know what they need and expect, and you can respond in a way that is most likely to leave them feeling seen, heard, and supported. And when you're the one who needs a little TLC, be sure you do the same. Expressing compassion is an inherently generous act, but there is also generosity involved when you open yourself up to receive compassion by letting your partner know exactly what you need in that moment. Not everyone sees compassion the same way, or gives it the same value, but together you can work to make compassion the bedrock of your emotional connection.

CHAPTER 9

Loving Behaviors

Love is a property that only exists through its manifestations.

—Jamshid Gharajedaghi[1]

"Wait a minute," you might be thinking, "I thought this whole book was about loving. If Emergent Love is the by-product of having all these individual and relational ingredients in place and functioning really well, then how can love itself be one of the ingredients?" Please be assured that I have asked myself that same question many times. One of the reasons I made the decision to differentiate *loving* from other aspects of Emergent Love is because loving has a quality to it that none of the other ingredients has, a tenderness and affection that you feel toward the person that is hard to deconstruct and even harder to describe. In this chapter, I'm going to attempt to do just that. For our purposes, I think of "being loving" as having two dimensions. First, it is a state of being where you have the capacity to cultivate love for anyone or anything. Second, it is the manifestation of love through specific actions directed at the beloved.

Being loving is an inside job; the capacity for love must exist internally, in the form of self-love, before it can be experienced with another person. This is a bit different from the self-love that has become a new trendy jargon in our society these days. Turning the focus outward, we'll look at how being loving toward a partner includes everything you do to show that you value your partner's unique presence in your life, and you appreciate the exclusivity of your bond (this is equally true if you are not in a monogamous relationship). Loving behaviors include how you express tenderness and affection, how you pay attention, and how you prioritize your finite resources—your time, attention, energy, and money—on their behalf. The person that we love has an unequal distribution of these resources to their favor. Loving also includes seeing your partner in the fullest sense of the word, as a differentiated being who is constantly evolving, and embracing all of the aspects of self that they bring to the coupledom.

Think, for a moment, about all the members of your inner circle, including your closest friends, your family of origin (if they are part of your inner circle), mentors, children (if you have them), anyone and everyone who occupies a central position in your life. All of the ingredients of Emergent Love that we have discussed so far apply in each of these relationships. You are attracted to these people in the sense that the relationships continue to draw you in and to serve you. You also, I hope, feel respect, trust, compassion, and commitment for and from each of them. All of the ingredients are there. So what, then, distinguishes your significant other from the rest of your inner circle? Many of you are probably thinking "Sex!" And you're right, sexual exclusivity is often (not always) a component of committed partnership and part of the boundary you draw around your coupledom. But even committed couples who practice non-monogamy have a boundary to differentiate their primary partner from others. So if it isn't sex, then what is it? Loving.

WHAT IS THE STATE OF BEING IN LOVE, REALLY?

Humanity has been grappling with this question for millennia, with mixed results. The distinction between *loving* someone and *being in love* traces its roots back at least as far as the ancient Greeks, who separated the passion of lovers (*eros*) and the platonic love of friendship (*philia*). Today we see this in the often-repeated pronouncement, "I love you, but I'm not *in love* with you." Teenagers call it "getting stuck in the friend zone," and adults often see it as a harbinger of separation.

As you may recall from chapter 1, the Greek philosophers recognized a number of other variations on the theme of love as well: *Agape* is love that is selfless (what could be felt toward any other human; it is universal in its nature); *storge* describes a devoted love (what a parent might feel toward a child); *pragma* is dutiful love (what a child might feel toward a parent); *xenia* is the love that a person feels for their guest that is shown through their act of hospitality; *philautía* is love of self (which the Greeks considered both necessary and positive unless it was egotistic, in which case it became negative); *ludus* (when you're not fully invested and just playing a game); and *mania,* which is the obsessive kind of love that tends to be possessive and all-consuming, and which destroys rather than creates. Love is a universal emotion, and understanding how love manifests itself seems to be a universal concern. Most cultures recognize that the word *love* holds a multiplicity of meanings, and they have words and phrases to describe all the nuances.

Yet there are also those who maintain that there is only one love— usually described as selfless and unconditional—and that anything less is not really love. Leo Buscaglia, in his bestselling book *Love*, argues that "there are degrees of love, but there's only one *kind* of love [emphasis mine]."[2] He goes on to explain that love in its purest form is freely given with no expectations—admittedly an almost impossible task, but a worthwhile goal. If it isn't *agape,* then it isn't really love. This idea of a transcendent and all-encompassing love—for self, for others, for a god, for life itself, for humanity—is more of a spiritual orientation than a relational one, and appears in one form or another in most of the world's religions. In our own research, altruistic love was mentioned primarily by couples who share a mutual devotion to a religious or spiritual faith tradition. For these couples, striving for the ideal of unconditional love toward their partners is part of how they practice their faith.

Erich Fromm writes, "Love is not primarily a relationship to a specific person; it is an *attitude,* an *orientation of character* which determines the relatedness of a person to the world as a whole, not toward one 'object' of love."[3] I agree with him. These are also the values I learned as a child. Growing up, I was taught that the capacity for loving is an aspect of the self, not an aspect of the relationship. If you want to love someone in particular, you need to know how to love in a universal sense. This, combined with learning how to manifest and express your love, makes it possible for you to love anyone and everyone. But there is an important qualification: You may be able to cultivate a loving attitude toward all of humanity, but this doesn't mean you can shape a thriving partnership with everyone. For Emergent Love to be present you need other criteria.

YOUR LOVE BLUEPRINT

Our first experience of love is with our primary caregivers. This is where we learn what it means to love and be loved. Developmental psychologists stress the importance of this first bond and argue that all of our future relationships are shaped by our primary experience of being loved. The adult's loving gaze lets the child know she is seen, she is here, she exists. That loving gaze is internalized and becomes the foundation for the child's sense of self. Our perception of self is formed when we recognize that another person sees us as a separate entity. French philosopher René Descartes famously said, "I think, therefore I am." We could amend that to say, "I am perceived, therefore I exist."

Infants experience this first as *being loved* (the act of being regulated and taken care of). This is long before they experience *feeling love* for another. Although many infants can feel and express their basic needs (for food, sleep, or comfort) these are not felt emotions. Instead, the infant becomes attuned to an other, someone outside themselves who is meant to ensure their survival. Later on we will feel love when we are held (emotionally and physically), comforted, and are provided with a context that gives us a sense of safety and belonging.

Understanding *how you were loved* will help you understand *how you experience love* today. For the record, adults who received perfect parental love and acceptance as children are rare. If you were not one of them, you are certainly not alone. We sustain all kinds of emotional injuries as children, some small and some more significant. If these injuries are internalized, they can interfere with a person's ability to experience self-love, which is an essential component of being able to love and to receive love from another.

In the last chapter we talked about how expressing compassion for others is difficult if you have no self-compassion. Well, the same thing is true for love. If you've ever tried to love someone who didn't love themselves, you know what happens. They don't believe you. They push you away in different ways, or sabotage the relationship, because deep down they don't believe they are lovable. Often, people who don't love themselves are anxiously on the lookout for their own sense of worth, and are eager to hand that job to anyone else, whether or not the other person is willing. How they feel about themselves becomes almost a full-time occupation for you. And no matter what you do, or how hard you work, the results are temporary and will vanish the moment you relax your vigilance. Then you will probably feel like you're not enough, or you're not doing enough, and you might start questioning your own self-worth. No one benefits from this dynamic. If you are having a hard time with the concept or practice of self-love, I encourage you to go back to the chapter on compassion and make self-compassion your first priority before you can cultivate self-love in a meaningful way.

Just to put your mind at ease, childhood hardships don't necessarily lead to a lack of self-love or adult dysfunction. In fact, hardship is often beneficial to child development. British psychologist and pediatrician Dr. D. W. Winnicott coined the term "the good enough mother" in 1953.[4] (Today we refer to "the good enough parent.") Winnicott observed thousands of babies and mothers before he concluded that babies and children benefit when their mothers fail them in manageable ways—ways that are not threatening to the existence of the child and don't overwhelm them emotionally beyond their level of tolerance. He explained that these seemingly negative events can build autonomy and resilience in young children, which later serves them in shaping healthier social bonds and adult relationships.

Thinking back to your own childhood, what are your memories of how love was experienced and expressed in your household? This exercise is designed to guide you with some relevant questions.

BUILDING BLOCK: YOUR LOVE BLUEPRINT

- What are your earliest memories of feeling loved, or of loving another? This includes feeling like someone truly cared about how you felt and was interested in you and your life, and not just in you as you related to them.
- What can you remember through your five senses? What are the touches you were given or allowed to give to express and receive love? Was there a particular facial expression that you associated with loving or being loved? What words did you hear? (These could be positively or negatively associated for you.) What do you associate with love through the senses of taste and smell? Was love expressed through play, or through food, or through other acts and rituals? Did you perceive it the same way that it was offered? (For example, if food was offered as a gesture of love, did you take it as such or did you see it as an act of imposition?)
- When you were growing up, did your family say "I love you" often?
- How did you know that you were loved, cherished, and special? By whom? To whom?
- Was love expressed as a reward for positive or desired behaviors like good grades, obedience, or being helpful?
- When you think about loving relationships today, either romantic or platonic, what behaviors do you associate with feeling loved?
- What was the energy around you when you felt loved or when love was taken away?

Mining your earliest experiences of giving and receiving love will help you understand how you receive and perceive love today. If you want to cultivate love in your coupledom, being able to identify the behaviors you associate with feeling loved is an important first step. Otherwise, your partner's best intentions and acts of generosity are likely to fall short of the mark.

LOVING: THE SECRET INGREDIENT

Etan and Anja had been married for twelve years when they came to my office complaining that they felt disconnected, disinterested, and numb. Anja explained, "I keep thinking to myself, 'Is this it? Just you and me in this house for the rest of our lives?' I love Etan, of course I do, but I feel like we're growing apart. And I know he feels the same way." Like a lot of couples, they had been passionately in love at the beginning of their relationship and felt like they couldn't get enough of each other. Over time, the passion had faded, but it hadn't been replaced by warmth and connection.

Etan's version of the current state of their marriage was much like Anja's. He said, "I knew that passion wouldn't last, and I didn't expect it to. I mean, it doesn't, right? But this is more than just sex. I feel like we're coworkers, or, like, she's this nice lady who lives in my house and sometimes I get to have sex with her but most of the time she's just sort of there, doing her thing. And I'm over here, doing my thing. We're together, but we're not *together*. You know?"

At first glance, Anja and Etan seem to have it all. She's a professor, he's a lawyer, they have a beautiful home, three kids, a dog, and two cats. They're a high-functioning couple, very organized and intentional when it comes to running their lives and getting things done. They take fantastic vacations. But when their eight-year-old asked, "Do you guys even love each other?" they realized that maybe their lives weren't as impeccable as they thought. (Remember the Leftover Couples from chapter 2? These are the ones who have a lot of independence but prioritize their resources toward each individual. The partnership gets the leftovers. Anja and Etan were perilously close to this.)

"I know relationships take work," Anja said, "and I'm willing to work at it. I'm a worker, it's what I do. I love to work…"

"She really does," Etan chimed in, as Anja gave him a sideways glance.

"But what is this mysterious work that we're supposed to do? I mean, how, *exactly*, do we do this? For a while we went on date nights, but it felt really forced and kind of stupid. We always ended up talking about operations—We have to sign Aiden up for soccer. Whose turn is it to carpool? What time is your dad coming over tomorrow? I'm flying to Belgium next Saturday, don't forget, so Mary is going to do school drop-off that week. Etc. etc. etc."

Anja and Etan had taken the Relationship Panoramic Inventory, and as we discussed the results of their assessment Anja began to fidget. She was moving around in her chair, crossing and uncrossing her legs, looking around the room, playing with her rings—all signs of discomfort. I invited her to speak about what was going through her mind in that moment. "Well," she began, "this sounds like we don't love each other anymore, and if that's true then it feels like we're doomed. But it's not like we're miserable. We hardly ever fight and when we do we resolve things pretty fast. I mean, we're on the same page with all this stuff—the values, the vision, our finances, how we want to live, how we parent; even our sex life is okay. I'm still attracted to Etan and we have a good connection sexually even if it is less frequent. But, you know, if we don't *love* each other then that's it, right? I mean, that's the most important thing, and we don't have it."

"First, let me be clear," I explained. "This is not a reflection of how much or how deeply you love each other, it's an assessment of how effectively you are expressing your love, and receiving Etan's expressions of love, so that you *feel* loved beyond just *knowing* that you're loved. It doesn't say that you don't love each other, it only suggests that you each might need to make more effort to express your love in ways the other person understands. You see the difference?"

"I do!" she said, relieved.

"So, tell me, do you love Etan?" I asked her.

"Of course I do. I do love you, Etan," she said, turning to him. "I can't imagine my life without you. The idea of separating fills me with dread and so much sadness."

"I'm not going anywhere," Etan reassured her. "I love you, too."

Not wanting to interrupt, I gave them a few moments to let those words sink in. Then, gently, I asked, "How do you know?" They looked at me with identical expressions, eyebrows knotted in confusion, and Etan said, "What do you mean?"

"How do you know she loves you?" I asked him. Then, turning to Anja, I repeated, "How do you know he loves you?"

"He's my husband, of course he loves me! We've built this whole life together, we show up for each other, we've got these amazing kids, we support each other in our work, he doesn't lie or cheat or flirt with other women or even look at other women. I know he's in this a hundred percent."

"Yes, all of that is very critical. You trust him. You respect him. You know he loves you, your rational mind knows he loves you, and he shows his commitment every day. But let me ask you this: Deep down in your heart, in the core of your being, do you *feel* loved?"

She paused for a moment. "I'm not sure."

Being able to express and receive love *for this particular person* is one of the defining features of coupledom. The love between partners is special, it is exclusive (unless you have agreed otherwise), and the way it is expressed should be unique, like no other relationship. Your physical touch, your words, the way you look at each other, the focus of your attention, the way you express your deep appreciation for this person, at this time, in this relationship, are all markers of the unique role your partner plays in your life. Their singular importance is also reflected in how you allocate resources of time, energy, attention, affection, and money. Many couples, like Anja and Etan, work well together in the sense that they function well as a unit. They get things done. These relationships are solid, but they aren't necessarily close, and they can degrade into the kind of platonic buddy dynamics that brought Anja and Etan to me.

When I was doing my research, I began to think about this as the difference between a stable and sustained relationship and one that is thriving. In a stable relationship, the partners share values and a vision for the future, and they experience and express a strong sense of commitment. Stable couples describe each other with words like "dependable," "reliable," "trustworthy," and "solid." There is a lot to be said for stability—relationships where basic relational needs are not met tend to be confusing and exhausting. Partners spend enormous amounts of energy trying to assess their value and importance to the other person. In stable relationships you're not confused about where you stand, you don't seek constant reassurance, and so your energy and attention are freed up for other, more important things.

Yet just because a relationship is stable doesn't mean that it is thriving, or even particularly intimate or close. For that, you need more. In our research, the couples who describe themselves as "thriving" are pretty versatile in the way they show up in their relational spaces, whether as friends, lovers, co-parents, partners in a project, companions on a spiritual journey, or any other aspect of themselves or their coupledom that is important to them. They experience points of connection in most, if not all, of these various roles. And, significantly, they are *intentional* and *specific* about what they bring to the table. Partners are able to distinguish among behaviors that are caring, respectful, sexy, loving, comforting, playful, reassuring, challenging, and others too numerous to mention.

Most of this seems to happen almost instinctively, below a conscious level of awareness. Yet, when questioned, these partners describe an internal process of assessment that includes the current context, the partner's verbal and nonverbal signals, and the wealth of information they have gathered about the partner over the course of their relationship. All of these bits of data inform the behavioral response they choose in any given moment.

Many of the couples that I know and work with, if they're lucky, come together for dinner, maybe watch something on TV, cuddle for a bit, and then they're out for the night. But when you're only together as a couple late at night, after you've put the children to bed or after a long day of work, do you really think that you are capable of giving each other enough to reinforce all of these roles that you have in each other's life? Where in this can you show tenderness, or celebrate the other for their specialness? Some couples preserve one night per week or per month, if at all, to dress up and go out with each other for a date night. And while it's nice to be served food without worrying about cleaning up afterward, and certainly lovely to be dressed up in nice clothes, many couples share with me that date night feels awkward. Sometimes they don't know what to talk about, or they get into an argument because they seize the moment to resolve an ongoing disagreement. Or they get drunk or high or into fights because one person thought the night would end with sex and the other didn't. Date nights are brilliant ideas if that is all you can manage, but there are so many other ways.

Let me give you an example. Eileen and Fred are in their seventies and have been married for forty-nine years. They came to me because they want to renew their vows for their fiftieth anniversary, and they wondered if there might be anything they could put into practice in this new phase of their marriage together. Eileen giggled a bit when she explained, "We didn't know about couples counseling back then, so here we are! Are we thriving? I'm not sure I'd use that word, but we're pretty happy together. At least, I'm happy. Are you happy, Fred?"

"If you're happy, I'm happy," Fred answered, smiling.

When I asked Eileen how she expresses love, she said, "Oh, I don't know. I just try to be nice. I think of what makes him happy. Sometimes I'll make beef Wellington. It's a pretty complicated recipe and he knows that I only make it for him, because he likes it so much. Or I'll buy him something special that I know he really wants but that he'd never get for himself, like good wool socks or a fly-fishing reel. I'm not a huge fan of fishing, but I go with him once in a while because I know he loves it, and I want to share that with him. And when I really want to let him know how much I love him…well, you know." Eileen blushed deeply, then stage-whispered, "We make love."

I asked Fred if he receives these as acts of love, and he confirmed that he did. He clarified, "Eileen also does a lot for the kids, and for my mother, who is ninety-nine years old! Those are loving, too, but it's more like I know she cares about me, she has my back, so to speak. The things she just listed, though, are definitely the things that make me feel special." Then I ask Fred how he shows his love for Eileen, and he said, "I rub her feet at night. I know she loves it and I am the only one who can do that." They both chuckled. I later learned that Eileen does not like her feet to be rubbed by or even seen by others—an old issue she has from childhood. Fred also explained that when he wants to kiss her he always asks her to come closer and never just grabs her, because she was assaulted when she was younger and she gets triggered by unexpected touch. At this point, Eileen reached out and held Fred's hand.

Next I asked Eileen if these are all acts of love from her perspective and she said, "Rubbing my feet definitely is. I feel special when he does that. But not sneaking up on me is more just being respectful and paying attention. But that's love, too, so maybe both?"

All of the acts of loving Eileen and Fred described share two things: They are intentional, and they are specific to the other. They make a *conscious effort* (intentional) to do *something that will bring the other joy* (specific). Let's take a closer look at what that means, and how it might look in daily life.

LOVING WITH INTENTION

Several decades ago, researcher Robert Sternberg created his triangular theory of love. You may remember from the chapter on shared vision that one of the vertices is commitment, which he describes as the cognitive component that involves decision-making and is most within our conscious control. The other two vertices are passion and intimacy. Passion refers to the physical and sexual drives that are the primary motivational factor in relationships, and can be thought of as the energy or life force in the relationship, Sternberg's version of *eros*. And intimacy includes feeling close, connected, and bonded, "those feelings that give rise, essentially, to the experience of warmth in a loving relationship."[5] So loving, this elusive quality, includes all the things you do on purpose, with intention, to cultivate feelings of closeness, connection, and bonding.

Let's return for a moment to Etan and Anja. When I asked Anja if she felt loved, she became confused. I explained, "Think about all the things Etan does with you and for you. Which of those behaviors lets you know that he sees you, he appreciates you, and he loves you?" Still, she looked puzzled. "What does he do that gives you the warm fuzzies?" She laughed, then started to really think about it. I gave them this exercise, which I invite you to do as well, to help identify and articulate the loving behaviors they each wanted to express and receive.

COUPLE'S TOOLKIT:
EXPRESSING AND RECEIVING LOVE

1. First, make a list of all the things your partner does that result in you feeling loved, appreciated, cherished, or seen. How would you complete the sentence, "I feel loved when my partner _____"? Think about how these messages are received through each of your five senses, and also through the atmosphere or energy between you.

2. Next, make a list of all the things you do to express to your partner that you love, appreciate, cherish, and see them. "I express my love for my partner by _____." Again, think of all five senses and also energy.

3. How are these different from the way you show your respect to each other? What about trust, commitment, compassion, and attraction?

4. After you've completed both lists, take turns sharing the first list only. Did you learn anything about your partner that surprised you? What were your reactions? Discuss any thoughts or feelings, positive and negative, that came up as you were writing your own list or listening to your partner's list. Try to keep it free of judgment and blame so it is a productive exchange of information.

5. Now take turns sharing the second list. Again, discuss thoughts and feelings that emerged while writing and listening.

As you do this exercise at home, try to keep the focus on your senses. This will help you differentiate between what you know and what you feel. How do you express or perceive love through sight? Do you maintain eye contact while holding a loving gaze, or give a secret wink of understanding when no one is looking? What about sound? Do you say, "I love you" or use other words to express your love? Is it different for different roles that you have in your coupledom? Does your partner call you by a pet name or nickname, or do you have a special song that transports you both back to a particular place and time? What are the specific ways you touch your partner, sexual and nonsexual, that are meant to convey love? What about taste and smell? Maybe you prepare certain foods or wear a cologne you know she likes. The idea here is that you want to shift your focus from the cognitive awareness of knowing you are loved to the felt sense of being loved right now, in this moment.

For the record, I have yet to see a couple whose lists are 100 percent in sync with each other, especially if it is the first time they're doing the exercise. The percentages go higher as you each continue to share and to learn about how you show up and how your partner receives what you put out there. The idea is to be proactively and continually open to showing each other the special place you hold in the other person's life. It's important to do these kinds of exercises to make sure that what you are offering to your partner is received the way you intend.

Anja and Etan worked on their lists separately between sessions, then brought them back so we could process what they learned. Anja began by telling me how challenging this exercise was for her. Reflecting back on her own experiences of love as a child, she explained, "My family was very oriented toward accomplishment. When I did well in school, when I won awards, when I made the softball team I was celebrated. My family was very WASPish, so there were never a lot of warm fuzzies." She recalled, as a child, overhearing her mother say, "If you tell someone you love them all the time, it cheapens it. Say it sparingly and it holds its value." Expressions of love were a reward for good behavior. "I knew I was loved because I had everything I needed, but I don't think I felt loved."

What helped Anja connect to the feeling of being loved were her memories of her aunt Coco. "Whenever she came to visit I would follow her around the house. I just adored her. And she adored me. She wanted to know everything about my life, and she'd ask me who my friends were, what books I liked to read, whether I thought high-heeled shoes were a patriarchal conspiracy against women. She was great. Even when

I made mistakes or did something wrong, she just sort of brushed it off and didn't pound me when she saw I was feeling bad already. She used to tell me that there was more to life than having a 4.0 GPA. I had no idea what she was talking about at the time, but I remember feeling so excited by the idea that there was a way of being in the world where *who you were* mattered more than *what you accomplished.*

Not surprisingly, Anja feels most loved when Etan tells her he loves her, reassures her that she doesn't have to be perfect or do it all, and willingly does more than his share around the house when she's feeling pressured or overwhelmed.

Etan grew up in a household where his parents, particularly his mother, were very involved in all aspects of his life, so much so that it felt suffocating. "I remember when I used to get phone calls—this was back in the days of landlines—and my mom would always get this urgent need to clean out the linen closet that was right outside my bedroom. I would get so mad at her, and she'd act all innocent and tell me not to be so *sensitive.* I think one of the things I really liked about Anja was that she gave me so much space. But these days it feels like a little too much space." Etan feels loved when Anja is playful with him, flirts with him, and lets him know she desires him. "There is a certain thing she does—I'm not going to tell you what it is—that make me feel kind of manly. Not like a caveman, or like some hyper-masculine goon, but like a provider, a protector. Competent. I'm not just a man, I'm *her* man."

When it came time to share the lists of what each partner does to express love, they both became a bit sheepish. "I hardly have anything on my list," Anja admitted, "and what's there has nothing to do with what Etan just said makes him feel loved. I guess I'm not very good at it. I just assume he knows I love him, like I know he loves me." Etan said much the same thing. I reassured them that 90 percent of the couples I see have exactly this issue. When they do this exercise, they realize that their partners very rarely receive the message they intended. For instance, one husband said, "I bring you coffee every morning because I love you. That's how I show love." His wife responded, "That's care, that's not love. But last week, when you took my mother to her doctor's appointment, that felt like love. I know what my mother is like. She's challenging. No one else would do that for me, and you wouldn't do that for anyone else."

Perhaps this is why Gary Chapman's book *The 5 Love Languages* has become so popular with couples; it gives us a language to understand that each of us receives love differently.[6] If you're struggling to understand what love feels like to you, or how to express love to your partner, Chapman's book might be a good place to start. One of the things I especially like about this book is how it underscores being intentional in the way you express love to your partner. It is not enough to express love in the way that makes you most comfortable—what you do has to resonate with your partner.

WHAT LOVING LOOKS LIKE: BE SPECIFIC

Loving includes everything you do to express love to your partner, but there is a caveat: Your partner has to recognize and receive the act *as an indication of your love*. Loving behaviors have to have meaning for the other person, or they fall short of the mark. They need to be not only intentional, but also specific. Let me give you another example.

Paolo is an executive at a multinational company based in New York City, and he travels a lot for work. Every time he comes home from a trip he brings his partner, Vincenzo, a gift—French linen dish towels, Turkish espresso cups, Tennessee bourbon. It is usually something small, but he always comes with something. Paolo thinks of these gifts as expressions of love, but for Vincenzo, "Every gift is like *un coltello nel cuore*—like a dagger to my guts!" Vincenzo wants something special, not something for the house. "Dish towels! Like I am a housewife and it is the 1950s. It is like you do not know me at all. In all the years you have known me I have never, *non una volta*, expressed any thoughts about dish towels! Do you even ask yourself if what you buy is something that I *want*, or you just grab the first thing from the airport gift shop?"

"What *do* you want?" Paolo asked, with genuine interest.

"From Paris? I want a silk tie that will go with my blue suit. You know I do not have a tie that looks good with it. I *like* silk ties. I also like the dark chocolate, Danish modern desk accessories, those socks with the diamond pattern, anything with coconut in it, and pictures of dogs who look like their owners." As an aside, to me, he explained, "In New York people get the dogs that look just like them. Do you think they do this on purpose?"

When Vincenzo brought something home for Paolo, it was always personal: a leaf he found that had turned the exact shade of burnt orange that was Paolo's favorite color, or a snapshot of a street scene that Paolo would find hilarious, or a pound of ridiculously expensive coffee that Paolo really wanted to try but refused to spend the money on. "My little offerings are always about you," he explained, "but yours are about nothing at all. They are about our house."

Being loving means knowing all of your partner's identities, embracing all of them, and appreciating them in ways that leave your partner feeling seen. It means that in this relationship every part of your partner's identity—all of the roles they play in their own life and in your coupledom, all of their likes and dislikes and preferences, what brings them joy or misery—is also a point of concern and thought for you. Remember earlier, when we talked about the loving gaze of the caregiver? When a child feels seen and loved for his whole self, beyond his flaws and strengths, eccentricities, vulnerabilities, and quirks, the result is a feeling of fulfillment. He is enough. That is what you want to bring to your coupledom.

The way that this manifests in everyday life and interactions is when you shine a light on these different roles and identities in various ways. It could be verbal (nicknames, compliments), visual (gifts, gestures), surprises that show them you know something about them that others don't necessarily, and so on. Buying gifts that highlighted Vincenzo's role as a house buddy who happens to do most of the cooking was interpreted by Vincenzo as an indication that Paolo only missed his home and the comfort of Vincenzo's cooking. Vincenzo wanted to be missed as a person, and specifically in his role as a lover and companion.

Here are some ideas for expressing love that thriving couples have shared with me:

- Seek the other person out even if you just give them a gentle kiss on the cheek and leave them to what they were doing.
- Send short texts to remind them of their importance in your life (and not just what is missing in the fridge).
- Send messages through channels that they don't expect, like a post-card through the mail (or anything other than the digital communication that most of us rely on today).
- Give a gift related to a hobby of theirs that you don't share (like Eileen's fishing reel for Fred) to show that you are interested in them as a person beyond the roles they serve in the coupledom.
- Do something you know will make their life easier.
- Put little notes for them in places that they don't expect.
- If you don't have anything to say, just sit beside your partner, look them in the eye, and touch them tenderly in a way you wouldn't touch another person.
- Create a loving language that you don't use for your kids, your pets, or other people in your life.

PAYING ATTENTION

Loving your partner in their entirety, and expressing that love in ways that are specific and meaningful to them, is what I mean by being loving. In order to do this, you have to know your partner very well. Loving with *intention* means paying *attention*. And you have to keep paying attention. This usually comes easily at the beginning of a relationship, and many people will say that they chose their partner because of their attentiveness. I have heard so many versions of this from my clients: "I had told him that I hate roses, and I really do, so when he bought me a dozen daisies on Valentine's Day, I knew he'd been paying attention." But over a period of time, and especially in long-term relationships, we often stop sharing and we stop asking. We operate based on our own assumptions. My client

Oscar told me that his wife has never bought broccoli in eleven years of marriage because when they were dating he told her that he didn't like broccoli. "I like it now, I've liked it for years, but it's like there's no more room in her brain for new information about me."

Being loving means maintaining curiosity and interest in the other as a person in their own right, separate from you. (To clarify, when I say "curiosity" I mean that you try to maintain an attitude of "not knowing" in regard to your partner: You let go of all your assumptions and preconceived ideas about who they have been and try to see them as who they are in the present moment. When I say "interest" I mean that you include everything you know about your partner, and you use that knowledge to pose meaningful questions.)

We spoke earlier about how romantic love is an illusion, an act of the imagination where we overvalue certain qualities in the partner, undervalue others, and in doing so we create a version of our partner that may or may not reflect reality. In the book *Can Love Last?* psychologist Stephen A. Mitchell makes the intriguing argument that security is also an illusion, "the sense of safety is not a given but a construction, the familiarity not based on deep mutual knowledge but on collusive contrivance."[7] We don't know our partners as well as we think we do. Even if we do, tomorrow will be a new day. Instead, for the sake of stability, we see only as much as we can tolerate. "We strive to fix the fluidity and multiplicity of the other into a predictable pattern."[8] Modern life is overwhelming enough; we don't want any surprises. Oscar doesn't like broccoli; no need to look there again.

The problem with assuming that we know everything there is to know about our partners is that we stop paying attention to their growth, their development, and the way their dreams and goals and expectations change over time. We stop trying to uncover their mysteries. And when we lose interest in our partner, there's a good chance that they will lose interest in us. We stop seeing them, they stop seeing us, and we both feel empty inside. Unfulfilled. When couples come to me complaining that they feel invisible to each other, it is often because the partners don't feel seen and loved. As Fromm explains, "If there were more depth in the experience of the other person, if one could experience the infiniteness of his personality, the other person would never be so familiar—and the miracle of overcoming the barriers might occur every day anew. But for most people their own person, as well as others, is soon explored and soon exhausted."[9]

This is why our manifestation of loving acts has to be specific, and not only in terms of the other's role as partner, husband, or wife, but in terms of all the roles they play, all that we value and they value.

COUPLE'S TOOLKIT: GETTING THE LOVE YOU WANT

Take a moment to review your love blueprint from page 216 and reflect on how and what you learned about love in your childhood and also later in your adolescent and adult relationships. How do you define tenderness, affection, and being loving? Now, ask yourself the following questions:

- How would you like your partner to express love for these various parts of yourself and the roles you play?
- Do they already express their love to you in any of those ways? When they do, or have done so in the past, how did you receive it? How did it make you feel? How do they know you appreciate them?
- How could they acknowledge, appreciate, celebrate, and reward each part of you in a way that is different from how they show you they trust you, care for you, cater to you, respect you? Are there overlaps?
- How are these different from what you give and receive in your other relational spaces (as a parent, friend, etc.)?

As you go through different stages in your relationship, it is important to stay connected to how you and your partner are both changing and evolving. You need to know and appreciate who she is today—what she is proud of, what brings her joy, what makes her feel loved and special to you in a way that no one else does.

We may be in relationships that satisfy our sexual needs, our need to be cared for, or our needs in terms of managing the everyday tasks and functionality of our lives. But if a relationship is going to be fulfilling we have to go much deeper than that. Radical acceptance of our partner doesn't mean it's okay for him to hog the remote control or chew with his mouth open. It means we get to know his multiple identities in ways that other people don't or won't. This is a privilege that we only honor within our committed coupledom. Remember the Venn diagrams from chapter 2 that describe different models of love in terms of the areas of overlap between two circles? And remember how Emergent Love has three circles, one for each partner and one for the relational space between them? This is where $1 + 1 = 3$. Being loving creates a conducive environment for love to emerge.

PART III

FROM LITERACY TO FLUENCY

CHAPTER 10

Navigating Conflict

The real art of conversation is not only to say the right thing in the right place, but, far more difficult still, to leave unsaid the wrong thing at the tempting moment.

—Lady Dorothy Nevill, *Under Five Reigns*[1]

Thank you for making it this far with me. It is my hope that you've learned a lot about yourself as you were reading, and also developed some literacy about how you show up in your relational spaces. Now that you're familiar with the building blocks of Emergent Love—attraction, respect, trust, compassion, shared vision, and loving behaviors—part three is about bringing everything together to develop fluency. It's like learning partnered dancing; first you learn the steps (literacy), and then you practice on the floor (fluency). But if you become preoccupied with your steps, stay in your head, and try to do everything perfectly, you will hinder the flow and step on each other's toes a lot! You need to practice them enough that they become second nature—like a muscle memory, your fluency and competence improve with repetition. In this section we'll look at how all these ingredients work in unison to sustain and nurture a relationship that has the potential for love to emerge.

For the remainder of our time together I want to do two things. First, we'll do some troubleshooting around two domains of coupledom where partners frequently become misaligned: conflict and sex. The chapters Navigating Conflict and Sexual Harmony will explain how to cultivate fluency in these areas using the ingredients of Emergent Love. The second thing I'd like to do is to leave you with a toolbox of techniques for checking in with your partner to make sure that your vision is in sync, you're clear about what's expected of you, and you connect in small and large ways every day, week, month, and year. Conflict, Sexual Harmony, and Check-ins are arenas in our coupledom that help us maintain the respective ingredients and are also a natural by-product of their health. It's a virtuous cycle.

Part of maintaining equilibrium as a couple is being able to move fluidly between and among your roles as partners, friends, confidants, co-parents, housemates, lovers, and any other roles you play in your relational space. You share your resources of time, energy, attention, and money in a way that feels equitable, though it might not always be completely equal (a lot of the time it is not). Sometimes one person needs a little bit more of something, and the partner gives generously because they know that they are investing in their shared interest (the relationship) and also they trust that when the roles shift, the same will be done by the other person. The important thing is to keep the balance, however you define it within your own coupledom.

Does this seem too good to be doable? I assure you it is not. At the same time, it doesn't happen overnight. Emergent Love is all about what you build with another person, and building anything takes time and skill. Remember the story of three little pigs? We are building a coupledom on a solid foundation, with building blocks instead of straw and sticks! The good news is that you are not at the mercy of the other person. There is a lot that you control and contribute from your own side to design the love you desire. Each of you has to be intentional about what you bring to your relational space, and for that you need insight into your own patterns of relating.

HAPPY COUPLES *DO* ARGUE

One of the great misbeliefs embedded in submergent love is that thriving couples never get into arguments. It's also one of the most damaging. People who see conflict as a sign that their relationship is in trouble will tend to avoid it at all costs. If your goal is to be totally enmeshed with your partner, it *would* be threatening to have conflict, because conflict means that there's friction and space between you. But if you avoid conflict by never addressing the behaviors that cause you discomfort, your partner is destined to repeat those behaviors over and over again, much to the detriment of your relationship. I am not talking about calling out every little discomfort, but when something keeps repeating itself, it's worth addressing. Having said that, there is a way to do it that is constructive and not destructive.

There is a concept in physics called "material fatigue." It goes like this: If you tap a quarter against a wineglass, nothing will happen. Usually. If you do it again, still, nothing will happen. But if you do it enough times, eventually that glass is going to break. With every tap, you create a tiny fracture in the structure of the glass, which ultimately causes it to become fallible and break. The same is true for your relationship. One little tap is hardly enough to cause any damage, but if you repeat it enough times it will end in a rupture that will be difficult to repair. When people refer to "the straw that broke the camel's back" this is what they're talking about. You can only take so much. That's one reason we talked about sensitivities, quirks, and pet peeves and why it's so important to clarify boundaries, and to address problems in as timely a manner (not necessarily as quickly) as possible, even if it's awkward or uncomfortable.

Knowing how to express anger, hurt, disappointment, or disagreement in a way that leads to resolution is a skill. Like all skills, it takes practice. Avoiding conflict makes conflict inevitable, and usually makes it bigger than it has to be. If you *never* argue, then when disagreements do arise, you won't know how to best show up. This is not to say that couples who argue *all the time* are necessarily experts, however. If you cannot maintain a reasonably calm presence in the moment of conflict, or if you continue escalating when you know the conversation has derailed, you're probably not going to walk away satisfied. People get triggered; they explode, or they shut down; they say things they will later regret; or they avoid the subject by avoiding the partner. Often, once tempers have cooled, the couple covertly or overtly agree to act as if it never happened. There may be apologies, but rarely the kinds of conversations that lead to resolution and repair. Instead, the issue gets shelved for another day, another fight, another round in the boxing ring.

It's important to underscore something: All couples have conflict. *All.* It is a sign that you have healthy boundaries and are not fusing or merging (or submerging). It shows that you are not indifferent, and you care about the quality of your coupledom. You are individual people with your own opinions, preferences, and ideas that sometimes differ from those of your partner. That is a good thing. When you become skilled at managing conflict you will be able to build resiliency, deepen your connection by learning something more about each other, and unlock your own potential and the potential of your romantic relationship and beyond.

UNDERSTANDING YOUR CONFLICT STYLE

We all have our own ideas about the best way to handle conflict in relationships, and a unique style for dealing with problems in general. For example, some people dive right in and may even enjoy a stimulating argument. Others have a hard time tolerating any signs of lack of harmony and tend to withdraw from arguments in an effort to keep the peace. The way you deal with each particular conflict will depend on many different variables.

A lot of my clients find it helpful to think of conflict as having two distinct dimensions.

There is the *conscious* or *cognitive dimension*, which has to do with the roles you play, sociocultural expectations of the self and the partner, and feelings of equity in the relationship. The cognitive dimension is usually about differences in what each partner perceives as equitable and fair. The ideal purpose here is to resolve the conflict and create a deeper connection; the less-than-ideal purpose is to "win" the argument by defeating the other (which could feel good in the moment but won't benefit you in the long run). The other dimension is *physical,* and includes everything that happens to and in our bodies during an argument. This has to do with how we respond to perceived danger physiologically. When our boundaries are crossed, whether intentionally or not, our bodies become alerted to the need to respond. The purpose here is to preserve survival and safety.

In part two we talked about the fight-or-flight response, which is how we describe typical reactions to perceived danger. You may remember that in fight mode you become aggressive and, in a way, mobilized—eager to engage and defend yourself or others. If your instinct is to look for the exit door and get away from the threat as quickly as possible, because in that moment you feel like you can't fight, or the threat is too dangerous to engage with, then flight might seem to be the better option. But what about when your body is unable to either fight or flee? In those times, you may freeze instead and respond to the threat by becoming very quiet and still. And sometimes the situation calls for de-escalating the threat by accommodating or becoming agreeable to appease the other's distress and ensure your own survival. Most people identify strongly with one of these responses (fight, flight, freeze, fawn)[2] but will react differently depending on the context. You might try to appease an employer or a police officer, for example, but you freeze when your partner raises their voice.

How you respond to a perceived threat has a big influence on how you deal with disagreements in your relationships. Of course, there are two of you, and you each have your independent nervous system responses to the given situation. How your responses intersect will have an impact on how you disagree. Often the cognitive aspect of the conflict—the actual subject under discussion—is eclipsed by the emotional and physical reactivity of the partners.

There are three main conflict management styles as I see them. Different people might label them in different ways, but I like to think of them as Net and Sword, Stallions, and Turtles. Net and Sword style describes the dynamic when one person needs closure and resolution while the other person needs space. One person casts their net to catch the partner and bring them close, while the other pulls out a sword to tear the net and get away. Think of it as one person in fight mode and the other in flight mode. The Net fears abandonment and feels an urgent need for resolution, closure, and connection—even if they have to scream and yell to get it. The Net might cry, block the other person from leaving the space, or use provoking words to have the partner stay: "You are not a man, you are a coward. You're a horrible person." The Sword feels an equally urgent need to get away from the partner, and fears being over-whelmed and smothered by what feels like unrelenting pursuit. Swords sometimes say very hurtful things as well and even throw down ultima-tums because they long to set themselves free in that moment in time: "What do you want from me? I can't do this anymore. Maybe we should get a divorce."

Stallion style is when both partners are in fight mode and go head-to-head until they're exhausted, then start all over again. Stallions are likely to dig in their (respective) heels and keep at it for as long as they can. Their positions often become so deeply entrenched that they lose sight of the subject of the argument and instead focus on not back-ing down or giving an inch. Compassion is noticeably absent, and respect could be, too. These arguments tend to be recurring, because partners are unable to regulate themselves enough to sit down, negotiate, and compro-mise. It's all about who has the last word and about winning.

The Turtle style is where both partners withdraw. They dislike con-flict equally. Partners often have difficulty setting clear boundaries for themselves, and when their boundaries are crossed, they have a hard time expressing that to each other (or even admitting it to themselves). The result is that injuries and breaches of trust are not repaired, and the behavior that caused the injury continues to exist. In this way, withdraw-ing to protect the self or the other ends up creating fissures between the partners that can quickly grow into chasms. Partners with these styles are often full of resentment, numb, or somewhere in between.

My clients Allie and Karen were a classic example of turtles. They were very careful not to say anything that would create tension and proudly proclaimed, "We don't argue!" When they did have a disagreement, they preferred to move past it quickly by pretending it never happened. This style worked for them for quite a while. What brought them to me was that they needed a third party to be able to discuss whether or not they wanted to start a family. Karen really wanted a child but thought, based on Allie's previous comments, that Allie didn't want to become a parent. As soon as they started to discuss the subject, they both felt uncomfortable, so they would divert by making a joke or postponing the conversation, so they didn't risk a possible disagreement. Karen revealed that she was holding back but simmering inside while Allie found herself walking on eggshells, knowing that something was wrong but not wanting to "break the dam."

You and your partner might identify with one of these conflict styles, or you might not. Each of us is unique, and the specific way you respond to a perceived threat is influenced by your culture, the messages you heard as a child, what you saw modeled by the adults in your life, and your own personal experiences with conflict, resolution, and repair throughout your life. Some of my clients tell me that they never saw their parents argue. Instead, the adults would have heated discussions behind closed doors so they could present a unified front to the children. Other couples, the majority, saw frequent arguments, sometimes very loud and hurtful, but they never saw or heard an apology or an attempt to repair. My client Jennifer, who is a self-identified "bully," told me that any time her parents had loud exchanges, her father would escape to another room, even as her mother continued to yell insults at him. Later they would all come together over the next meal as if nothing had happened. She adapted the same pattern, first toward her father and later her partners. It took Jennifer years to realize that not everyone is willing to take the bullets like her father did.

While there are people out there who grew up in households where conflict was managed with respect, in truth, I don't see a lot of them in my office. Adults who model constructive conflict to their children remain respectful even when expressing anger, they listen to what the other person has to say, they take accountability for their own role in the conflict, and they make a conscious effort to repair any harm they might have caused.

Knowing your personal style will help you to ask for what you need, whether it is space, more closeness, or more passion and engagement. Together you can strategize the best way to manage conflict to meet both your own and your partner's needs. Below is a self-literacy exercise to help you start thinking about your own conflict style.

BUILDING BLOCK: YOUR CONFLICT BLUEPRINT

- How was disagreement expressed in your household growing up? Did you ever see adults argue, or was it done behind closed doors?
- Was anger considered a dangerous emotion or something healthy that needed to be channeled appropriately? Was everyone allowed to express anger, or was that reserved for specific people like adults, women, or men?
- When people argued, were you afraid? Did they call each other hurtful names, or say cruel things? Did someone leave the house? Did they say these things to you or about you?
- When arguments erupted, were they later resolved and repaired or were they never spoken about again? Did your parents apologize to you or to each other when they said or did hurtful things?
- As a child, were you ever labeled as out of control, rageful, angry, mad, crazy, loud, or overly sensitive? Was someone else called these things?
- Were you allowed space when you needed to settle your emotions? Were you given too much space or sent to time-out when you needed to connect and process with another person around?
- Did you feel safe to feel your emotions including anger?
- Were you taught to take responsibility for your own contribution to a conflict, and did you see adults do the same? What did that look like?

In addition to thinking about your blueprint, I want you to take a moment and reflect on what you learned about emotions like anger, disappointment, and other feelings that might have been perceived as negative growing up. Do you bottle them up and then explode? Or do you bottle them up and then implode? For some people, getting it all off your chest by expressing your anger immediately and completely is a good strategy (as long as you do it in a way that preserves the dignity of the other person, and you make sure to offer and accept repairs afterward). Others need to step away and regroup; you're more comfortable expressing your anger when you are no longer actively feeling it. Some people need to stay in the conversation until it is resolved, they feel heard, apologies are given and/or received, and their bond is repaired. Others are more comfortable processing the aftermath in bits and pieces, taking breaks to reevaluate, and then coming together again to continue the process.

All of the above are viable strategies when it comes to engaging in conflict and processing it afterward. It is only when we fail to address the underlying conflict and fail to address the injuries caused to ourselves or to the other during moments of disagreement, that conflict becomes really problematic. We need to equally call out what bothers us and call in to invite a conversation and resolution.

CHANGING THE FRAMEWORK

When I talk about conflict in coupledom, I try to avoid the word "fight" as much as possible, because it automatically triggers black-and-white thinking. Fights have winners and losers, and who wants to be the loser? Practically no one. So we stand our ground, and we search for evidence to prove that we are right and they are wrong. When we fight, we are on opposite sides of an issue that may be more complex than either partner realizes. Philosophers call this a false dichotomy. When all options are reduced to two options, one right and one wrong, we effectively close the door on future dialogue and blind ourselves to any solution other than our own.

I prefer to think about episodes of conflict as arguments, tiffs, disagreements, or differences of opinion. You can be in an argument and still be on the same side. Instead of being *Me versus You*, it becomes *Us versus The Problem*. But this perspective is only possible when you have a clear sense of healthy separateness so you don't get overwhelmed or sucked into the issue. This is Emergent Love: You stay separate enough to stand side-by-side so you can solve the conflict for the sake of the relationship. Let me give you an example.

Althea's mother, Ruth, who is ninety-six, is still living independently but she needs a lot of help. For many years Althea stopped by once or twice a week to take her mother to appointments, bring in groceries, and help with the cleaning. But since her mother fell, she's been stopping by every day, at least once, and often for several hours. Sometimes she spends the night. Althea feels constant pressure to please everyone, so she promises more than she can reasonably accomplish. Her husband, Liam, is frustrated because she keeps dropping the ball and he has to cover for her. By the time they come to see me, they are having daily "fights" about whether or not to transition Ruth to a nursing home. Liam insists that it is the only solution, and Althea absolutely refuses to consider it. They are highly polarized, and their positions are entrenched.

In our work together, we began to talk about Ruth's need for care as a situation that impacts both of them in different ways. It is especially challenging for them as a couple because their whole system has become unbalanced. Althea was able to talk about the deep sorrow she feels when she thinks about her mother's death, and her desire to spend every possible moment with her while she is still alive. She explained, "I might have considered a nursing home before COVID, but now it terrifies me. If my mother died, I would never forgive myself." When Althea was able to show Liam her grief, and not just her anger, he was able to tap into his compassion and see why this was so important to her. Liam admitted that part of why he wants Ruth in a nursing home is because the prospect of her death is a painful reminder of his own losses. "She's our last surviving parent. When she goes, we become the old people. I know, we're already old, but we're not the *oldest*. When Althea comes home and talks about how frail her mother is, I can't take it. My mother died of cancer when I was in my twenties, and I've hated hospitals ever since."

When we shift from being on opposite sides of an argument to being on the same side, we have the opportunity to deepen our connection and have conversations about what really matters to us without feeling like we have to one-up the other person to win the argument or get the outcome that we want. Eventually, Liam and Althea were able to work together to come up with some solutions. Liam, who is a great administrator, reached out to a lot of the people who had offered to help. He figured out what each person could contribute, then scheduled help with meals, shopping, and visiting. Ruth was very social, and being stuck in bed had been hard for her. She was thrilled to see her friends and family, and Althea got a much-needed break without feeling guilty about leaving Ruth alone. Althea hired a weekly cleaner, arranged for daily meal delivery beyond what family and friends offered, and started to research home health aides. She was still committed to keeping her mother in her home but accepted that she couldn't do everything herself. Liam realized that he could be a part of the solution and contribute his time and skills in a meaningful way that also respected his vulnerabilities around illness and death. Althea also joined a caregiver support group, which offered her a much-needed emotional support, so she didn't have to use Liam as her go-to person for that.

Many of my couples ask me, "But what if I have a problem that was caused by my partner? How can we make that *our* problem?" The principles discussed here (the process) still hold true. The nature (content) of the problem is only one part of the whole mix. Objective problem-solving, free from personal biases or emotions, leads to better outcomes. Part of making the shift to a new framework in which you're on the same side includes paying attention to how you show up during conflict. The devil is in the details! The way you deliver the message is just as important as the subject. If you want to have a productive conversation, rather than an explosive one, you need to pay attention to your affect (emotional expressions including body language), content (subject matter), and tone (tone and volume of voice). The easy way to remember this is with the acronym ACT. These are all areas that make a huge impact on what the outcome of your argument looks like, how you land on a solution for the problem at hand, and how you both walk away from it. In fact, when you have a positive affect you have access to more creative problem-solving.[3] A valid point, made in a mocking or otherwise disrespectful tone, is less likely to be heard and more likely to escalate the conflict.

In addition to your ACT, the way you approach a difficult conversation is another often-overlooked factor in navigating conflict successfully. For those of you who dislike conflict of any kind, initiating conversations in which you need to ask your partner to amend their behavior can feel daunting. Many of my clients who feel this way have found it helpful to frame these conversations in terms of elements that feed into their shared vision. I've developed a simple guideline for bringing up a sensitive topic in this way. I call it the Four A's.

COUPLE'S TOOLKIT: THE FOUR A'S

- *Assess* your energy and intention, and the context in which you are going to have the conversation. Also assess whether your partner can give you the attention you need for this topic at this particular moment in time.
- *Announce* the issue. Try to keep to the point, and be concise and precise in your language. This is your opportunity to focus the issue, state the facts as clearly and succinctly as you can, and clarify what exactly you want to discuss.
- *Acknowledge* that this might be hard or sensitive for you and your partner, and make sure to let them know why this matters for you and how this conversation is going to serve your relationship in general.
- *Ask* for what you want and what you think would help in similar situations in the future. It is very important to be clear about what you are asking your partner to do. You don't want to be vague or leave them to their own devices to figure it out all on their own. Remember that assumptions create room for misalignments. Invite them to be a part of the solution.

When you are able to look at the conflict as objectively as possible, take responsibility for your own contributions, and ask for the specific actions that will help you to resolve the issue, your partner is more likely to feel respected and less likely to become defensive. They might not agree with you immediately or fully, but it's a good way to start the conversation and open the doors for collaborative negotiations.

Let's try another example. Luisa was surprised when she saw that her girlfriend, Iliana, had joined an expensive gym and used their joint credit card to set up monthly payments. She was angry, but she also knew that Iliana was having a hard time with her weight and was feeling desperate to do something about it. Luisa started by telling Iliana that she had something on her mind and she wanted to talk about it, and they agreed to sit together after the kids were in bed. When the time came, Luisa put her hand on Iliana's knee (a gesture of connection) and said, "I know you've been wanting to join a gym, and I really want to support you. The gym you chose is great, but it is also really expensive, and I was surprised when I saw the credit card charges. I know working out is a sensitive subject for you, just like money is a sensitive subject for me, and I really want to work this out so we both feel okay with it. We each agreed to put our individual expenses on our own cards. Since this is something that's just for you, and not part of our household expenses, I'd like you to use your own credit card. And, in the future, let's check with each other before we make purchases on the joint card that are for anything besides household expenses or beyond a certain limit. How does that sound?"

The way we approach our partner for these kinds of conversations has a direct impact on the success of the outcome. In his book *The Seven Principles for Making Marriage Work*, Dr. John Gottman talks about something he observed among real-life couples interacting in his Love Lab: The majority of times the course of a conversation is well defined before it even begins.[4] If Iliana had been working in her home office and Luisa barged in with the credit card bill clenched in her hand and shouted, "When did you decide to join a gym, and why didn't you tell me you were going to put it on our credit card! You are so irresponsible!" the conversation would most likely have escalated into an argument. By taking the time to assess the situation, Luisa had a much better outcome and was able to use the conflict to initiate a renegotiation of their shared vision going forward. This is what I call relational diplomacy: paying attention to the subtleties.

There is a lot of talk these days about authenticity. The meaning of the word is somewhat evasive but seems to include ideas about being true to yourself and your ideals, and bringing that true self into all of your relationships. Yet, in my experience, the idea is often misunderstood and misused. I see so many partners try to hide hurtful behaviors behind a screen of authenticity when they say things like, "I'm brutally honest," or "I always tell it like it is." The idea here seems to be that if you don't express your anger loudly and immediately you are being inauthentic or, worse, a pushover. Yes, relationships require honesty and authenticity, but they also require diplomacy and tact. You heard me right, my dear reader. You need diplomacy. Think of it as an outcome-based communication practice. Before you offer an "authentic" opinion, ask yourself, "What is my intention here? Would I achieve my goal by bringing this up now?" (Getting it off your chest, maybe, but being heard and creating a change in behavior, maybe not!)

The simple tools I have presented here can have a powerful impact on how, and how often, you and your partner disagree. Reframing the conflict from *Me versus You* to *Us versus The Problem* will help set you up for resolution rather than a competition that ends in winners and losers. Developing self-awareness around *how* you deliver a message (affect and tone) as well as the content of the message, calls upon the ingredients of respect and compassion, builds trust, and helps prevent unnecessary escalations. And thinking about a problem before you bring it to your partner, and choosing the best possible approach (Four A's), is much more likely to lead to a satisfying outcome for both of you.

You'll notice that all three of these interventions focus on resolving the cognitive dimension of the conflict while minimizing the physiological dimension. But what happens when it isn't possible to assess the situation? Sometimes conflict comes on suddenly. One minute you're having breakfast together, the next your voice is raised, your heart is racing, and you're primed to fight (or flee, freeze, or appease, depending on your situation). Let's turn our attention now to strategies for dealing with the physiological dimension of conflict.

GETTING FROM CLASHES TO CONVERSATIONS

The amount of time it takes for your brain to receive a message from the environment and respond to it is often very short. When the information coming in has to do with your sense of safety, the response can seem instantaneous. Learning how to slow down and make the best use of that short synapse of time will help you to *choose your response* rather than react instinctively. Awareness of your sensitivities comes in handy here.

The first step is simply to bring awareness to what is happening inside your body. In chapter 5 we talked about using your felt sense to identify and clarify your boundaries. Knowing when you're annoyed, uncomfortable, hurt, triggered, or offended is enormously helpful in real-time situations in which conflict has the potential to escalate. Our brain chemistry is altered by sudden, strong emotions, and critical thinking shuts down. You might also want to consider your context. If you just got off the phone with a nagging parent, had a difficult day with your child, or are still shaken up from being cut off on the highway, you're more likely to react negatively to any external stimulus, even if it is neutral.

If you aren't in a good space, you might want to pause the conversation for a moment, or for several moments, so you can down-regulate your emotions. Sometimes, for some people, anger has a mobilizing effect and helps them to think clearly and articulate more clearly. More often, though, it gets in the way of productive conversations and can leave a person feeling overwhelmed. I use the term "flooded" to refer to strong emotional states that overwhelm a person's ability to cope and can interfere with their capacity to think logically, or even to think at all. Usually, when emotions take over like this, it isn't just one feeling, either. A perception of threat can leave a person feeling angry, terrified, bereft, insulted, hopeless, and devastated all at once. As we discussed in the chapter on compassion, this is a good time to do yourself and your partner a favor and call a time-out. This is a great tactic, since we need to give our nervous system time to calm down from a place of activation. Later you can come back together and address whatever the issue was in a calm state when your cognitive mind is actually present, not when your system is still activated and will do anything to preserve survival and safety.

EMOTIONAL STRESS

Stress can be caused by a pleasant or unpleasant event. It is the arousal and activation of the nervous system. The meaning we attach to it determines how we perceive it and whether we look at it as an enhancer or an inhibitor in any given context. When cortisol levels rise in the bloodstream, the brain's sensory receptors trigger a "shutting off" response known as the negative feedback loop. This mechanism helps the body return to homeostasis, its stable and balanced condition. The time it takes for the body to calm down after an argument varies among individuals, influenced by factors like the argument's intensity, individual stress levels, and coping mechanisms. Physiological responses, such as increased heart rate and elevated cortisol levels, typically begin to subside within minutes after the argument ends. However, the emotional and psychological impact may persist for hours or even days, varying from person to person. Engaging in stress-reducing activities like deep breathing, meditation, or exercise can help expedite the calming process and promote emotional well-being post-argument. Engaging in physical exercises like walking or running, if feasible based on individual physical abilities and context, prompts the release of neurotransmitters that aid in stress reduction. Additionally, rhythmic movements, such as jumping or stomping in sync with mood-matching music, activate sensory receptors in the brain, leading to a calming effect. Moreover, relaxation techniques such as deep breathing, listening to soothing music, practicing guided meditation, or playing with soft objects can further assist in calming the body's physiological responses to stress. Some people also find it calming to receive a hug from their partner, their child, or their pet. These strategies contribute to the regulation of cortisol levels and facilitate the return to a balanced state of well-being. Anything that works to make you feel like you have gone through what you needed to and are back to being grounded and safely landed in your body is good. Emily and Amelia Nagoski's book *Burnout: The Secret to Unlocking the Stress Cycle* is a wonderful resource if you want to learn about this in more depth, or you can check out www.lovebydesignbook.com for additional resources.

There is a caveat here: Before you leave the conversation, you *must* explain to your partner that you need to take a break to cool down and give them an estimate of the amount of time you think you'll need. Respect comes into play here, too. Storming out, hanging up, slamming doors, or giving your partner the silent treatment is not the same thing as taking a time-out. It is disrespectful and damages trust. If your partner is the one who asks for a time-out to calm down, be respectful and honor their request. Following your partner from room to room to continue the conversation, or sending a thousand texts, or bringing the subject up again after three minutes won't be helpful or productive. Another addition here: If you are staying in the room physically but your body language says otherwise, please be aware of it and properly ask for space.

If your partner is the one who is flooded with emotion, this is a good time to call upon some of your compassion. Taking a compassionate stance means you step back from your own experience in that moment and lean in toward your partner. Focus on their experience, use your engaged listening skills, and give your partner the gift of your undivided attention. If you can let go of your own defensiveness and find even one tiny thing in what they're saying that you can agree with, even if it's just "You're right, it must have hurt" or "I could be a bit insensitive sometimes," the effect can be astonishing. We talk about going from zero to a hundred miles per hour in an instant. This tactic has the reverse effect. It's like slamming the brakes on their anger. When you agree with your partner, especially when they're really angry with you, it can empty their ammunition box in an instant. Of course, sometimes this doesn't happen. If they're really wound up and have been building their case against you all day, it might be too sudden for them to accept. You might want to acknowledge their anger and suggest a time-out so you can have a more productive conversation. Rage is often a mask for pain. When you show them that you aren't defensive, they can put down their weapons and give their pain a chance to show itself, which gives you a chance to practice loving behavior and participate in healing.

It's helpful to think of the time-out as a pause in the conversation, not an end. It's important to return at the appointed time. You don't necessarily need to finish the conversation, but you do need to re-engage and not leave the other person hanging. Let your partner know if you need more time to organize your thoughts, or if you'd rather finish the discussion at a specific future time under better conditions.

Most of you probably have a good idea of what it means to "fight fair," and taking a time-out is definitely a step in the right direction. For those who don't know what respectful conflict looks like, a quick internet search will yield thousands of results. Below is my own version, which I share with my clients. I call it "Rules of Row." Throughout our journey together, I've talked about interpersonal dynamics and how it is important to put emphasis on the reciprocal nature of all the ingredients that we have discussed. The idea here is to make sure that if you fall off the track, you can make your way back to it and keep building and rebuilding together. We often hear that you should avoid insulting your partner or hitting below the belt, so to speak, but there isn't much guidance around how *not* to do this, especially when emotions are high. Rules of Row is another tool in this chapter to help you avoid some of the most common behaviors that lead to clashes and more significant ruptures in your trust and respect. I offer it to all my couples as a way to explore recurrent issues in their ability to deal with conflict in their own relationship. I hope you find it helpful as well.

COUPLE'S TOOLKIT: RULES OF ROW

1. **Stay away from generalizations**. Stay away from hyperbole, generalizations, and absolute words like "never" and "always." When you make a global assessment of your partner's character, rather than addressing their behavior in the moment, they are more likely to feel insulted and become defensive.

2. **Stick with the problem at hand**. Don't link the incident to anything bigger or drag up evidence from the past to support your

position in the present. Don't wash all the dirty dishes at once. When you begin to reach into the past for evidence to build a case against your partner, you significantly decrease the chances that the current conflict will be resolved.

3. **Use "I" statements rather than "you" statements.** Own your feelings in the moment, and take responsibility for them rather than blaming your partner. Saying, "I'm so angry right now!" rather than "You make me so angry!" will help prevent escalation.

4. **No personal attacks**. Stay away from attacks on personal characteristics, extended family, professional status, or anything the other person associates with their identity that is not easily changed (national origin, ethnicity, family of origin, physical appearance, religion, income, education, and gender are a few).

5. **Avoid making ultimatums**. Refrain from threatening the worst just because you want to see a reaction or emphasize your distress. When you say, "I'm out of here" or "Maybe we should just get a divorce," you take the focus off the subject at hand, you introduce danger and uncertainty, and you effectively stop the conversation.

6. **Regulate, regulate, regulate**. Try to remain as calm as possible. If you are not able to do so, take a break.

7. **Ask for a break**. If you need to take a break, make sure you communicate that clearly to your partner by saying, "I am going to need to recharge and cool off a bit, let's check in again in twenty minutes." Do not simply storm out of the room or out of the house. Don't ask for space (pushing the other away), ask for a break to settle and recharge. Language has power.

8. **Watch for your affect, content, and tone.** Sneering, mocking, name-calling, or other disrespectful behaviors lead to escalation and away from resolution.

9. **Regulate your volume**. The moment you raise your voice, the other person will notice and react either by shutting down or by raising their own voice. This, too, will escalate the conflict.

10. **No hitting.** Check yourself for signs of physical aggression. This is important, and it is often overlooked. Physical aggression includes pounding the table, driving dangerously, punching the wall, or throwing anything (even if you are not aiming at your partner). It also includes invading your partner's personal space by towering over them, standing too close, or ignoring their request for a time-out. This can be especially important if one of you is significantly

larger or stronger than the other or has physical abilities that the other doesn't.

11. **If you hear a "but," pause. If you hear yourself say "but," pause.** Most likely it is not a good idea to go on with the conversation or argument. It means you have noticed that there is ground for escalation and you're choosing to ignore it. For example, "I know you are tired, but let's finish talking about the wedding and getting back to the planner," or "I know you had a long day and this is the last thing you want to talk about, but let's get it over with."

It can be helpful to review this list with your partner during a time that you are not in conflict. In the spirit of being accountable, always begin by acknowledging which of these is especially hard for you, rather than pointing out your partner's shortcomings. Ask for their feedback. Then invite your partner to do the same.

EMBRACE IMPERFECT RESOLUTION

People are often surprised when I say that not every disagreement has to end in seamless resolution. It doesn't even have to be discussed at length—or sometimes at all. This might raise an eyebrow for many of you reading this book, because the common belief (in our low-context social structure) is that we need to talk about everything. But talking isn't always the best option, and sometimes it's not even a good option. And this is coming from someone who talks with and listens to people professionally! Partners who spend a great deal of time processing things together can end up dreading being around each other because their conversations are frequently heavy and serious and cognitively engaging. They talk so much about their relationship and what could be improved that they forget to be in it, and often overlook the importance of cultivating joy. I am afraid many people in my profession fall into this trap in their own relationships. I have heard quite a few times, "It feels like we're in a podcast interview talking about someone else's relationship rather than ours."

Deep conversations can be exhausting, and there is no rule that says you have to keep at it until a decision is reached. Also, any topic of importance is bound to keep coming up again and again, so it is not like you resolve something and put it behind you and it will never show up again in some other shape or form. At the same time, our research data clearly indicates that thriving couples keep all channels of communication open (verbally and otherwise). Again, balance is the key here. You want to address serious issues in a timely manner without insisting on analyzing them at length until you are both exhausted. Many years ago my mother taught me a method to quickly decide if something is worth my emotional resources or not: In any given moment when you are upset, think about whether what is so upsetting to you is going to matter in five minutes, five hours, or five years. (This was years before Suzy Welch published her book *10-10-10: A Life-Transforming Idea*, which uses a similar strategy for decision-making.[5]) Your answer will give you some perspective by locating the current issue in the bigger picture of your vision for your life and your relationship.

For those of you who are looking for that happy medium between never talking and always talking, I recommend the Couple's Jar exercise. This is a tool I developed to help couples fine-tune the habit of open and timely communication.

COUPLE'S TOOLKIT: THE COUPLE'S JAR

Get a jar, and put it where both of you can see it. When you identify a topic that you want to discuss but you don't have the bandwidth or the context to have a productive conversation, write it on a piece of paper and put it in the jar. Be brief. Think "index card" rather than "essay."

Once a week (or more or less frequently as needed), depending on what your physical abilities and circumstances allow, either go for a walk or pick a time to sit together uninterrupted and go over the items in the jar. Be precise and stick to the point.

If the conversation lasts more than an hour, check in with each other to make sure you both have the energy and bandwidth to continue and agree over the time frame. Issues that are unresolved can either go back in the jar, or you can agree on a time to discuss them further.

Keep in mind that this is not a time to process things in your relationship in a general way. The goal of the Couple's Jar isn't to hash out old, unresolved issues, it's to create a space where you can address things as they come up. Maybe there is a quirk or an annoying habit your partner has that is beginning to turn into a pet peeve for you. Or it might be something more significant that could lead to a rupture in one of the fundamental dynamics like trust or respect. For example, if your partner has been promising things they can't deliver and you're beginning to lose trust in their reliability, write that down on a piece of paper and put it in the jar.

You might want to work through your feelings with a coach, therapist, or trusted friend, or write about it in your journal, or even just sit quietly and think about it, before the conversation. Go in with clarity about what is bothering you, why, and how you would like to move forward. The Four A's (assess, announce, acknowledge, and ask) are a good tool to have in your mind as you are organizing your thoughts for your conversation. If the conversation gets heated or derailed, just put it back in the jar for a few days. This way each of you has a chance to get some distance, process all the information, evaluate what your partner has said, and get creative about possible solutions.

You can also include things that are not potentially difficult or awkward, but are just things you haven't had a chance to discuss, like your next vacation or making holiday plans. Seeing the paper in the jar will help you not to dwell on it or carry it in your mind out of fear that you might forget about it later. You also avoid feeling like you're constantly asking to talk about something (or being asked by your partner) when the timing is inconvenient.

Many of the issues couples face require more than one conversation. Embracing imperfect resolution means that you avoid trying to force a solution and instead keep the lines of communication open even when a definitive solution hasn't been reached, unless there is a timeline that you need to resolve something by. Disagreements about significant life events are common—things like when and whether to have a child, leave a job, move to a new house, or assume caregiving responsibilities for an elderly parent. All of these will require ongoing negotiations as you fine-tune your shared vision going forward. Disagreements can (and probably will) arise, and sometimes they can get heated. When this happens, repairs might have to be made. Let's turn our attention now to that.

REPAIRING AND RECONNECTING

Making an intentional effort to come together and repair after a disagreement is crucial, yet it is often overlooked. We are so eager to move past the disconnection that we rush to return to a state of normalcy without giving ourselves enough time to restore our connection. This repair must happen cognitively and also at a more physical and primal level. Long-term couples regularly go through cycles of feeling connected and disconnected, and it's not always due to conflict. Sometimes it's just a matter of busy schedules, competing demands, long-term projects that absorb our attention, the care needs of children or other dependents, illness—you get the idea. Disconnection always requires reconnection, which is why I place such emphasis on being intentional in your coupledom. Reconnection and repair are especially important after conflict. I think of it as getting back on track after being on a dirt road for a while.

Before you can begin to repair your connection, take some time to check in with yourself, regulate your own emotional state, and make sure that you're ready to repair (and don't rush to re-engage!). Next you want to revisit what happened. If you want to do this verbally, you can use the A-ARM tool from chapter 6: *Acknowledge* what happened, *appreciate* the impact it had on you and on your partner, *reassure* each other that you are in this together, and offer a *mending* solution. Be sure to go through each step of this process, as it will help to restore your sense of connection and commitment.

Finally, take some time to repair the physical agitation and disconnection together. Again, conflict is both cognitive and physiological. When the resentments build up, and the little annoyances build up, you begin to feel physically alienated from your partner. In the heat of an argument, your body does not recognize their body as safe anymore. (Many times, when "sexless" couples come to see me, we discover that both are feeling a profound sense of what I call *body alienation*. It isn't just that they don't have sex, it's that they don't know how to be together physically even at a basic level.) This is why it's so important to repair the rupture physically, too. I'm not talking about makeup sex, though that could happen. I'm talking about reintroducing your nervous systems to each other incrementally.

To do this, I recommend that you sit side-by-side or back-to-back, and breathe. Hold hands, lie down next to each other, maintain eye contact for several minutes (it is okay to giggle or cry), or listen to each other's heartbeat. Again, whatever works to remind you that your body is safe with their body. Talking isn't necessary, and it might be counterproductive. Sometimes the body is the best pathway for connection.

I encourage you to practice this process of repair after any conflict, no matter how small. Even when you have agreed to postpone the conversation, repairing the rupture will make any future conversations easier. It builds trust by reinforcing the idea that conflict doesn't mean uncontrollable outbursts or the end of your coupledom. It will also leave both partners feeling seen and respected, which helps you establish a safe space to bring up a potential conflict in the future.

One final piece of advice? Once in a while, in a calm moment, go over something that you did not resolve well. A *do-over*, so to speak. Use the tools that you have learned here and see if you can apply them into that scenario and have a different outcome. This will create muscle memories for you so that you have a different default to go to in the moments of tension and when the emotional stakes are high.

There is an old Iranian saying about a couple's need for disagreement: We say, "Food has to have a little bit of salt and a little bit of pepper, otherwise it is tasteless!" Think of conflict as a sign of vitality in your relationship—it means you both care enough to engage with each other when times are hard. If you can keep the connectivity with your partner and move through conflict together, you are both more likely to walk away undisturbed, and even pleased, even if you still don't agree 100 percent. Managing conflict on this more sophisticated level requires leveraging the respect, trust, commitment, and compassion you have built up in your coupledom.

When respect is present and fully functioning, each partner knows and expresses their own boundaries and respects the boundaries of the other. If and when boundaries are crossed, the partners can address it in a way that is less likely to lead to escalation. We respect that our partner can handle their own part of the equation, so we don't need to protect them. Commitment shows up in conflict in much the same way: When we know what is expected of us, and we commit to a shared vision with our partner, if our behavior falls short there is a clear path for accountability and repair. Furthermore, commitment makes it easier to remind yourself that you are communicating with your partner, not a stranger, and that your communication is in service of your relationship.

Many people assume that conflict damages trust, but the reverse is actually true: Repair is possible only because there is a fundamental level of trust operating in the relationship. We trust that our partner will be mature enough to receive our opinion, that they are accountable, and that they will make the effort to repair if and when it is needed, and our partner trusts us to do the same. In fact, I would argue that a *lack* of conflict is more damaging to trust. A strong foundation in compassion—the ability to show up fully for our partner without taking on their feelings as our own—means that we can listen fully to their anger or their disappointment because we value them and want to learn about the nature of their pain to be a part of their solution. Conflict can sometimes injure the partner's sense of relational safety, but when we respond to conflict with compassion, we reinforce the sense of safety between us. As Dr. Harville Hendrix and Dr. Helen LaKelly Hunt, founders of Imago Therapy, put it, "every conflict could be an opportunity to get to the underlying emotional issues and patterns in a coupledom, and working through them in a healthy way leads to strengthening their overall relationship."[6]

CHAPTER 11

Sexual Harmony

I closed my mouth and spoke to you in a hundred silent ways.

—Rumi[1]

When you ask partners what distinguishes their committed couple-dom from other close relationships, the most common answer is "Sex." Of course, now that you know all about Emergent Love, you see the importance of expressing your partner's unique centrality through a variety of loving behaviors, but the physical connection you share with your partner matters. A lot. Sexuality, sensuality, and physical connection are commonly an important part of a couple's relationship.

The way you are together in your physical shared space is a manifestation of your overall relational space. When all the components of Emergent Love are functioning smoothly, this becomes a place of sanctuary where your physical connection has the potential to flourish, too. We can use our physical bond to express and receive so many different things. Sex can be passionate and intense, but it can also be playful and even silly sometimes, as well as warm and affectionate, slow and erotic, or quick and pragmatic. The point here is that sex doesn't play just one role in your coupledom; it plays many. What it means for each partner is highly subjective and influenced by circumstances. Sexual issues aren't always a reflection of other problems in the relationship; sometimes they are caused by organic problems like hormone levels, medical conditions, or physical and other conditions that are typical for the partners' age, health status, and stage of life.

We don't talk about it often, but our sexuality and sexual experiences naturally change in long-term relationships. We go through different phases in most areas of our lives and seem to accept them, so why not in sex? Our bodies change: We age, have a child, get in an accident, or find a newfound love for open-water swimming. Just as our physiologies change, so do our needs, wants, and desires. What we are attracted to in ourselves and our partners changes. Most importantly, the role and meaning of sex evolves for us over time. Submergent love emphasizes the central importance of sexual chemistry as the foundation for a lifetime of erotic satisfaction; in Emergent Love I would like to invite you to welcome sexual harmony instead.

When we tether ourselves only to our biology by overvaluing the idea of sexual chemistry, we limit ourselves to the fullness of what our lives—particularly our love lives—have the potential to be. Instead of relying on the primal reactivity of our brains to create and sustain "love," it's imperative that we move into something more empowering and something that we have more sense of agency over (like other elements of Emergent Love). In this view, our physical connection is a renewable resource that has the ability to be cultivated and calibrated over time. This is what I call "sexual harmony."

THE HALF-LIFE OF CHEMICALS

Zoey and John had been together for seven years and married for five when they came to my office seeking help. Their sexual connection had weakened over time to the point where they were both frustrated with the frequency and quality of their sex life. "When I first met Zoey it was like I couldn't get enough of her," John explained. "I wanted to be with her all the time; the sex was electric. She just had to walk into a room and I'd forget what I was doing. Now she could walk into a room naked and I probably wouldn't even notice her." Zoey added, "Yes! It's like I'm his pal in the locker room lately. To tell the truth, I don't even want him to look at me these days. I'm so tired by the time the kids are in bed that all I want to do is read a book and fall asleep. Sex is the last thing on my mind." Privately, both expressed concern that their diminished desire was an indication of a larger problem in the marriage. "I feel like she's avoiding me, like she doesn't want to be around me at all," John explained. Zoey admitted, "I love John but maybe I'm not *in love* with him? I don't know. I think what I'm really afraid of is that *he's* not in love with *me* anymore."

For more than twenty years I've sat in pain with couples who express distress over this apparent loss of desire. Usually (but not always!) the partners experienced intense feelings of sexual connection and desire early on in the relationship; they use words like *electric, amazing, hot, all-encompassing, intense,* and *mind-blowing* to describe early sexual encounters. They walked around in the heightened neurobiological state that we've come to know as the meeting of *sexual chemistries.*

When people talk about "seeing fireworks" they are not far off the mark. When the conditions are right, and the chemicals are all packed in the right amount, all you need is a match to set the night ablaze with a spectacular display of pyrotechnics. It's stunning, exciting, and awe-inspiring. The most obvious problem with relying on sexual chemistry as the foundation stone of erotic connection is that this state of bliss doesn't last forever. You may remember from earlier chapters that sexual infatuation lasts about two years on average—in evolutionary terms it lasts just long enough to make a baby and see it through the first year of life.[2] Relationships that make it past sexual infatuation generally shift from passion to attachment, a more practicable alternative. Still, when that intoxicating spell wears off, as it inevitably does, many couples feel adrift and unmoored.

Another significant problem that stems from relying on chemical reactions in the brain (that we do not and cannot control) to carry us through coupledom is that we never develop and hone the skills necessary to move away from performance (what sex *should be*) and closer to presence (what sex *is* in the dynamic of our coupledom) in order to get to a place where we can experience pleasure. Depending too much on the biological tide of these neurochemicals, our sexual repertoire becomes limited and narrow. We can recognize desire and arousal, *but we don't know how to create them.*

There are scores of books and articles out there that promise to help you *re-create* or *rekindle* your sex life. Most are written for couples like

Zoey and John: married, heterosexual, cisgender, monogamous couples who have experienced a waning of the intense sexual connection they once felt and want to get it back. You might find resources out there that could help you if that is your goal, but I want to have a different conversation. I want to talk about what it takes to build a mutually satisfying physical relationship that is intentional, intimate, and erotic, and not only sexual. I want to talk about the whole physical connection between two humans, whether they are male or female or non-binary, gay or straight or bisexual or pansexual, married or single or *monogamish*.

Some of you may be thinking, "How does this look if you don't happen to be anything like John and Zoey? If I can't relate to this heteronormative couple, will this still work?" Let me reassure you. I've used these same basic interventions with heterosexual religious conservative couples from Kabul to Los Angeles, queer couples in London, couples who practice non-monogamy, a Catholic couple in Cusco who've been married for forty-three years, and college sweethearts in New York who came to me for premarital advice, and many, many others besides.

Sexuality is funny this way: The way we think about sex might be infinitely variable, but the body behaves in predictable ways. The way you turn yourself on or off might be unique to you and your sexual blueprint, but the fact *that* you get aroused in the first place is part of your physiology. When we cultivate sexual harmony in our coupledom, we get to honor and celebrate the infinite variety of our own and our partner's sexuality, and at the same time we learn about the behaviors that will predictably lead to satisfying outcomes, however we define them.

But before we get into an in-depth conversation about sexual harmony, let's begin at the beginning and focus our attention on one of the essential elements of any physical relationship: It all starts with touch.

TOUCH 101: DEVELOP A TOUCH LEXICON

Physical connection is a critical component in coupledom. Think about it, our body language is our first language! For the majority of couples our partners are often the primary providers of physical contact in our lives.

And because, for most couples, sexual connection is an important part of physical connection, the two are often considered to be the same thing. Sexual connection then becomes the place that we go to seek connection, comfort, validation, release, attention, or reward. This is even more heightened when one person doesn't have other outlets to validate their multifaceted identities, affirm their good qualities, to feed their emotional needs, and so on. They experience *famine* in so many areas of their lives that when it comes to sex and sexual connection, they expect a *feast* to satisfy their needs all in one place and from one person.[3]

This may be even more true in the United States than elsewhere in the world. Whom we touch and are touched by, and how we touch, is largely circumscribed by our culture. Heterosexual men in many countries (in the Middle East, the Mediterranean, southern, central, and eastern Europe) greet each other with a kiss on the cheek to say hello and sometimes walk holding hands or arm-in-arm. Most heterosexual American men do not (unless they are from somewhere else originally). The sitcoms and movies portraying disgust by children catching their parents kissing are not present in other cinemas of the world. In fact the reverse is true: Adult affection is seen as something to aspire to. In the United States, adult men may continue to embrace their parents, siblings, or children, and adult women may add friends to that list or they may not. But for most of us, the only adult-to-adult relationship we can reliably turn to for regular physical connection is within our coupledom.

Yet when we reduce the entirety of our physical connection to sex, we do ourselves a disservice and limit the fullness of our expression. When we are in long-term partnerships we expand in our roles for each other—we become more than lovers and sexual companions, we become in-laws for each other's families, we become parents to children (and sometimes pets), we become social companions, business partners at times, public representations of the other, house managers, financial partners—the list is endless. One simple gesture or touch cannot encapsulate all the roles we fulfill for each other. For example, you pat your husband on the back and thank him for walking the dog, then pat him on the back again meaning, "Hey! Let's have sex!" You see the confusion that it could create? It is important that we connect with each other in ways that accentuate each of the roles we fulfill within our coupledom.

Lexicon is a linguistics term used to refer to all of the words in a particular language. You've probably heard that the Alaskan Inuit people have forty words for snow. A linguist might say that snow is represented forty times in the Inuit lexicon. I'd like to invite you to think of physical contact in the same way. How do you say, "I love you" or "I want you" or "I fancy you"? What about "I'm sorry," "You're pretty," "I see you," or "Thank you"? What is your touch lexicon?

One exercise I especially like, and my clients seem to agree, involves a consensual touching game in which each tries to guess the intention behind the touch of the other. I call the tools in this chapter "sexercises," although there is not much sex involved in many of them. Just one way to expand what you associate with sex! It goes like this.

COUPLE'S SEXERCISE: DEVELOPING A TOUCH LEXICON

Pick a time and space that is comfortable and neutral (as much as you can). Taking turns, each partner thinks of a type of touch—sensual, platonic, a teasing touch, a touch of comfort, a playful touch, or a tender one—then delivers that touch to the other without telling them what they had hoped to convey. The partner who receives the touch verbalizes how they received and interpreted it.

Some questions to reflect on are:

- How did this touch make you feel?
- What sensations did you notice?
- When was the last time you exchanged such a touch?
- What were your reactions?
- What do you think your partner wants to convey through their touch?
- Was there a memory associated with the touch?
- Which one of your roles in life or your relationship do you associate with this touch?

It is common for your body to react to these touches, especially if you are not used to them; giggles, tears, tingles are the common reactions.

Gauging these exchanges will help you begin to explore the preferences and existing confusions around each and, ultimately, create a more informed physical connection with each other, sexual and beyond. When sexual connection fades for a couple, it is very common for other forms of touch to fizzle out, too. I also want to bring a gentle reminder here about what we covered around consent earlier, and specifically invite you to think of the sexual menu as a dynamic, evolving, and ever-changing agreement between the two of you. This does not mean that you have to check every five seconds to see if everyone is okay and that you are on track! It does, though, mean even if you both agree regarding the general act, you still need to communicate with each other about your needs and boundaries as you go. Think of it this way: You have given your consent at a macro level and now you want to make sure that you have consent all the way through the interaction (and after) by communicating and negotiating microconsents as well.

You can do this through body language (this is especially common in long-term couples), or by using code words. Choose code words that you would feel comfortable saying and that wouldn't automatically disrupt the flow of your intimacy to represent your green, yellow, and red lights. Saying your "green" word affirms your consent. Your "yellow" word indicates you need to go slowly, renegotiate, or change course. And your "red" word means that you need to stop. If further discussion is needed, you can then discuss anything you want in a neutral setting. Again, I don't recommend having big picture discussions about your sexual needs, wants, or boundaries in the middle of sex! It's not an ideal circumstance for anyone, and often leads to hurt feelings and confusion. When in doubt, stop, and pick up the conversation later.

———

When Zoey and John tried this sexercise, they were surprised by what they learned. Earlier in their relationship they had enjoyed a lot of physical contact. Each was able to identify touches that conveyed sensuality and desire or were interpreted as such. But in the current state of their relationship, the majority of the touches given by one to the other as a representation of friendship, support, or tenderness were interpreted as sexual advances. This might be why they preferred to keep their hands to themselves so they would not send confusing messages to each other and could avoid rejecting the other person or being rejected. "So you think every time I touch you it's because I want to have sex with you?" John asked. "Apparently so and for me, too!" Zoey replied. "That explains a lot," he said. She agreed.

For Zoey and John, the only consistent touch they were receiving was from their children, and their *touch script* was limited to a few of the items in their touch lexicon because it was limited to their roles as parents. They had a bit of work to do to make full use of their touch lexicon and create a more expansive touch script that would be inclusive and descriptive of all their roles within their partnership.

One reason I like this sexercise so much is that it helps you make the crucial shift from what you *think* about your physical connection to what you *feel* with your senses. Touch is a language all on its own. It is the very first language we learn as infants, and can be a powerful connector. As the US came out of the strictest COVID-19 restrictions, many people felt starved for touch. One of my clients, a woman who lives on her own in Los Angeles, told me she hadn't been touched by friends or family in months. "Usually, I see my brother and nieces at least once a week, or I have friends over to watch movies or cook. I didn't realize how important that was until it was gone." There is a growing body of research that indicates the importance of physical touch on health. There is data to show that touch is linked to higher oxytocin levels, lower blood pressure, and better sleep as well as lower inflammation rates.[4] Physical touch may also buffer stress, which made prohibitions against physical contact particularly hard during the pandemic, when people needed relief from stress. Couples who exchange positive touches on a daily basis have better immune systems in comparison to those who don't.[5]

Once you have a wide-ranging physical connection, we can start speaking about sexual connection as a component in this mix. The language we use, touches we give, and our overall energy and actions around each other all come together to shape the communication channels needed to create sexual harmony. If you're kissing your partner's forehead, which may be what her father used to do when she was a kid, this could be a welcome gesture, especially if she is in pain or needs reassurance in uncertain times. But when you want to highlight the physical attraction you have toward her and want to invite her to interact with you as a lover, then a different kind of touch might be more inviting. Touches that remind a person that they are in a sexual relationship should be like no other. A kiss with a sense of anticipation—lingering your lips near each other without kissing for a few seconds, or even a little nibble of the earlobe or the back of the neck—might convey the message and be more of a reminder of your unique dynamic. A touch that you would not give to or receive from anyone else can be a powerful connector and a reminder of the unique erotic potential in your relationship.

LISTENING TO YOUR BODY AND COMMUNICATING FOR IT

Is there a part of your body where you don't like to be touched, or you don't like to be touched in a certain way? This is one question that I always ask my couples in each other's presence. There is nothing wrong with you if you don't want your feet to be touched, or your belly is too ticklish, or you hate having your face touched right after you've put on moisturizer. Not all touch feels good to us! Sometimes this is because of a past adverse experience, but more often it is just a question of personal preference. Being aware of what you like and dislike, and communicating that to your partner, helps you learn about each other rather than relying on assumptions or taking it personally when your partner avoids your touch. Remember the Platinum Rule? Treat others—touch others—the way they want to be touched, not the way you think they want to be touched. To do that, you have to know what feels good for each of you.

To frame all this and put it in the most memorable terms, the physical brain interprets only pain or pleasure. We naturally tend to be motivated to move toward pleasure and away from pain. This is true in all aspects of our lives, and it is part of how we learn about the world. Physical touch is no different. In the late 1990s researchers at the Kinsey Institute developed what they call the Dual Control Model of Sexual Response.[6] The idea is that we respond to sexual stimuli with either excitement or inhibition, depending on the context for the stimulus and our own unique sexual history. It's easier to conceptualize if you think of it like the pedals of a car: Pleasure pushes down on the accelerator while pain hits the brakes.[7] Part of nurturing your physical connection includes educating yourself about what excites you and what leaves you cold.

To demonstrate this idea, and also to help you understand your own physiology and history, I have a simple exercise about pleasure and aversion to share with you.

COUPLE'S SEXERCISE:
TASTE OF PLEASURE AND AVERSION

- Think of two foods, one you love and one you hate.
- Beginning with the food you love, use your imagination to picture it. What does it look like? How does it smell? Imagine yourself eating it. Visualize placing the food in your mouth, chewing, and swallowing.
- Now do the same for the food you hate. Picture it in your mind: what it looks like, what it smells like. Imagine placing the food in your mouth, chewing, and swallowing.
- What did you notice about your bodily reactions—Did saliva build up in your mouth? Did you feel any tingling sensations? (acceleration) Or, alternatively (usually for the food you don't like), did you feel your jaws tense? Did you shiver? Did you experience a dry mouth? (brake)

The brain reacts to physical cues (like touch) in much the same way as it reacts to taste. Does your body tense when your partner touches you in a certain way? Are your palms sweaty? Do you feel uncomfortable?

Or are you calm? Anticipating an exciting time? Are you feeling aroused? Relaxed? Invited? Turned off? Repulsed? These responses indicate how your brain interprets certain stimuli, which can be used to assess how your brain might be reacting to physical cues including the ones that could lead to a sexual interaction. A word here about grooming: Your partner might not want you to touch them intimately (or at all) if you have dirty or jagged fingernails, haven't showered in a few days, or just finished mowing the yard and are covered in sweat and tiny pieces of grass! Sometimes we hit the brakes because of reasons like these that could be rectified so easily.

After doing this sexercise, Zoey reflected that when John approaches her she has the "yuck" response. Not because she doesn't love him, and not because she finds him unattractive. Instead, it's because at this time in her life, with a part-time job, a son who is still nursing, and a four-year-old preschooler, "It feels like everyone needs a piece of me, of my physical body, every waking moment of my life and sometimes in my sleep. So when John approaches me I feel like, *Oh God, not you, too?* I just can't meet one more person's needs right now or I will collapse. And then I feel guilty, so I'll talk myself into sex, and it's usually good and I'm glad I did it, but it's also very much something I do for John, not for myself."

John realized that feeling rejected by Zoey had a big impact on his own feelings around sex. "She was always so receptive before, and when she first started telling me that she was too tired for sex I felt like I was doing something wrong. It reminded me of all the movies that I have watched where the woman fakes a headache, etc. After a while of trying and being shot down I sort of just stopped trying. I am not one of those men who imposes himself on a woman. I want her to want me. So I sort of have the 'yuck' response, too, when it comes to initiating anything." He continued, "With all this confusion it's no wonder that we stopped touching each other altogether!"

If sexual encounters are undesirably painful in any form (physically, emotionally, or otherwise), and even if they're simply awkward and unpleasant, the part of the nervous system that is supposed to be responsive to sexual cues begins to shut down. This is sometimes true when there has been sexual trauma of any kind, but it can also happen under ordinary circumstances. Aging, pregnancy, childbirth, or other changes in physical health can turn activities that were once pleasurable into uncomfortable experiences. For example, some people report having a difficult time sexualizing a pregnant partner; nursing mothers might feel uncomfortable having their breasts touched in a sexual way; and men with erectile dysfunction might need encouragement to engage in sexual activity that doesn't include penetration.

Understanding what accelerates your desire and what slams on the brakes is only a first step (both internally and externally). Now you need to communicate this to your partner. It's important to do this in a loving way that leaves your partner feeling encouraged rather than criticized. Don't just say, "Be more tender"; actually take their hand and show them how you want to be touched. Let them know when they're doing it right! You also need to communicate firmly, rather than in a joking way, if you want your partner to take it seriously. You might even want to use the scoring system we talked about in the chapter on respect. "When you tickle me as part of foreplay it's distressing to me on a scale of ten out of ten." Preferably, don't say this in the middle of sex. Bring it up another time when you both can pay attention.

YOU AS A SEXUAL BEING

As important as it is to acknowledge what is happening in your body during sex, your body isn't the only thing you bring to the bedroom! Now let's move out of the realm of touch, pleasure, and pain on a physical level and into understanding the messages you've learned about sex, sexuality, and yourself as a sexual being.

Your individual sexual blueprint is the culmination of all your formative experiences around sex, sexuality, sensuality, attraction, desire, and lovemaking. I like the garden metaphor that my friend Dr. Emily Nagoski uses in her book *Come as You Are*. She tells her readers to imagine that their sexuality is like a garden they're given at birth, "a little plot of land, slightly different from everyone else's, and uniquely yours." When you're young, your family, community, and culture put in the foundation plants and take care of them. But as you age you're expected to tend the garden yourself. Your garden keeps evolving but your blueprint, if unexamined, will remain the same and will dictate how you show up in your interactions, what you are drawn toward and what you want to escape. Sometimes the foundation plants put in place by others aren't really a reflection of what you want today.

As we begin to explore some of your earliest memories about sexuality and sensuality, please keep in mind that your sexual blueprint includes not only what you were taught about sex, but also what you experienced. For this reason, the following exercise consists of two parts: what you think and what you feel. When you understand where your ideas about sex originated, you can make the shift from what you think you're *supposed to* feel or expect in the physical aspect of your relationships and step into who you *are* and what *is*.

BUILDING BLOCK: YOUR SEXUAL BLUEPRINT

- How did you learn about human sexuality? Reproduction? What did your parents and caregivers tell you about sex?
- Did you grow up in a house where your parents showed each other physical affection, or were they more reserved in front of you?
- If you were raised within a particular religious tradition, what were the values around sex that were communicated to you?
- How did your culture view sex and sexuality? What were the messages you received as a child and later in your life about the role and purpose of sexuality, both within and outside of committed coupledom?
- What were you taught about masculinity/femininity and physical attractiveness?
- Were sex, sexual pleasure, and physical pleasure considered a normal part of life, or was there a sense of secrecy attached to it? What about shame?
- Was everyone seen as equally deserving of sexual satisfaction, or was that reserved for a particular group? Some examples of these

groups might be: men, people who are married to each other, people who are young, people who are beautiful, people who are thin.

- When you became sexually active (not necessarily intercourse), was it a cause for celebration, a cause for shame, or neutral?
- What did you call your genitalia when you were growing up?
- Up to this moment, have your genitals been places of shame? pride? liability? confusion? or pleasure?
- Do you know your sexual, gender, and relational orientation?
- Has this been information that you were comfortable sharing with anyone, including your partner?

As you considered the questions above, did anything surprise you? Often, when I do this sexercise with couples, one or both of them will have an "Aha!" moment, when they connect the dots between what they were taught about sex and how they experience sexuality in their relationship today.

While talking about sex is certainly important, involving the body also is necessary for tangible fluency. The next sexercise, which includes all five senses, not only helps individuals to focus on their own garden, it also helps them to hone in on their partner's. It is a formative sexercise for tapping into our sexual blueprints. I call it the Five Senses Exercise.

BUILDING BLOCK: THE FIVE SENSES EXERCISE

Think of your five senses—touch, taste, smell, sight, and sound. Now write down the first time you received any information that was sexual or sensual through each of these senses. For each one, answer the following questions. Think about the context and the energy that you felt in that moment, too.

- How old were you?
- How did it make you feel, and what did you think?
- Who else was there?
- What was their reaction?
- What was your reaction to this?

- How does it feel to remember this now?
- How do you think it shaped your ideas and ideals around your sexuality?

To make this more practical and memorable, feel free to download the five senses cheat sheet at www.lovebydesignbook.com. It includes a set of images representing each of the senses to make it easier to reflect. Then set aside some time during the week to do this exercise alone. It is fine if you both wish to share the results, but this is often deeply personal, and each person should only share what they wish with no pressure. If you don't want to share what you have learned with your partner immediately or at all, you might want to reach out to a professional to help you process what came up for you. Later, they can also help to facilitate a conversation with your partner if you choose to have one. The idea here is that you need to understand your sexual blueprint before you try to sort out which parts will be most relevant and helpful to bring to your partner.

Once you're in touch with some of your first experiences around sex, take a moment to consider how those formative experiences make you feel today. Do they have any overt relevance for your coupledom? How was it to recall them? Were you surprised by being able to recall the memories? Now that you are not a child anymore, how do you react to similar stimuli? Setting aside sexual or sensual touches, think about how you were comforted by touch as a child. The need for safety and comfort is a primal need for a child. Finally, did someone ever touch you, or ask to be touched by you, in a way that made you uncomfortable or scared?

SEXUAL TRAUMA, SELF AND RELATIONAL CARE

When your formative experiences were not positive, consensual ones, this sexercise can sometimes reveal past situations that made you feel uncomfortable, humiliated, unsafe, or threatened. Depending on how you respond, more work may have to be done on an individual level to help you understand, manage, and/or heal these negative sexual associations.

If, at any point in this chapter, you find yourself feeling angry, confused, irritated, frightened, or otherwise agitated, try to identify what triggered this response. Only share these details with your partner if you think it will feed into your sexual intimacy. If there is anything you are unsure about sharing, it would be a good idea to consult a professional before bringing it into your coupledom. Your partner, as understanding as they might be, is not a trained professional and often not the best person to process these matters with you.

Every person deserves to feel safe. If you don't, help is available. In the United States, resources like the National Domestic Violence Hotline (800-799-SAFE), the National Sexual Assault Hotline at 800-656-HOPE, and the Trevor Project (www.thetrevorproject.org/) are available to you 24/7.

If you're looking for ongoing support and finances are an issue for you, I recommend reaching out to an organization, an institution or university, or even a group practice, where an experienced professional is supervising interns. The American Association of Sexuality Educators, Counselors and Therapists (AASECT) could be a good resource to find qualified professionals. You can find additional resources on the *Love by Design* website at www.lovebydesignbook.com.

I've had clients who shared that their first experience with sexual stimuli was when they accidentally found their father's *sexy* magazines, watched a TikTok video, or saw a pop-up ad online. Some felt proud and giddy, and some felt ashamed of the arousal they experienced. Some men recalled the first porn they watched secretly with friends and how it made them worry that their penises were too small or their ejaculation didn't shoot far enough. These and many other questions related to "am I normal" were among the frequently asked questions that I received when I hosted my show on the BBC. Many people remember the first time they pleasured themselves and how exciting and confusing it was. I've heard from women who still remember the sensation of their first kiss by a tentative lover, or the water pressure of the bidet that felt so good they continued until they couldn't anymore, the whisper of a loving word, the smell of a cologne. I also heard how some people felt aroused when they sneezed or rode on their bike or sat on their grandmother's lap. However you first experienced your introductory pleasurable sensations, you are most likely not alone.

For Zoey, who had always thought of herself as a sexual and sensual being, the feeling of not wanting to be touched was disturbing. Then she remembered hearing her mother yell, "Get out! Get out!" when she was six and accidentally walked in on her parents having sex. Why were her parents doing something she wasn't allowed to know about? Who was being bad, them or her? Exhaustion wasn't the only thing causing her to turn away from John. She was responding to some old messages about having sex in a house with children.

John recalled learning about sex from his beloved uncle Jo, who acted as a surrogate father after his own father died. Jo was really successful with women, and had a string of girlfriends before he married. "I felt like I had to be like him or I wasn't a real man. Growing up without a dad, I worried a lot about being manly enough." When Zoey avoided him, John experienced it as failure.

As individuals we learn something from our formative experiences, and what we learn consciously and unconsciously shapes our unique path to arousal. Recalling these earliest lessons helps individuals and couples understand why one interaction is arousing and satisfying while another is not. It can also help them to reshape the path of arousal for themselves so it is not rigidly scripted by their sexual blueprint.

Once we have a good idea about what excites us and what leaves us cold, and we understand where our ideas about sex originated, we can make the shift from what we think we're *supposed to* feel or expect in the physical aspect of our relationships and step into who we *are* and what *is*. Exploring early memories around sexuality through the lens of the body also helps individuals understand what sex means for each of them and what role it plays in their lives today.

THE ROLE AND MEANING OF SEX

As we talked about briefly before, the *meanings* we attach to sex are usually personal and have to do with the way that we connect with our own sense of sexuality. Our perception of the *role* of sex has to do with the way it serves us in our relational spaces with others. The questions I encourage you to ask yourself are: What is the purpose of sex? What's it for? How do you hope it will make you feel? How do you think the other person feels when in that interaction with you? What is the currency that you are exchanging when having sex? Is it love, affection, making babies, financial security, improving your mood, repairing after conflict, or something else? Let me clarify here that people have sex for different reasons. The idea that sex is for mutual physical pleasure might not resonate with everyone. The reward might come in different forms and shapes, physical, emotional, relational, spiritual, or however else you might define that reward system for yourself.

For some, sex is an opportunity to feel comforted, taken care of, and loved. For others sex is an expression of vitality, a life-affirming celebration of their physical being. Some see sex as a channel for play and self-expression, others as an opportunity to communicate all those feelings that words often fail to capture. Some people engage in sex when they are mourning, or when they get bad news from a doctor, as a way to feel alive and in touch with reality. In similar situations, others might feel depressed, despairing, and detached from anything that might remind them of feeling and being alive, including sex. Still others see it as a question of morality, and engaging in sex during or around times of grief and loss feels inappropriate.

For John, sex was primarily a way to feel close to Zoey. It was also an affirmation of his manhood. When Zoey recoiled from him, it hurt. He felt isolated and alone, especially since he saw her touching and holding the kids all the time. Meanwhile, Zoey was having her own problems reconciling her sexy and playful self with this relatively new role as a mother. "When I'm in mommy mode and John approaches me as a lover, I feel so alone. It feels like he has no idea who I am anymore and no idea how I need him to show up for me."

Before becoming parents, this couple had a powerful physical connection that was almost entirely sexual. But as their lives shifted and changed (as lives inevitably do), that sexual connection was no longer enough. Like many heterosexual couples who have a hard time connecting after children enter the picture, one partner is skin flooded (i.e., too much physical contact that emphasizes a very particular role, usually the mother) while the other becomes skin hungry (too little contact, usually the father). This same dynamic exists when traditional gender roles are reversed, and is also true for same-sex couples when one partner takes over infant care.

Being able to acknowledge, appreciate, and work with a shift from one form of physical connection to another is crucial in coupledom, especially when the role and meaning of sex has changed with changing circumstances. Couples who do not invest in developing a large repertoire in their touch lexicon often suffer more when their interpersonal dynamics change because of a life-altering situation such as becoming parents, adopting a pet, going through physical injuries, or aging. In much the same way that mutual attraction and being loving are fluid concepts that have to be flexible and meaningful to the other in the present moment, so too does the role of physical connection.

Zoey longs to be seen and appreciated by John *as a mother*. "The idea of being a sex object or even just having a quickie is too much for me right now, but there are lots of times when I crave the feeling of John's body. I love when he hugs me really tight. It's so different from how I feel with the kids. I love the sheer size of him. He's got these muscles and this great man-smell which is familiar and safe. I feel like I can let go of my protective, mama bear status and just be there in a protected zone of my own. His hands are strong and capable and almost never covered in strawberry jam."

Sometimes what one person is looking for is not sexual pleasure; they just want to feel safe and comforted. Not everyone strives for pleasure all the time. I had to mention this here because the opposite of pleasure is not pain, it is comfort! Insisting on giving pleasure to one's partner is often experienced as pressure to perform the act of sex, which is not going to serve anyone involved.

When Zoey said this during our session, John visibly relaxed. He craves feeling connected to Zoey as a lover and a partner. And while he's not exactly happy to forgo penetrative sex, he is more than willing to work with Zoey to come up with new ways of expressing and experiencing physical connection. At the same time, his sense of himself *as a man* has expanded beyond a vague notion of sexual prowess to include this new feeling of being a solid and grounding presence for his wife. If you're thinking, "This sounds like they just negotiated a shared vision for their sexual bond," I applaud you. You are spot-on!

Understanding the role and meaning of sex in their coupledom can also help partners know how to show up for each other in different ways and in different contexts. Let me give you another example.

When Darian and Jerome first came to see me, they were having some serious problems. We had been working together for a couple of years, and making progress, when Darian's mother was in a fatal car accident. He was devastated. Jerome helped Darian arrange the services and stayed by his side while family and friends gathered to mourn their loss. When they came home from the funeral, Darian wanted to have passionate sex with the man he loved. Jerome was horrified. They brought their fight into my office.

"I cannot *believe* you want to have sex while your mother's body is still fresh in the ground! Have you no respect for her at all?" Jerome demanded. Darian, confused by his outburst, replied, "What are you talking about? I love my mother, you know that. You love her, too. Where is this anger coming from?"

When I asked each of them what sex would mean in this particular situation, what role it would play in their grief, Darian explained, "I want to feel alive, I want to be comforted by my husband and know that I am not alone in the world." Jerome was surprised. He replied, "For me, sex is a place to play, and it's naughty but in a good way. When I'm mourning a loss and wearing my big-boy pants to be present and represent myself as your partner for your family and friends, which by the way is not always easy to do, I cannot possibly bring myself into that space. It feels disrespectful and greedy to want sex when your mother just lost her life."

After hearing the other articulate the meaning and role of sex for him at that time, their argument quickly dissipated. Darian felt appreciation for the effort Jerome had made on his behalf. Jerome understood Darian's need for comfort and the life-affirming release of sex. They used this moment to start talking about Darian's mom, what her role was in their lives, and how happy she was when Darian finally found someone to share his life with. They could access their source of compassion for each other, and their solution was to grieve together by intentionally comforting each other physically—they would breathe together and use their tenderest touches in a way that would leave them both feeling connected and seen. This solution neither deprived Darian of comfort nor pressured Jerome into a sexual encounter that would not feel welcome.

Gestures that reinforce physical connection can take many forms. In creating or re-creating this sense in your coupledom, I suggest that you work together to find small ways to remind each other through touch that you are safe, loved, cared for, seen, wanted, and celebrated in all the roles you each fulfill, including as a lover and sexual being. Then watch the dynamic shift. This is not always easy, but the dividends are usually high.

WALKING AWAY SATISFIED

Before we get into a discussion about cultivating sexual harmony, let's pause here for a moment to talk about what satisfaction means, since many people equate satisfaction with orgasm. For some people it is, and if you and/or your partner want to experience orgasm in every sexual encounter, then that's very important information to share with each other. But many people do not require an orgasm to walk away satisfied. Also, a hint here for people who chase orgasm: The more you chase it, the less likely you can catch it. Pressuring your partner to "achieve" orgasm also makes it less likely for them to experience it. (As a side note, in our book *Orgasm Answer Guide*, I was joined by three of my esteemed colleagues to answer the eighty most common questions about orgasm. If you want to learn more, pick that one up!)

For example, knowing that your husband loves receiving oral sex or a hand job, and taking a break from your busy day to surprise him with some expert fellatio on your lunch hour, can be immensely satisfying to some partners even when he, she, or they don't receive the same sexual act in return. The currencies exchanged don't have to be the same. If you enjoy giving oral sex, you will certainly walk away satisfied. But you can also be satisfied just knowing you've been sexually generous and made a significant contribution to the overall sexual goodwill of your partnership. This is an overlapping gesture with loving behaviors, since one of the criteria is to demonstrate tenderness, exclusivity, and attentiveness in a way you don't with anyone else.

The important point here is that each of you comes out of the experience satisfied, sexually or otherwise. Why is the satisfaction piece nonnegotiable? Think about the foods you love and the foods you hate. If you go into an experience expecting satisfaction and come out not satisfied, or even worse with unwanted pain, then your brain starts to go into protective mode. When you have sexual encounters with your partner that are not fulfilling, over time the brain stops getting excited about sex. Many people who come to me with decreased sexual desire are among this group. For one reason or another, they've experienced little to no reward from their sexual encounters, and this inevitably leads to a downward spiral of decreasing sexual desire. This is why it's important to make sure your bodies "like" and feel safe with each other if you want desire to be sustained over time. Keep in mind that each physical interaction should have an introduction, a middle, and an end. For example, if your hands feel sweaty or you feel off-balance, or for whatever other reasons you want to let go of your partner's hand as you are walking down the street, first giving their hand a bit of squeeze, or saying why you are going to let go, or even giving a little kiss on their hand before letting it go goes a long way. Every attempt to connect is an invitation to receive, decline, or defer as you do according to your manners elsewhere. Make sure you close the experience positively to create an accelerator for your next experience.

CULTIVATING SEXUAL HARMONY

Sexual harmony does not look to rekindle the initial spark; it involves more than grasping at a euphoric past experience. Nor does it rely on spontaneity, intensity, and a final orgasm as the marker for intimacy and satisfaction. If sexual chemistry is a firecracker, sexual harmony is more like composing a piece of music—one person plays a note, the other listens to it, picks it up, and continues to build on it. Every subsequent interaction co-creates a well-aligned harmony. Couples who strive for sexual harmony seek to create a melody using everything available: all five of the senses, plus the imagination, and the understanding of what your partner wants and needs *in that moment*. Together, partners connect with each other's voice, body movements, and gaze; they pay attention to the sight of each other's face, the taste and smell of each other's body, the subtle and unsubtle shifts in energy that indicate arousal. It could be as quick or as lengthy as the two of you desire, but the elements remain in place.

Often in a harmonious sexual interaction couples feel *with* each other, sharing what is known as a sexually empathic experience, almost as if each has access to the other's nervous system. This is one place in coupledom where empathy is very much welcomed. In an empathic state, partners move together and experience a multitude of emotions together. In this way, each person in the partnership can get lost in the other while still remaining grounded in their own senses and imagination. In this space, mind, heart, and body all are present and interacting. And though the partners may experience orgasm, it is not the goal of the encounter. Presence and pleasure are the goals.

Sexual harmony is founded on the idea that sexual connection and sexual intimacy are teachable skills and a mutual frame of mind. Instead of seeking the surge of chemicals, sexual harmony allows us to connect and reconnect with our partners in a way that is personally meaningful. Sexual harmony is a multilayered dynamic through which each person engages with the other using the whole self, all of the various identities that define and shape us both as individuals and as a couple. In this way, sexual harmony is a channel for increased intimacy. Or, "into-me-I-see," and "into-me-you-see." Fulfilling connection, partly born from the mastering of sexual harmony, allows for a deep, resonant exchange with each other. Because we evolve and change as individuals over time, having this deep and empathic sexual connection means that there are always new aspects of the self and the coupledom to be explored. It is a powerful corrective to the monotony of a sex life that relies solely on chemistry.

This does not mean that both parties need to have the same level of desire or enjoy the same things. One of my favorite tools to help cultivate sexual harmony is to have couples develop their own unique sexual menu: a list of individual, action-oriented preferences that bring them fulfillment or that they might like to try. Like improvisational jazz, the rules are pretty flexible, but there are guidelines that, when followed, allow for a more pleasant harmony. The menu provides you with a variety of self-selected options and the language to talk about what you want without being heavily burdened by expectations, shame, fear of rejection, or performance anxieties. Connection, physical and otherwise, thrives on consistent and open communication about the content that serves the process. And though talking about sex can be awkward at first, research suggests that the more couples talk about sex openly, the more successful their sexual connections are all around.[8] Creating a sexual menu is one place where talking really matters. By establishing a mutually agreed-upon list, I have seen that couples feel freer to engage—they've determined a foundation for their sexual encounters and can refer to it whenever necessary. Also, because they know that their partner's preference does not have to become theirs, they are more relaxed about accepting the other person's inclinations. This next exercise will provide the self-literacy you need so you can know how to be fluent with each other when it comes to creating sexual harmony.

COUPLE'S TOOLKIT:
CREATING A SEXY TIME MENU

This is most effective as a written exercise, so grab some paper or open a new document on your laptop, if you have the ability to. If not, consider recording a voice memo, or using a voice-to-text function on your phone.

Now, think about mood enhancers and diminishers when it comes to sex. Think about your five senses and the information you receive through them; think about the context and about the energy (yours and the other person's). Then make a list of physical behaviors, including but not limited to sexual acts, that you currently engage in with your partner or would like to try. Be creative. Your list can include anything from a back rub to penetrative intercourse to having your partner wash your hair.

Share your list with your partner. This is the time to talk about any items that might not be agreeable to the other. If you want to experience a ménage-à-trois, or sex with a person of a different gender than your partner, that might have to be negotiated. The decision to keep it, modify it, or omit it will be made together and based on your agreed-upon boundaries.

The only requirement is that each item on your list must be fulfilling, in some way, for you.

Some examples of what might be listed on a sexual menu include:

- A thirty-minute foot rub
- A fifteen-minute ear rub
- Oral sex
- Taking a shower together
- Sixty-nine
- Looking into each other's eyes and breathing together
- Prostate massage
- A ten-minute back scratch
- Using sex toys
- Blowing gently on the back of the neck
- Anal stimulation
- Premium massage
- Bondage
- Tickling
- Holding hands, playing with each other's hair, or kissing in public
- Spanking
- Little kisses on the lips while the other only receives
- Gentle love bites
- Brushing or washing the other's hair
- Licking different parts of the body
- Eating food off of each other
- Role playing
- Dressing up
- Acting out a fantasy
- Narrating an erotic story
- Being fed something delicious
- Any of the above while blindfolded

Being creative is really helpful here. I encourage you to use your imagination—something that can be hard for adults! You can start by thinking about what kind of material you find arousing. If you watch porn, what kind do you watch, and what about it is arousing to you? For example, I've heard heterosexual, cisgender men and women share that they like gay porn. When I ask them what components they find arousing, usually they say the equality of the parties, the same level of pleasure that they both seem to be experiencing. Some male clients like gay porn because they identify with the masculinity and the power that the actors might represent. If you read erotic literature, ask yourself the same questions. These all could become elements of exploration for the couple's sex life.

If you're still having trouble imagining what you might want to include on the menu, or what would feel exciting to you, I invite you to do the Fantasy Lover exercise. It goes like this.

SEXERCISE: FANTASY LOVER

Imagine you could be anywhere in the world and could have sex with anyone you wanted. Where would that be, who would it be, and what would you be doing together? Consider what emotions, feelings, and fantasies this brings out in you. Some questions to reflect on might be: What do those fantasies reveal about your path of attraction, desire, and arousal? What do they reveal about your past and present partner(s)? Can you/do you want to cultivate elements of it in your coupledom and with your partner?

I also recommend seeking out a stimulus that might act as inspiration for creativity. If you are comfortable with the idea, visit a sex store, read or listen to erotica, sign up for apps that offer recommendations and even send you toys to experiment with, or purchase ethical porn* of your liking, or engage in other experiences that might inspire your imaginative side (for some suggestions check out the resource page at www.lovebydesignbook.com).

The human brain lacks the capacity to differentiate between something

---

* Ethical porn is a type of pornography produced and consumed with a focus on responsible and respectful practices. It prioritizes consent, fair treatment, fair compensation, diversity, transparency, safer sex, and often, environmental considerations.

that felt real and something that actually happened.[9] This means the imagination is an incredibly powerful tool, capable of relieving stress and even alleviating physical pain. It is also capable of conjuring pleasure. It is a reservoir of untapped sexual curiosity and yearning. As adults, we often lose touch with that playful, creative energy, or we become afraid to engage in that space. When used correctly, the imagination nurtures desire and arousal, but in a much more sustainable way.

Another key component to the sexual menu is that the items listed do not have to lead to a sexual encounter (depending on how you define sex). This is so important I'm going to say it again: The sexual menu can and should include items that do not have to lead to sex. Of course, many of the options will be different forms of sex, or sensually engaging, or more obviously sexual in nature, but that is certainly not a requirement. A sexual menu can contain any type of act that involves the body, directly or indirectly, and nurtures intimacy and connection.

Alone and together you each get to choose items based on your preferences and abilities. Long hugs or kisses—six seconds or more—have been shown to foster bonding.[10] Sometimes, one person might not be "hungry" at all, so to speak, but is happy to serve the other or just be there while the other enjoys their meal. Sometimes both will enjoy sitting together and poring over the menu, trying to decide which options might work best together. Sometimes both partners are interested in the same option. And there will also be times when you choose something solo from the menu that you'll enjoy if your partner is not available, tired, or not able or willing to join you. In any given interaction, you don't have to pick the same items. It's very much like when you go out to eat together: Every person eats as they please and walks out satisfied in their own taste. If all this seems too out of reach, you might consider contacting a professional to facilitate your reconnection. You can find additional resources at www .lovebydesignbook.com.

For Zoey, the sexual menu allowed her to ask for what she wanted very specifically: "Good hugs, back rubs and foot rubs and ear rubs, and reminders that I'm beautiful even when I have macaroni in my hair. Maybe *especially* when I've got macaroni in my hair. Oh! And also sensual touch that doesn't always lead to sex. If you want to go there, please be clear from the get-go." Knowing that Zoey welcomed his touch and sincerely wanted to engage with him helped John to articulate some wishes of his own. "Sometimes I do really just want to cum, and I don't want to do it alone in the shower." Together they came up with "collab-o-rama masturbation." John would masturbate while Zoey was present with him with words and touch. And though she was more than welcome to join him, it was also fine if she didn't. Zoey liked the idea of participating in John's experience without having to play a starring role. They would then join together and cuddle for a bit.

Items on your sexual menu don't have to be especially complicated or involved. They can be more like what I call chitchat sex, where you just say, "Hello, I am here, how are you?" and you're gone. You can also include longer experiences that involve a buildup of anticipation, sexting, hotel rooms, hours of conversation, or whatever it might take for you to have what I call a heartfelt and more intimate encounter. Both are necessary in long-term relationships.

This is the part that I promised was coming. So sexual harmony allows for both chitchat and heartfelt sex to be satisfying while recognizing that spontaneity is more present with chitchat sex, and anticipation is a key element of a heartfelt sexual encounter. One makes sure that the mechanics are in place and the connection remains, while the other guarantees that the couple does not take each other for granted and sex does not become dull and disconnected over time.

Months after our first meeting, I saw Zoey and John for a virtual session. In our initial sessions, I walked them through each sexercise. Together, they began to develop a shared language around touch, sex, and physical intimacy. The sexercises allowed them to become more intimately familiar with each other, discussing and processing each person's thoughts, perceptions, expectations, and experiences around various forms of touch including sex. This helped to inform the sexual and sensual beings that they presently became in their relationship. They began to occupy their relationship more actively—talking about how to cultivate their sex life, improve it, and incorporate a deeper level of intimacy within their partnership. Most important, they no longer felt passive, caught up in the tides of biology and the central role sexual chemistry once played in their lives. The last time I saw them, Zoey reported that they had discovered levels of orgasm that she didn't know existed. She called it "the cherry on an already yummy cake."

As with all the ingredients needed to cultivate Emergent Love, I urge you to remind yourselves that everyone is deserving (not a word I use lightly) of fulfillment—whether that be physical, sexual, or otherwise. Our bodies, minds, and hearts tell the unique story of who we are; if we want to experience fulfilling coupledom, we must let those stories be heard and known by the people that we trust and choose to share these with. When we learn how to create and cultivate Emergent Love, we move away from unrealistic expectations and toward actual fulfillment in the real world.

CHAPTER 12

Check-ins and Checkups

Chains do not hold a marriage together. It is threads, hundreds of tiny threads which sew people together through the years.

—Simone Signoret (about her marriage to Yves Montand)[1]

It would be wonderful if I could give you a Certificate of Completion at the end of this book, something to hang on your wall and admire for years to come. But that's not how this works. There is no graduation. Emergent Love, as you know by now, is more of a process than a goal. Instead, designing a relationship where love emerges as a natural by-product is a lifelong project. You have to pay attention, then calibrate and recalibrate your relational dynamics as your life shifts and moves around you. Emergent Love is about moving flexibly within your relational space depending on the roles you each are playing, the needs and requirements of the moment, and the capacities of each partner.

This chapter is all about fine-tuning the vision of the future we discussed in detail in chapter 7: Shared Vision. As you saw in the last chapter, your physical connection is one area where a regularly discussed and negotiated shared vision will serve you well, but there are many, many others. Sometimes you need to become very specific about what has to happen in the next few hours. Other times you will talk about your dreams and long-term goals. There will be times when you need to touch base to problem-solve, to share if there is a change to your boundaries or express when one has been crossed, or to highlight a particular behavior that is troubling to one or both of you. But it's not all about highlighting or solving problems. You also need to come together intentionally in ways that are meaningful to each of you and to you as a couple. Cultivating joy is just as important as managing conflict, and often it is more important. The Emergent Love research was born because I didn't want to focus on just taking people's pain away or labeling what their problem was. I wanted to see what thriving couples do that we all can learn from and live by. Below I will offer some tools to check in yearly, monthly, weekly, and daily. They cover everything from whose turn it is to make the lunches to how you're progressing in your dreams of a lifetime. They are designed to help you stay connected, reconnect, and repair when—not if—you begin to feel disconnected. I hope you find them helpful as you design the love you desire.

ANNUAL CHECK-INS:
FINE-TUNING YOUR SHARED VISION

In both my practice and my research, I have seen over and over again that couples who dream together stay together. Understanding how to set realistic goals for yourself and your partnership, and how to go about achieving those goals, will help both partners feel that they are active agents in their own lives.

Take a moment to think about the love you are creating and cultivating with your partner, and your shared vision for your life together. Remember 1 + 1 = 3? This is the 3 in the equation. The goals are the fun part: They're the reason you partnered with this person in the first place, and what you imagined when you thought about building a life together. Your rituals, habits, and behaviors are what feed that vision.

Before we begin, I want to make sure we are sharing a similar language about what we are aiming for by clarifying three terms: *goal*, *strategy*, and *tactic*. I define a *goal* as anything that you want to bring into being in your life: developing a closer relationship with your mother, finishing your dissertation, moving to a warmer climate, becoming a better tennis player, or exploring an interest that you never seem to have the bandwidth to pursue. A *strategy* is the overall plan that will help you accomplish that goal. So if your goal is to develop a closer relationship with your mother, your strategy might be to spend more time with her doing things that she likes to do. When it comes to taking specific actions to realize your goal, we're talking about *tactics*. If your mother is passionate about gardening, your tactic might be to go to her house once a week to help her with her garden. If you live too far away for that, your goal and strategy will be the same, but your tactics will be different: A weekly video call and a monthly visit will be more realistic.

I've developed an exercise, Roles and Goals, designed to help you think about and prioritize how you want to spend your finite resources of time, energy, attention, and money. Don't worry: The purpose of this is not to give you more work! Nor do all your goals have to be about accomplishing things, getting promoted, advancing your career, or making more money. Your goal might be to spend more time with family (and less time at work). Goals can also be about slowing down, cultivating serenity, strengthening friendships, or just doing more of the things that bring you joy.

In this exercise, we will go through your roles (current and aspirational), your intention for each of them, and the resources needed to get you from point A to point B by the end of next year. I ask all my clients to do this exercise on an annual basis, so they don't leave too much to chance. I invite you to do the same, too. The point isn't that you have to stick to your vision come hell or high water (or a global pandemic). You will always get to refashion and renegotiate that vision. But having one in the first place will help you have a sense of agency around creating the life you desire.

EXERCISE: ROLES AND GOALS

1. Make a list of all your main roles, both current and aspirational. Get a piece of paper or open a document and create three columns. In the first column list all of the roles that you currently have. Skip over the middle one for now. In the third column list only the roles that you would like to keep; leave a blank space for those you no longer want, and add new roles at the end of the column.

2. Clarify goals: For every role in the first column, create one goal (aka intention) in the second column. If it is a role you would not like to keep, add that as your intention.

3. Create tactics and strategies. In a separate space below the three columns, for each of your roles, write down your intention and then work backward to put action items toward that goal. Begin with your overall strategy, then attach tactics in the form of positive actions you can take.

4. Think of the resources required. List the resources of time, energy, attention, and money that each action item requires.

5. Understand expectations surrounding the role. These include your expectations of yourself, the expectations of others who are involved in or impacted by that role, and the expectations from your blueprint of what this role is supposed to look like.

6. Repeat steps 2–5 for every role.

Below is an example of what your Roles and Goals worksheet might look like. For the record: Kevin, his wife, Karen, and their daughter, Iris, are purely fictitious. They are an amalgamation of many of the couples I see. I'm bringing them in here as a way to demonstrate what this exercise can look like, and the kind of perspective it offers.

KEVIN'S ROLES AND GOALS WORKSHEET

1. Make a list of all your roles, both current and aspirational.

2. Clarify goals for each person.

Current Roles	Goals	Future Roles
Husband	Feel closer to Karen	Husband
Employee	Advocate for more interesting projects	Employee
Father	Work on my temper	Father
Son	Set better boundaries, especially with mom	Son
Friend	Make more time to see the guys	Friend
Church Leader	Give up some responsibilities at church	
Musician	Play every day	Musician
	Coach Iris's softball team	Coach

3. Create tactics and strategies.
   Role: Husband
   Goal: Feel closer to Karen

Strategy: Spend more quality time together

Tactic/Action Items:

    a. Set up a weekly date night for just the two of us and take turns organizing what we do

    b. Spend time with other couples we both like

    c. Plan some physical activities together, skiing or running or hiking, since we really do well together when we're doing something physical

    d. Have sex more often

4. Understand the resources required.

    a. Money for babysitter, time to make plans (15 min?), time to go out (3 hrs?), enough energy

    b. Money for babysitter, time to make plans, time to go out, enough energy

    c. Time to run together (1hr)

    d. Energy, time. (>15 min!)

5. Understand expectations surrounding the role.

    Self: I expect to feel really close to Karen, have a decent social life, and have sex twice a week. I feel guilty, and like I'm not doing marriage right. I've stopped expecting Karen to manage our social life.

    Karen: Karen says she's just exhausted. If I want to do more, I have to plan it, because otherwise it feels unfair. Karen expects me to initiate sex, which feels like pressure.

    Blueprint: Everyone says that couples need to make time for each other. My mom stayed home full-time and organized dates and got babysitters. She threw parties and managed everyone's schedule in the house. I assumed my life would be a lot like my dad's life, and that Karen would just take care of this. But she works, too, so that's not very realistic. I don't know where I got the idea that only men are supposed to initiate sex, or where Karen got that idea, but it really isn't working for us.

6. Repeat steps 2–5 for every role.

After you've finished writing everything down, you can share it with your partner. Then, together, you can discuss how to prioritize your resources so that you, your partner, and your coupledom (all three of you; remember, 1 + 1 = 3) feel fulfilled about committing to your shared vision for the upcoming year.

One of the wonderful things about this exercise is that it both reflects and supports the components of Emergent Love. They all come into play, and not just when you're talking about your role as a partner. You see your partner in their totality when they show you what is important to them and what they value about themselves, what roles they consider significant for themselves, and how they prioritize their resources for them, which strengthens mutual attraction and trust. You express your respect for your partner when you recognize them for who they are outside the relationship. Trust and commitment underscore the whole exercise: You trust that they will honor your vision, that your arrangements will feel equitable, and that your partner will show up reliably and consistently in the arrangements you negotiate together. You express compassion when you listen to your partner's goals and dreams from a place of generosity and non-judgment, and you allow their dreams to be about them, not about you. And understanding your individual and mutual goals will help you to express your love in ways that are specific, intentional, and meaningful for the other person.

When it comes to your goals for your role as a partner, check with each other to make sure that your strategies and tactics are aligned. Let me give you an example. Karen might respond to Kevin's goals as a husband by saying, "I also want to feel closer to you. But I'm so busy already, we both are, that even thinking about going out once a week is too much. I don't know if it would make us feel closer or if it would just add to the pressure. What I'd really like to do is sit in the living room with a pot of tea and talk to you. I'd love it if we put our phones and computers and tablets on silent mode in another room and just sat together. Can we schedule some time to *do nothing* together?" Kevin agreed that it sounded incredible. The goal (bonding) and strategy (spending time together) remained the same, but the tactics shifted to accommodate their circumstances.

As you go through this exercise, there are a few things to keep in mind. First, when it comes to conceptualizing your goals, try to be sure that what you've written is what you actually want. In business there is a problem-solving technique called 5 Whys that helps companies discover the root cause of a problem, rather than just treating the symptoms.[2] It works for setting goals as well. Here's an example:

Angela: My goal is to pick up my child from school three days a week.
Dr. Sara: Why?
Angela: Because I want to spend more time with her.
Dr. Sara: Why?

Angela: Because I love her!

Dr. Sara: Of course you do. But *what do you hope to accomplish* by spending more time with her?

Angela: She tells me she misses me when I work late. I want to show her that I love her in a way she's going to understand. I want her to feel safe and close.

Dr. Sara: So your goal is to bond?

See how this works? Picking up her child is more of a tactic than a goal for Angela. The goal is bonding, the strategy is spending time together, and the tactic is picking her daughter up from school and reading her a bedtime story. When you write down a goal, make sure to ask yourself why, then dig deeper to really understand the outcome you want. This is the exact same exercise I do with corporate groups when they want to set their annual goals and three-year strategic plans.

Second, when you're exploring the expectations you have attached to the goal, think about your larger circle and see whose voices you recognize in the mix. For example, "A good mother is...," "A healthy relationship is...," "Husbands are supposed to..." This recognition will help you to clarify whose voice you're hearing and whether or not you actually agree with it. Then you can proceed with a sense of agency and awareness, rather than just going with the flow or fulfilling other people's expectations without knowing if they are actually meaningful to you.

I also invite you to share this with other family members as well, like children, depending on their level of maturity, siblings, parents, and so on. This is very similar to the exercise I do at companies when they want to make sure that everybody is on the same page, they are all working toward the same goals, and they want to offer support to one another. When we know where the other person wants to go, it's much easier for us to offer a hand when we can or when they need it. If you need more help with this, go to www.lovebydesignbook.com for a step-by-step video of the Roles and Goals exercise.

Another annual check-in is the Bucketing, Rebucketing, Planting, and Pruning exercise that I promised in chapter 7: Shared Vision. This one is designed to help you and your partner have a common vision when it comes to cultivating social capital for yourselves and your coupledom. Though partners fulfill many roles for each other, it isn't fair to expect your partner to meet all of your emotional and relational needs. Feeling a sense of belonging outside of the relationship, and having places to go for specific supports that your partner can't provide, is an important part of both relationship satisfaction and also life satisfaction in general. The Harvard Study of Adult Development, which has been ongoing since 1938, continues to find that healthy and satisfying relationships of all kinds are incredibly important to physical and emotional health in all stages of life.[3] Taking time each year to reassess your social capital can have enormous benefits.

BUILDING BLOCK:
BUCKETING, REBUCKETING,
PLANTING, AND PRUNING

For this exercise you will need a comfortable place to sit, small pieces of paper, a writing instrument, and a collection of small containers. On each piece of paper, write the name of a person with whom you have a relationship.

> Bucketing: Label each bucket with a specific type of relationship you currently have, or would like to have, in your life, such as "friend," "acquaintance," "colleague," "family." Place each name in its corresponding bucket.
>
> Rebucketing: Now, evaluate. Are any buckets overflowing? Are any empty? Should any names be shifted from "friend" to "acquaintance" or vice versa?
>
> Planting: Are there any relationships you would like to have that you don't currently have? Any empty buckets?
>
> Pruning: Are there any relationships that were fulfilling at one point in your life but that you have now outgrown? These are all candidates for pruning—either cutting back or uprooting entirely.

You don't have to sit on the floor here or use actual buckets. Coffee cups, jars, anything you have handy is okay to use. Once your buckets are full, you can shift things that need to be shifted, fine-tuning the importance of each person and the role you would like them to play in your life (and you in theirs). The next step is to consider areas of your social life where you feel dissatisfied and would like to build or shift some capital. Maybe you need an exercise buddy, someone to trade babysitting with, or a banjo player for your bluegrass band. If you've recently moved you might need a close friend or two who doesn't live halfway around the world, or a handful of playmates for your child.

Finally, are there any old high-school friends, people from the parents' group you joined fifteen years ago when your daughter was a newborn, or family obligations that demand more time and energy than you are willing to give? What about people who are actively problematic, like neighbors who drop by unannounced or high-maintenance friendships that require lengthy conversations and bring unwanted drama into your life? This is a good time to reevaluate, dig deep, and use those boundaries.

Once you have an idea of what you want your individual social circle to look like, think about who you want to mingle with together. What would that look like? This is the time to let your partner know what's important to you, and to identify any tricky areas.

Both of these annual exercises are fairly involved and require some time to complete. I like to do them during the winter holidays, as a way to reflect on the year that has passed and to plan for the year that is to come. Remember, it doesn't matter how good your ladder is if you don't know which roof you want to climb.[4]

MONTHLY CHECK-IN

I cannot tell you how many times partners come to me and report, "I'm drowning over here and she doesn't even care!" or "He said he'd do the drop-offs this month, but he's always got some reason why he can't!" Usually the other partner responds with, "Why didn't you tell me you felt that way?" or "You never asked for my help. I didn't know." Simply by checking in with each other we can prevent the slow drift apart and alienation that plagues so many couples. The reason I urge you to assign time every month for this is because, well, who are we kidding? It doesn't matter how much we talk about giving and receiving help, or meeting each other's needs, it's still very difficult for most of us to find the time. Waiting for your partner to ask you if you need anything, or waiting for the right opportunity (when neither of you is overworked or overwhelmed or you feel comfortable enough to approach and ask for the resources) means waiting for something that might never come. Before you know it months have passed, you feel unsupported, and resentments are born. If you can prevent all this with just one monthly check-in, why wouldn't you?

One tool I especially like for the monthly check-in is an exercise I designed to assess the perception of fairness in your relationship and the balance (or imbalance) among the multiple roles each of you plays. I call it the Resource Pie.

EXERCISE: RESOURCE PIE

1. With paper and pen, draw four large circles. Label one Time, one Attention, one Energy, and one Money. Then draw pie slices to represent where your own individual resources go over the course of a typical month.
2. Now take a clean sheet of paper and do the same thing, but this time divide the pie to reflect what you would like these slices to look like (instead of what they actually look like).
3. Share with your partner, and see if you can come up with a strategy that will bring each of you closer to your ideals.

Remember: The first set shows the *current* distribution and the second one shows the *desired* distribution.

For some couples it is easy to be precise about this; for many others just a rough estimate is enough. You don't have to be perfectly accurate, but it is important to be realistic and not exaggerate. Sometimes our perceptions are influenced by emotion. It might *feel* like you're washing dishes *all the time* (or walking the dog, changing diapers, etc.) when in reality it only takes about an hour a day. If you see that you are struggling with this exercise, it could be a sign of being exhausted, overwhelmed, and having too much to unclutter in your mind before being able to organize your life. Or maybe this simply is not your thinking style, so don't be harsh on yourself. See if the suggestions below could help to get you started:

- Time: Paid work, unpaid work (operations, childcare), quality time with kids, sleep, exercise, self-care, couple time, time with friends, recreation, extended family obligations, hobbies, screen time, _____ _____.
- Attention: Any kind of mental preoccupation that you might have.
- Energy: Paid work, unpaid work, operations, providing emotional support, quality time with loved ones, worrying, screen time, _____.
- Money: Budgeted and unbudgeted items (housing, food, utilities, transportation, childcare, etc.), hobbies, entertainment, discretionary spending, _____.

This exercise should help you to quite literally see any discrepancies between your current life and the one you desire when it comes to what you give and receive (the various currencies that are at play). Some might even overlap with one another. For example, worrying about your son's performance at school might occupy your attention a great deal and deplete your energy, too. It might also motivate you to take action to change things for him. Putting it all in front of you, in black-and-white and side by side, takes it out of your brain and gives you a different perspective. Rather than ruminating on vague feelings of unfairness, you can examine the facts and come up with a plan to make your arrangements more equitable. This is also a great way to show each other how you see your life, priorities, and resources. For example, if you have a tiny slice of energy left for self-care in the current diagram and in the desired version it is a substantial slice, it shows a discrepancy and lack of balance in your life. Many of my couples shift their lifestyle and priorities and show up in significantly supportive ways for each other after seeing what the other person drew.

Another benefit is that you and your partner will be able to see the currencies each brings to the table. This is especially helpful if there is conflict around fairness or equity in the relationship. For example, Peter felt it was unfair that he had to pay for everything while Carrie stayed home with the kids (six and three years old at the time). When they did this exercise, they both realized that Carrie spent eighty hours a week on unpaid labor (operations and childcare), while he spent a total of sixty hours a week on paid labor, childcare, and operations, and he began to have more compassion for her and appreciation for her contributions. When they experimented with how their resources would look if Carrie took a full-time job, both quickly realized that it was not a viable alternative at this time. It might mean more money, but it would also mean more expenses, more unpaid labor for Peter, and less time for each other and for their family.

Reallocating resources and solving for these kinds of operational relationship problems can take time, which is why these conversations are rarely a one-and-done deal. Our priorities might also shift and change over time. Carrie, for example, might decide at some point that she wants to work outside the home, so the couple will have to recalibrate to make that possible. Or Peter might want to spend more time with the children and less time at a job that demands sixty hours a week. This is a very cliché example but still more common than you think. Checking in every month will give you an opportunity to evaluate your progress and ongoing needs as a couple, and practice that *Us versus The Problem* attitude we discussed in the Navigating Conflict chapter.

RETHINKING EQUITABILITY

Domestic arrangements are often drawn along gender lines. Historically, unpaid labor has been performed by women; in much of the world it still is. The idea that "women's work" is less valuable has been deeply ingrained in us. So it is particularly interesting to see what happens in same-sex couples, or in couples where traditional gender roles are reversed, when one partner takes on the burden of financial responsibility and the other takes on the burden of care. Vincent and Tony are a couple in their early forties who recently became parents to twins through a surrogate. They had agreed that Vincent would quit his part-time job as an actor to stay at home, and Tony would continue working full-time as a lawyer. They came to their first consultation just after the twins turned one. Vincent was depressed, resentful, and exhausted, and had gained twenty pounds in a year. Tony didn't understand why. "This is what you always wanted, and now you have it and you're so unhappy. I just don't get it," Tony said.

"It's like this," Vincent explained, "these kids are a ton of work. I'm on my feet and on duty from the minute they get up until they go to bed at night. Plus, I'm doing all the other stuff—buying groceries, feeding them seventy-two times a day, doing laundry, cleaning, making sure we all get outside at least once a day. I know you work hard, Tony, and I'm grateful for it. But of all the work that we both do each day, your work is paid, it's recognized, you get to talk to grown-ups, and you get more valuable and more marketable over time. My work is not seen as important, in fact most of it is pretty menial, my day never ends, everything I do has to be done again tomorrow, and the longer I'm home the less marketable I become, and my prospects for earning actual money are getting smaller and smaller. It's like your life is growing and mine is shrinking. Except for my stomach. But that's a whole other thing."

All of this is to make the point that domestic arrangements have to be perceived as equitable, and those negotiations must include the impact on each partner's development, professionally and otherwise.

The perception of equitability is fundamental in creating a shared vision, and there's a good reason for this. Unfair arrangements are more likely to be experienced as sacrifices rather than compromises. And sacrifice weakens all the ingredients of Emergent Love, some more than others. It's hard to feel attracted to a partner when you feel unseen and taken for granted (whether or not you actually are). When you think your partner takes more than he gives, it's easy to see it as disrespectful. When your commitments start to feel like sacrifices, you're more likely not to honor them reliably, and when you stop doing what you say you'll do, trust is eroded. You see how this works? The ingredients are all interconnected, and when one is damaged, the others start to fall like dominoes.

Hence, the monthly check-in. And it's not only about domestic arrangements, either, though that is often a part of it. The monthly check-in is a time to bring everything out into the open, lovingly and firmly. This is where you can have the time and space to really address the more serious issues, like boundary violations, breaches of trust, and relational injuries to any of the fundamental ingredients of Emergent Love. It's also a good time to express some appreciation for the elements that are in place and working well, as in, "When I was racing to meet that deadline and you brought me a sandwich without me asking, it was incredible. I felt so loved and supported in that moment." "I'm really proud of you for committing to an exercise routine and sticking with it. I can see the change in you. You're so much calmer and happier. I know you don't do it for me, but I'm definitely benefiting right alongside you."

If you are noticing any tension in your own relationship I encourage you to try the monthly check-in, and keep all the elements of Emergent Love in mind. Some of my couples go away for a night or two for their monthly check-ins. If you have the means and the support, why not?

WEEKLY CHECK-INS

We are busy. We are all busy, all the time, and every day the list of items on our agenda seems to grow exponentially. That in itself is a problem and deserves its own book. Many have been written. In *this* book, I am telling you lovingly and firmly that if you don't carve out some time for your relationship, put it in your schedule, and prioritize it, then it isn't going to survive, let alone thrive.

Three areas of coupledom that are easily overlooked when things get busy are operations, sex, and important conversations. In order to remedy this, I invite couples to have three forms of check-in on a weekly basis.

Operations: Once a week, on a Sunday or any other day that works for you, sit down and talk about all the actual tasks that have to be done for the household to run smoothly in the coming week. Some of my couples call this the "Team Meeting." Make sure to leave some room for things that erupt during the week unexpectedly as well. Who will stay home if a child gets sick? No task is too small to go on this list. Grocery shopping, meal planning, meal prep, cleanup, laundry, drop-offs and pickups, cleaning the house, watering the plants, car maintenance and bill-paying, scheduling care—all of it has to be addressed and discussed. If you have children, and they are old enough to participate, please include them as well.

If you only have time for one check-in each week, make it this one. The admin meeting is essential. I would even go so far as to say that this one is non-negotiable. In my observations of couples I've found that it is usually these daily tasks, and each partner's perception of fairness, that ultimately causes conflict. Try to be realistic about your list and talk about the resources you each need. One week one of you might have more bandwidth and the other less. You might end up bringing in help or even finishing tasks from each other's list because your half-day meeting on Wednesday got canceled. The list has to be visible to you both (a shared online calendar with different color coding, for example).

When Pejman and I have our meetings, we add things in our calendars according to a color code. I use purple for my client meetings and other time-bound activities (these can only be canceled or interrupted if something very urgent comes up), red for personal errands (which can be moved around if need be), and orange for the family calendar. Pejman uses yellow for his hard-to-move meetings and blue for his personal and movable tasks. When I am going grocery shopping I use red, which means that I will do it on that day at some point. When he has laundry on his list he uses blue so I know I don't need to worry about it and on Monday we will all have clean clothes for the week! Over a period of time a lot of things become kind of automatic and some tasks only have to be discussed when there is a change (for example when Pejman cannot do laundry on Sunday, or I cannot do the grocery shopping on Wednesday).

The weekly admin meeting is also a good time to bring up any things you would prefer not to do—I call these your "pain points." If you really dislike washing dishes or making lunches, see if you can negotiate a different arrangement. Be honest and transparent about your capacities and abilities, and communicate them as soon as possible to your partner. They may be disappointed or annoyed, but it will be far worse if you drop the ball completely. Annoyance and disappointment can be rectified, but if you're constantly dropping the ball, your partner will see you as unreliable, and the trust between you will be shaken. That is much harder to repair. If neither of you wants to or can be on top of a task, maybe it is time to get creative or delegate it, depending on what it is and if that is possible. For example, invest in having a dog walker or arrange a carpool to pick up your child from school once a week while you go grocery shopping. These are all possible if you know about them in advance!

Sexy Time: In the last chapter we discussed physical connection in some detail, so just a friendly reminder to mention that your physical connection must be prioritized with regularity. I refer to these check-ins as "Sexy Time" because it suggests a lightness and playfulness that we so often lose sight of in our most intimate bond. One of my clients even writes it in her schedule with an exclamation point that acts as a visual reminder that Sexy Time! is something she looks forward to, and that she always leaves feeling satisfied in one way or another. For Sexy Time you decide in advance on a time and context to physically connect with your partner. It doesn't matter what you do during that time, as long as both of you walk away satisfied in whatever way each of you defines satisfaction in that context. One person might feel satisfied that they connected with their partner; the other might have really enjoyed the orgasm they experienced. Selecting an item from your sexual menu can help you to match each person's desires with the activity that is most likely to lead to a positive experience in your current context.

Couple's Jar: We talked about the Couple's Jar at length in chapter 10: Navigating Conflict, so I won't go into too much detail here. Just a quick reminder: You have a jar in which you drop pieces of paper with written messages to "talk about x." It could be about your next vacation, or about something that happened during the week that you didn't get a chance to talk about for whatever reason, or about anything at all that doesn't fit easily into your operations or sex check-ins. Admin time is for distributing tasks and planning for the week ahead, so conversations about vacation planning, looking for a new babysitter, or feeling annoyed because you hate raking leaves and want to hire someone this year are all topics for the Couple's Jar. And Sexy Time is for connecting physically, not *talking about* connecting physically. So if you want to add items to your sexual menu, or you want to go over something that you especially enjoyed (or didn't enjoy), or you need to figure out a new form of birth control, write it down and put it in the jar. Remember, couples who regularly talk about sex tend to experience more satisfaction in that arena.

You don't necessarily need to have these conversations every week, or even set aside a regular scheduled time to engage with each other. But keeping this option open can help you to address things that have to be discussed in a timely manner without having to wait for the monthly check-in.

DAILY CHECK-INS

Ideally, you act intentionally to express attraction, respect, trust, commitment, compassion, and love to your partner, and your partner does the same, every single day. The daily check-in isn't meant to replace intentional behaviors, it's designed to support them. There are no shortcuts or quick-fix prescriptions for creating a thriving relationship. But here are some ideas for strengthening your bond every day.

Routines and Rituals: Emergent Love is all about what you do every day to express and receive attraction, respect, trust, commitment, compassion, and loving behaviors. When these dynamics are healthy and functioning, each of these elements is present every day. But that takes effort and intentionality, especially in the beginning when you are learning these skills and incorporating these principles into your daily life.

Take a moment to think about the things you and your partner do every day. Maybe you wake up early and make coffee for your husband, or you pack a lunch for your wife. Maybe you scratch her back before you both go to sleep. Take a look at your daily routines and see if there are any opportunities to add a little extra something that could make your partner smile, or feel special and seen. Your daily routines are perfect places to manifest loving behaviors. Maybe you send a little "rise and shine" text every morning (even when you are working in the next room), or you both agree to have coffee together before the rest of the household wakes up. If you share a living space, pay attention to how you acknowledge your partner as you move through the day and the house together. A quick kiss before you leave for work or to your corner of the house, a smile when they enter the room, or an affectionate touch as you pass each other in the hallway all make a difference. These little gestures communicate tenderness for the partner by acknowledging, "Hey, hello, I see you. I am here with you."

If you share a religious ritual or spiritual practice, try doing it together. Research indicates that couples who pray together report greater trust and a stronger sense of unity than couples who do not.[5] If sharing a spiritual practice is something you have in common, you can express your commitment to that shared value together. If your version of prayer is meditation, or sitting on the beach contemplating the vastness of the universe, that works, too.

When you go to bed at night you might want to try some back-to-back breathing or front-to-front eye gazing. Again, this is a small change that can have big results. Anything and everything that you can add to your daily routine that will increase the points of contact between you is beneficial.

Earlier in the book I talked about how we spend 80 percent of our energy on things that matter only 20 percent. Understanding the little things that leave your partner feeling loved, cherished, and special, and working them into your daily routines, will definitely pay off. Remember, the goal is to spend 20 percent of your energy doing what matters 80 percent.

Oys and Joys: Every day, at least once and preferably at roughly the same time of day (I prefer dinnertime) share the Oys and Joys of the past twenty-four hours.[6] The oys of the day include anything that brought you down, made you upset, or impacted you in a negative way.[7] The joys of the day include anything that brought a smile to your face or joy to your heart—it could be a video clip that you watched, a person who smiled at you in the drugstore, your child uttering her first words (or doing some other ridiculously cute thing), and so on.

The purpose of this check-in is to make sure that you keep the window of intimacy open between you, so please don't turn this into a coaching or therapy session or an extended conversation about problem-solving; otherwise you and/or your partner could start to resent these conversations and try to avoid them. I'm talking about sharing something that touched you in a meaningful way. The point is to get a little beyond just the "What did you do today?" report and connect about each other's emotional experiences, large and small. By sharing your day with each other you're sending an invitation to your partner to be a part of your journey. It also makes it more equitable, because in many couples one person tends to share more and the other ends up just listening without having a chance to share their own inner world with their partner.

This is important, because every one of us is exposed to so much during the course of a single day. Even during the pandemic when most of us were stuck at home, we turned to our devices to connect us to the world, other people, and different realities and states of being. And we didn't have to move a muscle or leave our bedrooms to do it! Most couples today live in separate worlds when they're outside of the home, and even sometimes when they're in the home. At work we're in daily contact with people our partner has never met, doing things our partner doesn't know about. We have friendships and hobbies that predate our relationship and often don't include the partner. We do different things, read different books, consume different media, and don't even necessarily watch the same shows on television.

When it comes to the people, voices, and ideas that influence us, partners have very different inputs. Although most of us are attached to our devices and have the illusion of connection, we really don't share intentionally about the things that genuinely move us. These are all the things that might not seem significant in the moment, but they determine the trajectory of our thinking and state of being in the long run. Anything that leaves an emotional mark on any given day will create some sort of adjustment in how we see ourselves or the world, and that is something our partner needs to know if we are to remain close. We need a time to come together to share about our day. When people grow apart, it is often because they lose track of what is happening in the other's life; this is one way to help prevent that from happening.

One last thing: Make sure to share the oys before the joys. When you finish the conversation, you want to have a positive image in your mind to activate the reward circuit of the brain (much like walking away from a Sexy Time satisfied) so you have positive associations with daily sharing.

FUN, PRN

PRN stands for *pro re nata*, a Latin term used in medicine for prescriptions that are to be taken "as necessary." In addition to the yearly, monthly, weekly, and daily check-ins, there are some points of connection that happen on an "as needed" basis. Dealing with conflict is one of these, especially if you can't prevent the conflict beforehand, and having fun is another. I don't ascribe to any hard-and-fast rules when it comes to how often a couple should have fun together—the very idea of rules seems counterintuitive when it comes to play. Instead of telling you *how* to have fun, I want to talk about *why* to have fun. Let's start by talking about play.

Even before I became a mother I always liked watching children play. There's something so authentic about the way human beings interact before they've really been socialized. Some approach quickly and ask, "Want to play?" Others are a bit slower to ask but will usually join when invited. This requires a basic level of trust and begins a mutual process of constant negotiations and renegotiations about the rules of engagement with one another, always with the assumption that both are after the same thing: a positive experience. When something isn't working, they're quick to point it out. "No *I'm* the teacher. *You're* the baby." "I don't want to be the baby!" "Okay, after I'm the teacher you can be the teacher." "I know, let's get Ralphie to be the baby and we can have two teachers."

Children are often *self-centered*, meaning they pay more attention to their own experience than the experience of others, but they're not necessarily *selfish*. If they're not having fun, or the rules don't favor them (e.g., "You *have to* be the baby or you can't play with us!") they might still join the game, but only until they can find a better option. "This isn't fun. I'm playing tag." Children actively seek out positive, playful, joyful experiences. We should, too.

When two people are building a life together, trying to make time for each other, and running a household, there is a tendency to lose sight of joy. Everything becomes logistical, all conversations are about operations, and opportunities to be light and playful with each other, to make mistakes and be goofy and imperfect, become few and far between. "We are not laughing together anymore" is something I hear often from couples who are questioning their bond. When we talk about thriving couples, this lightness and playfulness is present, and when we talk about joyless relationships this is usually the part that is missing. For some people sex falls into the category of playfulness, but not for everyone. When you have a long list of tasks that have to get done before you can allow yourself time to play, then guess what? Play goes out the window, because there is always more work to be done. The whole "work first, play later" mentality is a little bit detrimental here. Instead, I recommend that you include play as an item on your to-do list, rather than a reward at the end of it.

When I talk about play, I am not referring to just setting aside a few hours to be out of the house together. For so many couples "date night" means going down the street to the same restaurant where you eat pizza with the kids on Fridays, eating that same pizza without the kids, and talking about the kids the whole time. It's not hard to see why this isn't restorative or even very fun. On a side note, I often tell my couples they cannot go to restaurants for date nights (to just eat and drink) unless they have other experiences before or after it, too!

Date nights are essential not luxury, although many couples really cannot make them happen for multiple reasons. If you can make them happen, here are some tips to make them count: It's important to organize your dates in a way that allows you to experience a variety of states of being around each other. When you choose an activity, think about where it falls in the continuum between novelty and familiarity. Taking lessons in a kind of dance that neither of you has ever done before would be novel for both of you (novel/novel), which means you would be on equal footing (no pun intended). Some couples even keep a list of things each partner would like to try, then take turns organizing outings (look how many elements of Emergent Love are packed in this one action: respect, compassion, attraction, loving behaviors, and shared vision). This can be anything from skydiving to square-dancing, attending a livestock auction to going to a ropes course, bowling, driving a go-cart, playing mini golf, or attending the opera. The idea here is to get you out of your comfort zone and get your adrenaline flowing. Have a brand-new experience. The novelty—and all its attendant neurochemicals—will become something you share with each other. If you are playing a game of pickleball with another couple, you might not be good at it or win, but you experience each other as a teammate beyond managing a household. Your body will recognize their body as a place of fun and excitement, which can have a very positive impact on your physical connection. You also get to see your partner in a different light, beyond being the father of your children or the person who forgot to put the toilet seat down.

If one of you has a hobby or interest, try an outing where you share that with your partner to see if they might also enjoy it (familiar/novel). But please keep in mind that you don't want to make it a bad experience for them by organizing the date as a way of showing off (i.e., expert/beginner rather than familiar/novel). I've had couples come back from a tennis session, skiing, or a camping trip with a lot of tension. If you want to share your love of tennis, don't play to win. And if you want to share your love of the great outdoors, make sure to ask your partner before you set out on a twenty-mile hike! If you want to go camping in a tent and your partner's idea of it is glamping, then we have an issue. It's also important to take turns as novice and expert. If you always want your partner to join you, but you resist activities that they want to share with you, it won't feel equitable and might be an indication of other, more serious imbalances in the relationship.

Sometimes you can choose activities that are familiar, and that you both love, but that you don't get a chance to do very often (familiar/familiar). This can act as a restorative when the relationship starts to feel more like a small business than a loving partnership. When couples come to me worried about boredom or monotony in their relationship, I usually suggest a weekend away together, or even just one night, to do something they know they both will enjoy. If you can't make it happen (many people can't), make it a day or even half a day. Many couples come back amazed that they still really like each other's company—they laughed and talked and actually had fun together—and they want to know how to keep that alive in their relationship going forward. For these couples, the challenge is to intentionally create shared experiences outside of the daily routine of chores and operations—to spend time together as human *beings* rather than human *doings*. This requires planning ahead. Again, nothing you learn about in this book should be left to chance. It is all about choices.

As I've said throughout this book, part of building a thriving relationship involves finding ways to acknowledge and appreciate all the roles you and your partner play for each other and also in your individual lives. This chapter is about moving with fluidity within your relational space depending on the roles each of you is playing, the needs and requirements of the moment, and the capacities of each partner. In this space you want to be sure to recognize that there are differences between admin time and sexy time, date night and couple's time. Each serves a unique purpose in your relationship. Admin time helps you build something together; sexy time maintains your physical connection; date night brings novelty, bonding, and excitement into the partnership; and couple's time helps to maintain and deepen intimacy. Trying to muddle all this together in every interaction, or attending to things in a piecemeal fashion as they crop up, is a far less effective strategy than incorporating separate times for each.

Conclusion

At the beginning of this book, I promised that your life and your pursuit of love would never be the same. I hope that promise has come true for all of you who have joined me on this journey. Be patient and keep going back to various sections of the book as need be. As you know by now, I don't subscribe to the fairy tale of submergent love. Most of the clients I see no longer subscribe to it, either, though many of them did when they first entered my office. Through our work together, they are reminded that we all have so much more agency in love than we have been taught.

The idea that thriving relationships are essentially a passive experience—a matter of luck, or timing, or chemistry—is deeply entrenched in our society. It is also profoundly damaging. The intimate, passionate, devoted coupledom you desire is not something that will just happen to you; it is something you build slowly, over time, in hundreds of thousands of actions and interactions both large and small. You cultivate it every day by choosing to act in ways that will strengthen your bond, that contribute intentionally to your coupledom, and allow yourselves space to flourish. Emergent Love is all about creating and sustaining partnerships that are based on a solid foundation of attraction, respect, trust, shared vision, compassion, and being loving.

This book was designed to give you a toolkit and a set of skills to build your own loving relationship. Those of you who have practiced these skills along the way know how to deepen your intimacy by acknowledging and appreciating the qualities you value in your partner, and also the qualities your partner values in themself. You are aware of your own boundaries and those of your partner, know how to communicate them, you know how to make repairs when those boundaries are crossed. You understand that trust must be earned by keeping your word and being reliable and consistent about the things that matter most. You know how to create a shared vision, and how to negotiate that vision on an ongoing basis so that your arrangements continue to feel equitable and mutually satisfying. You honor your commitments and know that they are promises you make to yourself to align your behavior and your values, even when it isn't easy. You understand that compassion is an essential component of safety and trust, and you accept that sometimes you need to dig deep to express compassion for your partner, especially in moments of discord. And you make an intentional effort to appreciate the special and exclusive role your partner has in your life every single day.

When you chose this book, you set your intention to take an active part in creating the love that you desire and deserve, and I would like to acknowledge and celebrate your belief in your own worthiness to have a loving and fulfilling relationship. What you learned throughout our time together in this book may not feel natural to you yet, but in time it will. If you keep practicing, these ingredients can come together into a feast greater than the sum of its parts—one that will nourish your love and your coupledom through all of life's seasons. It takes courage to hold such a belief, and your conviction inspires me. I hope you will join me in my mission to create world peace, one relationship at a time. On that note, let me not hold you any longer, you have a love to create. I hope our paths cross again and I get to hear your love story!

Acknowledgments

The creation and realization of this book took a village. I have been informed and touched by so many events and individuals in my life and career that I cannot even fit them into a book on its own let alone on a page. Here is my attempt to highlight a few:

My generously kind clients and research participants from all corners of the world. Your trust and willingness to share your stories have been both humbling and inspiring. I feel so privileged that you allowed me to hop on the train of life with you and be your thinking partner for a while. You might not recognize your stories because I rearranged the narratives, interweaving them to safeguard your confidentiality, but your experiences have shaped the insights and perspectives within these pages. I hope the positive karma comes back to you and your loving relationships.

A.K.A., for being my youngest thinking partner and the unquestionable joy of my life. Your presence and enthusiasm have brought immense inspiration to my work.

Dr. Beverly Whipple, for your unwavering love and informed mentoring for the past twenty years; Dr. Pepper Schwartz, for your generous spirit and guidance about the publishing process; Jamshid Gharajedaghi, for brilliantly teaching me about systems thinking and emergent properties; Dr. Christopher Walling, for your kindhearted presence and wisdom. Other individuals that I would like to acknowledge publicly for their support and thoughts during the whole process of putting this book together, from researching to getting it into your hands: Todd Shuster, Dr. Donna Sheperis, Sebene Selassie, Susan Quilliam, Dr. Stephen Snyder, Esther Perel, Dr. Jennifer Freed, Dr. Betsy Thom, Kim Wallace, Dr. Jane Greer,

Ann Peacock, Dr. Karen Rayne, Dr. Alex Terreau, Dr. Barry Komisaruk, Jacklyn Friedman, Francisco Ramirez, Heather Corinna, and Dr. Peggy Kleinplatz.

Hannah Robinson, for your grace, brilliant vision, and extraordinary editorial skills and for offering *Love by Design* a nurturing home within Hachette. To the remarkable team at Balance, I am so grateful for all your efforts and creative ideas on how to make my message seen and heard. Sarah Manges, for your phenomenal editorial skills and thinking partnership, I owe you a debt of gratitude. Sarah Phair, for diligently getting my work into the hands that mattered and your committed support throughout the process. Rachel Ayotte, for your editorial supports when the book was in its infancy. Dr. Emily Nagoski, for being there for me on multiple fronts throughout this process (remember the first time that I drew the Venn diagrams for you on a napkin at breakfast?!).

Those who hold my heart in their love's embrace: Alex Kayson, Farideh, Houshmand, Haana, Foad, Saba, Shahrzad, Amit, Nazila, Eilecia, Serin, Lily, Mojgan, Bahareh, Ellie, Farah, Minoo, Nivaan, Nikki, and Samvir.

The audience of my talks and trainings and our global community over the past two decades, I extend my deepest gratitude to you. Your willingness to share vulnerably and trust in our collective journey has been a profound source of inspiration. I will forever cherish our connection and send you light to brighten your days.

Palo Alto University, for providing me access to their extensive research archives as an alumnus. While we are on the topic of research archives, I didn't spell out every resource that I used within the text to keep the flow going but I tried to capture all the works that were directly used to inform *Love by Design* in the reference part of the book. More resources are captured on www.lovebydesignbook.com. Please accept my earnest apology for any errors or omissions that I might have made in this process.

Last but not least, I would like to acknowledge the shoulders that I am standing on. It is not possible to name everyone here (albeit throughout the book they pay visits): mainly Dr. Ellen Berscheid and Dr. Elaine Hatfield, for their pioneering efforts in scientific study of love, and John and

Julie Gottman, whose extensive research has legitimized couples therapy. Drs. Ellyn Bader and Peter Paterson, your innovative approaches have brought new dimensions to our field. Esther Perel, your efforts in destigmatizing couples' dynamics have been particularly significant. My hope is to further democratize relational science and the experience of love for all through *Love by Design*.

Notes

Introduction

1. Janice K. Kiecolt-Glaser and Stephanie J. Wilson, "Lovesick: How Couples' Relationships Influence Health," *Annual Review of Clinical Psychology* 13 (2017): 421–443; Daniel N. Hawkins and Alan Booth, "Unhappily Ever After: Effects of Long-Term, Low-Quality Marriages on Well-Being," *Social Forces* 84 no. 1 (2005): 451–471.
2. Paul R. Amato and Juliana M. Sobolewski, "The Effects of Divorce and Marital Discord on Adult Children's Psychological Well-Being," *American Sociological Review* 66 (2001): 900–921.
3. Demie Kurz, *For Richer, For Poorer: Mothers Confront Divorce* (New York: Routledge, 1995).
4. US Census Bureau, Decennial Censuses, 1890–1940, and Current Population Survey, March, and Annual Social and Economic Supplements, 1947 to 2022. https://www.census.gov/newsroom/press-releases/2021/marriages-and-divorces.html.
5. Jamshid Gharajedaghi, *Systems Thinking: Managing Chaos and Complexity*, 3rd edition (New York: Elsevier Publishing, 2011).

Chapter 1. *Modern Coupledom*

1. Yann Dall'Aglio, "L'amour—Vous le Faites Mal" [Video]. TED Conferences. February 2014. https://www.ted.com/speakers/yann_dall_aglio.
2. George Lakoff and Mark Johnson, *Metaphors We Live By* (Chicago: University of Chicago Press, 2003).
3. Mandy Len Catron, "A Better Way to Talk about Love" [Video]. TED Conferences. November 2015. https://www.ted.com/talks/mandy_len_catron_a_better_way_to_talk_about_love.
4. Lakoff and Johnson, *Metaphors We Live By*.
5. Serge Brand, Matthias Leuthi, Anina von Planta, Martin Hatzinger, and Edith Holsboer-Trachsler, "Romantic Love, Hypomania, and Sleep Pattern in Adolescents," *Journal of Adolescent Health* 41 no. 1 (July 2007): 69–76. DOI: 10.1016/j.jadohealth.2007.01.012.
6. Rayana Khalaf, "14 Stages of Love According to the Arabic Language," Stepfeed, February 10, 2017. Accessed November 10, 2022. https://stepfeed.com/14-stages-of-love-according-to-the-arabic-language-1371.
7. Domenic Marbaniang, "Specific Words in Hindi for LOVE," Domenic Marbaniang (blog), November 13, 2011. Accessed November 10, 2022. https://marbaniangdomenic.wordpress.com/2011/11/13/specific-words-in-hindi-for-love/.
8. "Love Hurts," performed by Nazareth, written by Felice and Boudleaux Bryant and first recorded by the Everly Brothers in 1960.
9. David Roberts, *British Hit Singles*, 14th edition (London: Guinness World Records Limited, 2001), p. 332.
10. Catron, "A Better Way to Talk about Love" [Video].

11. Mark Manson, "A Brief History of Romance (And Why It Matters)," Mark Manson (blog), accessed January 23, 2023, from https://markmanson.net/history-of-romance.

12. Helen Fisher, *Why We Love: The Nature and Chemistry of Romantic Love* (New York: Henry Holt & Co, 2004).

13. D. Marazziti, H. S. Asiskal, A. Rossi, and G. B. Cassano, "Alteration of the Platelet Serotonin Transporter in Romantic Love," *Psychological Medicine* 29(3) (May 1999): 741–745.

14. Fisher, *Why We Love*, p. 83.

15. Ann Swidler, *Talk of Love: How Culture Matters* (Chicago: University of Chicago Press, 2001).

16. Simon May, *Love: A History* (New Haven: Yale University Press, 2011), p. 4.

17. Laura Kipnis, *Against Love: A Polemic* (New York: Pantheon Books, 2003).

18. US Census Bureau, Decennial Censuses, 1890–1940, and Current Population Survey, March, and Annual Social and Economic Supplements, 1947 to 2022.

19. US Census Bureau, Decennial Censuses, 1890–1940, and Current Population Survey, March, and Annual Social and Economic Supplements, 1947 to 2022.

20. Michele Scheinkman, "Intimacies: An Integrative Multicultural Framework for Couple Therapy," *Family Process* 58 no. 3 (2019): 550–568.

21. Anthony Giddens, *The Transformation of Intimacy: Sexuality, Love and Eroticism in Modern Societies* (Stanford, CA: Stanford University Press, 1992), p. 58.

22. Stephanie Coontz, *Marriage, A History: How Love Conquered Marriage* (New York: Penguin Books, 2005).

23. May, *Love: A History*, p. 4.

24. Douglas R. Hofstadter (1996), "Preface 4 the ineradicable eliza effect and its dangers, epilogue." In D. R. Hofstadter (Ed.), *Fluid concepts and creative analogies: Computer models of the fundamental mechanisms of thought* (pp. 155–169) (New York: Basic Books).

25. Barry Schwartz, *The Paradox of Choice: Why More Is Less*, revised edition (New York: Ecco, 2016).

26. Jeffrey Simpson, Bruce Campbell, and Ellen Berscheid, "The Association between Romantic Love and Marriage: Kephart (1967) Twice Revisited," *Personality and Social Psychology Bulletin* 12 no. 3 (1986): 363–372. https://doi.org/10.1177/0146167286123011.

Chapter 2. *A New Model: Emergent Love*

1. Jorgen Elofsson and John Reid/Kelly Clarkson, "A Moment Like This," 2002, RCA.

2. The first formal presentation of the findings of my retrospective study was at the World Sexual Health Day at Stanford University in 2017; Sara Nasserzadeh, "Turning Love on Its Head, an Antidote to Love Confusion!," *International Journal of Sexual Health* 31 no. 2-4 (Oxon, England: Routledge Journals, Taylor & Francis Ltd, 2019).

3. Leo Tolstoy, *Anna Karenina*, translated by Constance Garnett (New York: Random House, 1950).

4. For those interested in learning more about the research, please visit https://relationship-panoramic.com/About/#Science.

Chapter 3. *What We Bring to Love*

1. Carl Jung, *Psychology of the Unconscious: A Study of the Transformations and Symbolism of the Libido* (New York: Moffat, Yard and Company, 1916).

2. Alexandra H. Solomon, Carolina Martinez, and James Wren, "Becoming What You Are Seeking: Building Relational Self-awareness in Emerging Adults," *Family Process* 60 no. 4 (December 2015): 1539–1554.

3. If you'd like to learn more about Dr. Walling's work, check out his website: https://somapsychology.com/.

4. Personal conversation with Dr. Christopher Walling, July 2022.

5. John Bowlby, "The Nature of the Child's Tie to His Mother," *The International Journal of Psychoanalysis* 39 (1958): 350–373.

6. Amir Levine and Rachel Heller, *Attached* (New York: Jeremy P. Tarcher, 2010).

7. Stan Tatkin, *Wired for Love: How Understanding Your Partner's Brain and Attachment Style Can Help You Defuse Conflict and Build a Secure Relationship* (Oakland, CA: New Harbinger Publications, 2011).

8. Erin Meyer, *The Culture Map: Decoding How People Think, Lead, and Get Things Done Across Cultures* (New York: Public Affairs, 2016). The idea of high context and low context cultures was first introduced by Edward T. Hall, *The Silent Language* (New York: Doubleday, 1959).

9. Michele Scheinkman, "Intimacies: An Integrative Multicultural Framework for Couple Therapy," *Family Process* 58 no. 3 (2019): 550–568.

10. Aaron Beck, "A 60-year Evolution of Cognitive Theory and Therapy," *Perspectives on Psychological Science* 14 no. 1 (2019): 16–20. For more information about CBT, see Judith Beck, *Cognitive Behavior Therapy, Basics and Beyond*, 3rd edition (New York: Guilford Press, 2020).

11. Though the concept of unrealistic optimism had already been explored by psychologists at least as early as 1980, the term "toxic positivity" first appeared in Jack Halberstam's *The Queer Art of Failure* (Raleigh, NC: Duke University Press, 2011).

12. Tara Brach. *Radical Compassion: Learning to Love Yourself and Your World with the Practice of RAIN* (New York: Viking, 2019).

13. Michael Gilead, Nira Liberman, and Anat Maril, "From Mind to Matter: Neural Correlates of Abstract and Concrete Mindsets," *SCAN* 9, (2014): 638–645. DOI:10.1093/scan/nst031.

14. Jean Piaget, *The Origins of Intelligence in Children*, translated by Margaret Cook (Madison, CT: International Universities Press, Inc., 1952), p. 332.

15. This quote is often attributed to Albert Einstein, though he never actually said it. For an interesting discussion I recommend the commentary by Sid Kemp on Quora. You can find it here: https://www.quora.com/Did-Albert-Einstein-ever-say-write-that-We-cant-solve-problems-by-using-the-same-kind-of-thinking-we-used-when-we-created-them-If-so-where-and-when-did-he-say-write-so?share=1.

Chapter 4. *Attraction*

1. Hermann Hesse, *Demian: The Story of Emil Sinclair's Youth*, translated from the German by Michael Roloff and Michael Lebech (New York: Harper & Row, 1965).

2. Dale Carnegie, *How to Win Friends and Influence People* (New York: Simon and Schuster, 1936), p. 58.

3. Shanhong Luo and Guangian Zhang, "What Leads to Romantic Attraction: Similarity, Reciprocity, Security, or Beauty? Evidence from a Speed-Dating Study," *Journal of Personality* 77 no. 4 (2009): 933–964.

4. Rajiv Jhangiani and Hammond Tarry, *Principles of Social Psychology*, 1st International H5P edition (British Columbia, Canada: BC Open Campus, 2014). https://opentextbc.ca/socialpsychology/chapter/initial-attraction/.

5. Robert Zajonc, "Attitudinal Effects of Mere Exposure," *Journal of Personality and Social Psychology* 9, no. 2 (1968): 1–27. https://doi.org/10.1037/h0025848.

6. Marjolijn Antheunis, Patti Valkenburg, and Jochen Peter, "The Quality of Online, Offline, and Mixed-Mode Friendships Among Users of a Social Networking Site," *Cyberpsychology: Journal of Psychosocial Research on Cyberspace* 6 no. 3 (2012), Article 6. https://doi.org/10.5817/CP2012-3-6.

7. Richard Crisp, Russell Hutter, and Bryony Young, "When Mere Exposure Leads to Less Liking: The Incremental Threat Effect in Intergroup Contexts," *British Journal of Psychology* 100 (2009): 133–149. DOI:10.1348/000712608X318635.

8. D. Watson, E. C. Klohnen, A. Casillas, S. E. Nus, J. Haig, and D. S. Berry, "Match Makers and Deal Breakers: Analyses of Assortative Mating in Newlywed Couples," *Journal of Personality* 72 (2004): 1029–1068. DOI: 10.1111/j.0022-3506.2004.00289.

9. Jhangiani and Tarry, *Principles of Social Psychology*.

10. Ramadhar Singh and Soo Yan Ho, "Attitudes and Attraction: A New Test of the Attraction, Repulsion and Similarity-Dissimilarity Asymmetry Hypotheses," *British Journal of Social Psychology* 39 no. 2 (2000): 197–211. See also: Donn Byrne, *The Attraction Paradigm* (New York: Academic Press, 1971).

11. Gillian Rhodes, "The Evolutionary Psychology of Facial Beauty," *Annual Review of Psychology* 57 (2006): 199–226.

12. Barnaby Dixson and Robert Brooks, "The Role of Facial Hair in Women's Perceptions of Men's Attractiveness, Health, Masculinity and Parenting Abilities," *Evolution and Human Behavior* 34 no. 3 (May 2013): 236–241.

13. Bridget Murray Law, "Hormones Associated with the Menstrual Cycle Appear to Drive Sexual Attraction More Than We Know," *Monitor on Psychology* 42 no. 3 (March 2011): 44. https://www.apa.org/monitor/2011/03/hormones.

14. Helen Fisher and J. A. Thomson, "Lust, Attraction, Attachment: Do the Side Effects of Serotonin-Enhancing Antidepressants Jeopardize Romantic Love, Marriage and Fertility?" In Steven Platek, Julian Paul Keenan, and Todd Shackelford (eds.), *Evolutionary Cognitive Neuroscience* (Cambridge, MA: MIT Press, 2007), pp. 245–238. https://helenfisher.com/downloads/Do-side-effects-of-ssris-jeopardize-romantic-love.pdf.

15. Christian Crandall, Angela Nierman, and Michelle Hebl, "Anti-Fat Predjudice," in T. D. Nelson (ed.), *Handbook of Prejudice, Stereotyping, and Discrimination* (New York: Psychology Press, 2009), pp. 469–487. See also: J. Hönekopp, U. Rudolph, L. Beier, A. Liebert, & C. Müller, "Physical attractiveness of face and body as indicators of physical fitness in men," *Evolution and Human Behavior* 28(2) (2007): 106–111.

16. George Homans, *Social Behavior: Its Elementary Forms* (New York: Harcourt Brace Jovanovich, 1964).

17. Social exchange theory is a broad term that refers to a large area of scholarly work. The term itself is usually attributed to Peter Blau. See Peter Blau, *Exchange and Power in Social Life* (New Brunswick, NJ: John Wiley & Sons, Inc., 1964). See also G. C. Homans, "Social Behavior as Exchange," *American Journal of Sociology* 63(6) (1958): 597–606. For a complete discussion of social exchange theory, see Karen Cook, Coye Cheshire, Eric Rice, and Sandra Nakagawa, "Social Exchange Theory," in John DeLamater and Amanda Ward (eds.), *Handbook of Social Psychology* (Dordrecht, The Netherlands: Springer, 2013).

18. Jhangiani and Tarry, *Principles of Social Psychology*.

19. Karen Dion, Ellen Berscheid, and Elaine Walster, "What Is Beautiful Is Good," *Journal of Personality and Social Psychology* 24 no. 3 (1972): 285–290.

20. Tony Alessandra and Michael O'Connor, *The Platinum Rule: Do Unto Others as They'd Like Done Unto Them* (New York: Grand Central Publishing, 1996).

Chapter 5. *Respect*

1. Sara Lawrence-Lightfoot, *Respect* (New York: Perseus Books Group, 1999), p. 10.
2. Joseph DeFeo, *Juran's Quality Handbook: The Complete Guide to Performance Excellence*, 7th edition (New York: McGraw-Hill, 2017).
3. Bessel van der Kolk, *The Body Keeps the Score: Brain, Mind and Body in the Healing of Trauma* (New York: Viking, 2004), p. 239. Van der Kolk was referring here to a conversation between Jerome Kagan and the Dalai Lama that took place at the Massachusetts Institute of Technology in 2006. http://www.mindandlife.org/about/history/.
4. The term "triggered" is often overused. Intense reactions of this kind are often associated with past events, usually ones that were traumatic at the time. Trauma is different for everyone. In my work I use Dr. Peter Levine's definition: Trauma is a fact of life, and what determines whether it becomes problematic is the way that we perceived ourselves in that moment in time. If we felt that the incident that happened was beyond our control and level of comprehension, it will leave us feeling traumatized. What one person experiences as trauma might not be traumatic for another person in that same situation. See also Peter Levine, *Healing Trauma: A Pioneering Program for Restoring the Wisdom of Your Body* (Boulder, CO: Sounds True, 2005).
5. Having the couples stand at the same level and talk was something that I observed in a film from a training that was done by the amazing Virginia Satir (the mother of family therapy).

Chapter 6. *Trust*

1. George MacDonald, *At the Back of the North Wind* (Horse's Mouth, 2014).
2. Jack Barbalet, "The Experience of Trust: Its Content and Basis" in *Trust in Contemporary Society*, Masamichi Sasake, ed. (Leiden, The Netherlands: Brill Publishing, 2019), pp. 11–30. https://www.jstor.org/stable/10.1163/j.ctvrxk3cr.6.
3. Adam Phillips, *Terrors and Experts* (Cambridge, MA: Harvard University Press, 1997), p. 53.
4. van der Kolk, *The Body Keeps the Score*.
5. van der Kolk, *The Body Keeps the Score*.
6. Hillary Clinton, *Living History* (New York: Simon & Schuster, 2003).
7. *Force Majeure*, directed by Ruben Östlund, 2014; Paris and Copenhagen; Coproduction Office.
8. Brené Brown, *Rising Strong: How the Ability to Reset Transforms the Way We Live, Love, Parent, and Lead* (New York: Penguin Random House, 2015).
9. You can download Brené Brown's "The Braving Inventory" here: https://brenebrown.com/resources/the-braving-inventory/.
10. M. Gómez-López, C. Viejo, R. Ortega-Ruiz, "Well-being and romantic relationships: a systematic review in adolescence and emerging adulthood," *Int. J. Environ. Res. Public Health* 2019 16: 2415. https://doi.org/10.3390/ijerph16132415.
11. R. Mora-Ripoll, "The therapeutic value of laughter in medicine," *Altern Ther Health Med.* 16(6) (2010 Nov-Dec): 56–64. PMID: 21280463.
12. K. Melton, M. Larson, & M. L. Boccia. "Examining Couple Recreation and Oxytocin via the Ecology of Family Experiences Framework: Oxytocin in Couple Leisure," *Journal of Marriage and Family* 81(1) (2019): 123–145. DOI: 10.1111/jomf.12556.
13. Jamie Ballard, "Sorry, but 24% of Americans Apologize for Something Outside of Their Control at Least Once a Day," Society (May 8, 2023), YouGov.com. This Daily Questions

survey was conducted online on April 11–12, 2023, among 9,594 US adults. The sample was weighted according to gender, age, race, education, US census region, and political party. https://today.yougov.com/topics/society/articles-reports/2023/05/08/sorry-americans-apologize -something-out-of-control.

Chapter 7. *Shared Vision*

1. Translated by Sara Nasserzadeh from the original text in Farsi: *The Dīvān-e Shams* ("The Collected Poetry of Shams"). For people who are interested, they can access a version of an English translation of the book here for free: https://www.academia .edu/31881025/Divan_e_Shams.
2. Pejman Azarmina, https://thinkocrats.net.
3. Bill Burnett and Dave Evans, *Designing Your Life: How to Build a Well-Lived, Joyful Life* (New York: Knopf, 2016).
4. John Gottman and Julie Schwartz Gottman, *Eight Dates: Essential Conversations for a Lifetime of* Love (New York: Workman, 2019).
5. Robert Waldinger and Marc Schulz, *The Good Life: Lessons from the World's Longest Scientific Study of Happiness* (New York: Simon & Schuster, 2023).
6. John Gottman and Nan Silver, *The Seven Principles for Making Marriage Work: A Practical Guide from the Country's Foremost Relationship Expert,* revised edition (New York: Harmony, 2015), p. 137.
7. Dr. Emily Nagoski, *Come Together: The Science (and Art!) of Creating Lasting Sexual Connections* (New York: Ballantine Books, 2024).
8. Robert J. Sternberg, *The Triangle of Love: Intimacy, Passion, Commitment* (New York: Basic Books, 1988), p. 97.

Chapter 8. *Compassion*

1. His Holiness the Dalai Lama, *The Dalai Lama: His Essential Wisdom*, ed. Carol Kelly-Gangi (New York: Fall River Press, 2007), p. 15.
2. Judith Schore and Allan Schore, "Modern Attachment Theory: The Central Role of Affect Regulation in Development and Treatment," *Journal of Clinical Social Work* 36 (2008): 9–20. https://doi.org/10.1007/s10615-007-0111-7.
3. Frans B. M. de Waal, "The Antiquity of Empathy," *Science* 336 no. 6083 (May 18, 2012): 874–876.
4. Robert L. Katz, *Empathy: Its Nature and Uses* (New York: Free Press of Glencoe, 1963), p. 1.
5. Alessandra and O'Connor, *The Platinum Rule.*
6. Sean Illing, "The Case Against Empathy: Why This Yale Psychologist Thinks You Should Be Compassionate, Not Empathetic," *Vox*, January 19, 2017. Accessed January 16, 2023. https:// www.vox.com/conversations/2017/1/19/14266230/empathy-morality-ethics-psychology -compassion-paul-bloom.
7. C. Joinson, "Coping with Compassion Fatigue," *Nursing* 22 (1992): 116, 118–120.
8. O. Klimecki and T. Singer, "Empathic Distress Fatigue Rather Than Compassion Fatigue? Integrating Findings from Empathy Research in Psychology and Social Neuroscience." In: B. Oakley, A. Knafo, G. Madhavan, et al., editors, *Pathological Altruism* (New York: Oxford University Press, 2011).
9. Olga M. Klimecki, Susanne Leiberg, Matthieu Ricard, and Tania Singer, "Differential Pattern of Functional Brain Plasticity after Compassion and Empathy Training," *Social Cognitive and Affective Neuroscience* 9 no. 6 (2014): 873–879.

10. The compassion training used in this study is described below, in a passage accessed January 13, 2014, from the Klimecki article cited above, at https://www.ncbi.nlm.nih.gov/pmc/articles/PMC4040103/: "Compassion Training: The practice of loving kindness or compassion aims at fostering an attitude of friendliness towards oneself and others. After a theoretical introduction, participants were guided to visualize their own past suffering and to relate to it with feelings of warmth and care. Sentences like, 'May I be sheltered by compassion' or 'May I be safe' aided this practice. This caring affective experience was then sequentially extended towards a close person, a suffering person, a neutral person, and finally towards strangers and human beings in general. The ultimate goal of this training was to foster the capacity to experience care and warmth, even when faced with one's own suffering or the suffering of others. Both the empathy and the compassion training practices were carried out in silence and participants practiced either in an upright, seated posture or while walking. Guided training periods typically lasted between 15 and 30 min."

11. Klimecki, Leiberg, Ricard, and Singer, "Differential Pattern of Functional Brain Plasticity after Compassion and Empathy Training."

12. Katz, *Empathy: Its Nature and Uses,* p. 9.

13. Sebastian Rich. https://sebastianrichphotography.com/Artist.asp?ArtistID=42032&Akey=Q446SBG6.

14. Joseph Bailey, *Slowing Down to the Speed of Love: How to Create a Deeper, More Fulfilling Relationship in a Hurried World* (New York: McGraw-Hill, 2004), p. 66. Italics are mine.

15. D. L. Stoewen, "Moving from Compassion Fatigue to Compassion Resilience Part 4: Signs and Consequences of Compassion Fatigue," *Canadian Veterinary Journal* 61(11) (2020 Nov): 1207–1209. PMID: 33149360; PMCID: PMC7560777.

16. Kristin Neff, *Self-Compassion: The Proven Power of Being Kind to Yourself* (New York: William Morrow, 2011).

17. C. Rogers and R. E. Farson, *Active Listening* (Martino Publishing, 2015, reprint of 1957 edition).

18. C. R. Rogers, "Empathic: An Unappreciated Way of Being," *The Counseling Psychologist* 5(2): 2–10. https:// journals.sagepub.com/doi/abs/10.1177/001100007500500202.

19. Thich Nhat Hanh, *The Art of Communicating* (New York: HarperOne, 2014).

20. Gene Knudsen Hoffman, "Compassionate Listening—First Step to Reconciliation?" a talk by Gene Knudsen Hoffman given November 25, 1997, at University of California at Santa Barbara; https://communication-skills.net/resource-library/gene-knudsen-hoffman-articles/compassionate-listening-first-step-to-reconciliation/.

Chapter 9. *Loving Behaviors*

1. Jamshid Gharajedaghi, *Systems Thinking: Managing Chaos and Complexity: A Platform for Designing Business Architecture*, 3rd edition (Burlington, MA: Morgan Kaufmann, 2011), p. 13.

2. Leo Buscaglia, *Love* (New York: Fawcett Crest, 1978), p. 96.

3. Erich Fromm, *The Art of Loving* (New York: Harper & Row, 1956. First Harper Perennial edition, 1989), p. 42.

4. D. W. Winnicott, *The Child, the Family, and the Outside World*, 2nd edition (Classics in Child Development) (New York: Perseus Publishing, 1992).

5. Sternberg, *The Triangle of Love*, p. 119.

6. Gary Chapman, *The 5 Love Languages: The Secret to Love that Lasts* (Chicago: Northfield Publishing, 1992).
7. Stephen A. Mitchell, *Can Love Last?: The Fate of Romance over Time* (New York: W. W. Norton & Company, 2002), p. 43.
8. Mitchell, *Can Love Last?*.
9. Fromm, *The Art of Loving*, p. 48.

Chapter 10. *Navigating Conflict*

1. Lady Dorothy Nevil, *Under Five Reigns* (London: Methuen & Co, 1912), p. 126.
2. Peter Walker, *Complex PTSD: From Surviving to Thriving* (CreateSpace Independent Publishing Platform, 2013).
3. K. Fiedler, "Affective Influences on Social Information Processing." In J. P. Forgas (ed.), *Handbook of Affect and Social Cognition* (Mahwah, NJ: Lawrence Erlbaum Associates Publishers, 2001), pp. 163–185.
4. Gottman and Silver, *The Seven Principles for Making Marriage Work*.
5. Suzy Welch, *10-10-10: A Life-Transforming Idea* (New York: Scribner, 2009).
6. Harville Hendrix, PhD, and Helen LaKelly Hunt, PhD, *Getting the Love You Want: A Guide for Couples,* 3rd edition (New York: St. Martin's Griffin, 2019).

Chapter 11. *Sexual Harmony*

1. Jalal al-Din Muhammad Balkhi (also known as Rumi), *Masnavi-ye-Ma'navi*, Towfiq Sobhani (ed.), (Tehran, Iran: Rowzaneh Publisher, 2019). Persian text translated by Sara Nasserzadeh.
2. Fisher, *Why We Love.*
3. Eric FitzMedrud. *The Better Man: A Guide to Consent, Stronger Relationships, and Hotter Sex* (Vancouver, BC: Wonderwell, 2023).
4. P. A. Thomas and S. Kim, "Lost Touch? Implications of Physical Touch for Physical Health," *Journal of Gerontology Series B, Psychological Sciences and Social Sciences* 76(3): e111–e115. DOI: 10.1093/geronb/gbaa134. PMID: 32845008; PMCID: PMC7499739.
5. B. Ditzen et al., "Positive Couple Interactions and Daily Cortisol: On the Stress-Protecting Role of Intimacy," *Psychosomatic Medicine* 70(8): 883–889.
6. J. Bancroft and E. Janssen, "The Dual Control Model of Male Sexual Response: A Theoretical Approach to Centrally Mediated Erectile Dysfunction," *Neuroscience and Biobehavioral Reviews* 24(24) (2000): 571–579.
7. Emily Nagoski, *Come as You Are: The Surprising New Science That Will Transform Your Sex Life* (New York: Simon & Schuster, 2005).
8. Allen B. Mallory, Amelia M. Stanton, and Ariel B. Handy, "Couples' Sexual Communication and Dimensions of Sexual Function: A Meta-Analysis," *Journal of Sex Research* 56:7: 882–898. DOI: 10.1080/00224499.2019.1568375.
9. David Hamilton, *How Your Mind Can Heal Your Body* (Carlsbad, CA: Hay House, 2008).
10. Gottman and Silver, *Seven Principles for Making Marriage Work.*

Chapter 12. *Check-ins and Checkups*

1. Simone Signoret, "Simone Signoret Talking to David Lewin," *Daily Mail*, July 4, 1978, p. 7 col. 3. (*Daily Mail* Archive: Gale NewsVault).
2. Taiichi Ohno, *Toyota Production System: Beyond Large-Scale Production* (Portland, OR: Productivity Press, 1988).

3. Robert Waldinger and Marc Schulz, *The Good Life: Lessons from the World's Longest Scientific Study of Happiness* (New York: Simon & Schuster, 2023).

4. Stephen Covey wrote: "It's incredibly easy to get caught up in an activity trap, in the busy-ness of life, to work harder and harder at climbing the ladder of success only to discover it's leaning against the wrong wall. It is possible to be busy—very busy—without being very effective." Stephen R. Covey, *7 Habits of Highly Effective People: Powerful Lessons in Personal Change* (London: Simon & Schuster, 1989), p. 98.

5. Nathaniel Lambert, Frank Finchan, Dana LaVallee, and Cicely Brantley, "Praying Together and Staying Together: Couple Prayer and Trust," *Psychology of Religion and Spirituality* 4 no. 1: 1–9.

6. Several years ago I came up with this exercise, but could never find a good name for it. To give credit where it is due, the term "Oys and Joys" was given to me by a beautiful woman named Shay. Shay, wherever you are, thank you!

7. Oy is short for *oy vey iz mir* which translates from Yiddish as "Oh! Woe is me" but is often used with a touch of humor. I first learned it from one of my wise clients and continued using it. See also: Oy vey! Oy vavoy! Oy vey iz mir! Oy gevalt! Or quite simply: Oy! Rachel Scheinerman and Ben Harris, from the website My Jewish Learning, explain it this way, "*Oy* is an iconic Jewish expression that conveys the weariness of a people overly familiar with hardship and oppression, as well as the resilience of a people that finds hope and sometimes even humor in catastrophe. It's both heavy and light. It's tragic and funny. It's so much better with a thick Yiddish accent." Accessed February 19, 2023, at https://www.myjewishlearning.com/article/the-story-of-oy-vey/.

About the Author

Dr. Sara Nasserzadeh, PhD, DipPST, CSC, is a world-renowned social psychologist, psychosexual therapist, and relationship expert. She has over two decades of experience working with thousands of individuals and couples across forty countries. Widely respected by her peers for her research, powerful keynote speeches, popular Instagram page, and numerous publications, her groundbreaking work has garnered global attention with media outlets such as NPR, BBC, *Harper's Bazzar, USA Today*, CNN, and Goop. Learn more at www.Sara-Nasserzadeh.com or follow her @dr.saranasserzadeh.